CÓMO HACER

tecni-ciencia libros
C.C.C.T. (02) 959.0315 / 959.5547
C. Lido: (02) 952.2339
C.C.G. Prados: (02) 975.1841
Valencia: (041) 22.4860
C. Sambil: (02) 264.1765

Si está interesado en recibir información sobre libros empresariales, envíe su tarjeta de visita a:

Gestión 2000
Departamento de promoción
Comte Borrell, 241
08029 Barcelona
Tel. 93 410 67 67
Fax 93 410 96 45
e-mail: info@gestion2000.com
www.gestion2000.com

Y la recibirá sin compromiso alguno por su parte.

CÓMO HACER NEGOCIOS EN INTERNET

Joint Ventures, Alianzas Estratégicas, Transferencia de Tecnologías y Know-how a través de Internet

Eduardo Paz

Quedan rigurosamente prohibidas, sin la autorización escrita de los titulares del «Copyright», bajo las sanciones establecidas en las Leyes, la reproducción total o parcial de esta obra por cualquier medio o procedimiento, comprendidos la reprografía y el tratamiento informático y la distribución de ejemplares de ella mediante alquiler o préstamo públicos.

© Ediciones Gestión 2000, SA, Barcelona, 1998
Primera edición: octubre de 1998
ISBN: 84-8088-283-2
Depósito legal: B. 37199-1998
Diseño cubierta: Manuel Couto/ASÍ Disseny Visual
Fotocomposición: gama, sl
Impreso por Romanyà-Valls, SA; Capellades (Barcelona)
Impreso en España - *Printed in Spain*

A Clara

Índice

Introducción 15

Capítulo 1. Formación de Joint Ventures Internacionales 19

1.1. *Razones y etapas para la formación de una Joint Venture Internacional* 19

1.2. *Etapa de Diagnóstico y Selección* 21
    1.2.1. Elaboración del Plan Estratégico de Internacionalización .. 21
        1.2.1.1. Diagnóstico de la empresa y determinación del perfil del socio potencial 21
        1.2.1.2. Plan de Actuación 22
    1.2.2. Estudio del Mercado del país de destino y de implantación 22
    1.2.3. Identificación del Socio Potencial 25
    1.2.4. Aproximación al Socio Potencial 26

1.3. *Etapa de Pre-Venture* 28
    1.3.1. Plan de Viabilidad y Fijación de Objetivos Comunes 28
    1.3.2. Análisis de la financiación y de la posible ayuda por parte de Organizaciones de Cooperación financiera y técnica ... 29
    1.3.3. Negociación de la Alianza o cooperación empresarial 30

1.4. *Etapa de Joint Venture* 33
    1.4.1. Definición contractual de la Joint Venture 33
        1.4.1.1. Confección y firma del contrato principal
              y accesorios 34
        1.4.1.2. Constitución de Sociedad Mercantil 35
        1.4.1.3. Permisos administrativos para funcionar 36
    1.4.2. Principales Disposiciones legales para la formación
        de Joint Ventures en la Región de Shenzhen (China).
        Caso práctico 36

1.5. *Etapa Operacional de la Joint Venture* 38
    1.5.1. Organización y seguimiento de la relación 39
    1.5.2. Rol de la gestión de la Joint Venture 40

**Capítulo 2. Fuentes de apoyo financiero y jurídico para
           la formación de Joint Ventures internacionales** 43

2.1. *Fuentes de cooperación de la Unión Europea para la formación
    de Joint Ventures* 43
    2.1.1. Euro Info Centres (EICs) 44
    2.1.2. Oficina de Cooperación Empresarial / Bureau de
        Rapprochements des Entreprises (BRE) 44
    2.1.3. Red de Cooperación Empresarial / Business Cooperation
        Network (BC-NET) 46
    2.1.4. Europartenariat 47
    2.1.5. Iniciativa de fomento de la cooperación entre empresas
        y servicios en Europa (INTERPRISE) 47
    2.1.6. Programa Europeo para la Financiación de Joint
        Ventures / European Community Investment Partners
        (ECIP) 48
    2.1.7. Iniciativa ADAPT 50
    2.1.8. Programa Phare de Joint Ventures / Joint Venture Phare
        Programme (JOPP) 50
    2.1.9. EU-USA Transatlantic Business Dialogue (TADB) 51

2.2. *Programa para la cooperación y acciones conjuntas entre
    empresas de la Unión Europea y América Latina (AL-INVEST)* 52

2.2.1. Red de cooperación económica con América Latina
 (Coopeco) 53
2.2.2. Red de Eurocentros (ECE) en América Latina 53
2.2.3. Red de la Asociación Latinoamericana de Bolsas
 de Subcontratación (ALASUB) 56
2.2.4. Sistema de promoción de Informaciones
 tecnológicas (Programa TIPS) 56

2.3. *Instituciones financieras de países europeos para el Desarrollo
e Inversiones de Cooperación con Mercados Emergentes* 57

2.4. *Fuentes de Cooperación Española para la formación de Joint Ventures* .. 60
 2.4.1. Dirección General de Política de las PYMEs (DGPYME) ... 60
 2.4.2. Instituto Español de Comercio Exterior (ICEX) 60
 2.4.3. Agencia Española de Cooperación Internacional (AECI) .. 61
 2.4.4. Red de Fundaciones Universidad-Empresa de España 61
 2.4.5. Compañía Española de Financiación del Desarrollo
  (COFIDES) 62

2.5. *Fuentes Internacionales de Cooperación Empresarial, financiera
y técnica* 63
 2.5.1. Instrumentos de Cooperación del Banco Mundial 63
 2.5.2. Instrumentos de Cooperación Empresarial en Estados
  Unidos y Canadá 67
  2.5.2.1. Overseas Private Investment Corporation (OPIC) .. 67
  2.5.2.2. The Bulgarian American Enterprise Fund
   (BAEF) 68
  2.5.2.3. Central Asian - American Enterprise Fund
   (CAEF) 69
  2.5.2.4. Export Development Corporation (EDC) Canadá .. 70
  2.5.2.5. The Canadian International Development
   Agency (ACDI-CIDA) 70
 2.5.3. Agencia Alemana de Cooperación (GTZ) 71
 2.5.4. Instrumento de Cooperación del Banco
  Interamericano de Desarrollo - Programa Bolivar 72

2.6. *Cuestiones legales relacionadas con Joint Ventures y transferencia de
tecnología y Know-how. Fuentes de información en Internet* 73

Capítulo 3. Transferencia de Tecnología y Know-how 77

3.1. *La Licencia como forma de explotación comercial de un Patrimonio Tecnológico* 77
    3.1.1. Valoración del precio de la tecnología y Know-how 80
    3.1.2. Royalties o regalías 81
    3.1.3. Valor equitativo de la regalía en transferencia de tecnología y Know-how. Caso práctico 82

3.2. *Fuentes internacionales y universitarias de cooperación para la transferencia de tecnología e envestigación y desarrollo tecnológico* ... 85
    3.2.1. Transferencia de tecnología e investigación y desarrollo tecnológico en el marco de la cooperación de la Unión Europea 85
        3.2.1.1. Servicio de información de la Unión Europea para la investigación y el desarrollo / The Community Research and Development Information Service (CORDIS) 86
        3.2.1.2. Red de centros de transmisión de innovación de la Unión Europea (IRCs) - Network of Innovation Relay Centres (IRCs) 88
        3.2.1.3. Cuarto programa marco / Fourth Framework Programme (FP4) 89
        3.2.1.4. Quinto programa marco / Fifth Framework Programme (FP5) 91
        3.2.1.5. Centro de investigación conjunta / Joint Research Centre (JRC) 93
        3.2.1.6. Fuentes de información en Internet sobre la Cooperación de la Unión Europea en el Sector de IDT 94
    3.2.2. Transferencia de tecnología e investigación y desarrollo tecnológico en el marco de la cooperación de España y América Latina 98
        3.2.2.1. Puntos de contacto en España de los Programas específicos del IV Programa Marco de IDT 100
        3.2.2.2. Red española de centros de enlace para la Innovación y Unidad coordinadora española de Centros de Enlace. Contactos en Internet 101

3.2.2.3. IBEROEKA Instrumento para la cooperación
tecnológica y empresarial en Iberoamérica 102
3.2.3. Transferencia de tecnología e investigación y desarrollo
tecnológico en el marco de los Países de la APEC 104

3.3. *El rol de las universidades en la transferencia de tecnología
e investigación y desarrollo tecnológico. Principales sitios Web* 105
    3.3.1. Transferencia de tecnología en universidades
norteamericanas. Contactos en Internet 106
    3.3.2. Transferencia de tecnología en universidades de Canadá.
Contactos en Internet 110
    3.3.3. Transferencia de tecnología en otras universidades del
mundo. Contactos en Internet 111

3.4. *Propiedad intelectual, marcas, patentes y modelos industriales.
principales sitios Web* 113

**Capítulo 4. Promoción internacional de ofertas y demandas para
la formación de Joint Ventures, transferencia de
tecnología y Know-how técnico y tecnológico** 117

4.1. *Selección de las mejores fuentes de información y sitios Web para
la promoción de propuestas de Joint Ventures, transferencia de tecnología
y Know-how* 117
    4.1.1. Recursos de Internet específicos para el intercambio de
información para la creación de Joint Ventures, Alianzas
estratégicas, transferencia de tecnología y Know-how 118
    4.1.2. Recursos de Internet para la promoción global de
oportunidades comerciales generales de productos
y servicios, incluso Joint Ventures, transferencia
de tecnología y Know-how 151
    4.1.3. Recursos de Internet en Europa para la promoción
de oportunidades comerciales generales de productos
y servicios, incluso Joint Ventures, transferencia de
tecnología y Know-how 159
    4.1.4. Recursos de Internet en América Latina y América
Central para la promoción de oportunidades comerciales

generales de productos y servicios, incluso Joint Ventures,
transferencia de tecnología y Know-how 163

4.1.5. Recursos de Internet en América del Norte para la
promoción de oportunidades comerciales generales
de productos y servicios, incluso Joint Ventures,
transferencia de tecnología y Know-how 167

4.1.6. Recursos de Internet en Asia y Oceanía para la promoción
de oportunidades comerciales generales de productos
y servicios, incluso Joint Ventures, Transferencia
de tecnología y Know-how 172

4.1.7. Recursos de Internet en África para la promoción
de oportunidades comerciales generales de productos
y servicios, incluso Joint Ventures, Transferencia
de tecnología y Know-how 177

4.2. *Páginas Amarillas electrónicas y directorios de empresas exportadoras
de todo el mundo* 173

4.3. *Sitios Web útiles para actividades comerciales y negocios de carácter
internacional* 177

Anexos

Anexo 1. *Formulario oficial de solicitud de ingreso al sistema de promoción
de negocios del programa BRE de la Unión Europea* 179

Anexo 2. *Formulario oficial para solicitud de información sobre el
programa ECIP de la Unión Europea* 185

Anexo 3. *Modelo de formulario a enviar al Mailing list de TradeWinds* 187

Glosario 189

Bibliografía 197

Introducción

Las Pequeñas y Medianas Empresas juegan un papel fundamental en el espectro industrial de los países desarrollados y, más especialmente, en los países en vías de desarrollo. En la Unión Europea (UE), por ejemplo, el 99,8% de todas las empresas son de pequeña magnitud, esto representa aproximadamente 16.000.000 de empresas y sólo 30.000 son grandes compañías. A pesar de la importancia de este tipo de estructura empresarial, la mayoría de las empresas tienen serios problemas a causa de los bajos niveles del contenido tecnológico de sus productos, intensidad de capital o posibilidad de auto-inversión, volúmenes de producción y niveles de productividad. Es muy difícil que esa falta de adecuación se revierta si las empresas se mantienen encerradas en las metodologías productivas que alguna vez les fueron útiles o persisten en ser conservadoras en su orientación al mercado.

El incremento de la competitividad global y el desenfrenado crecimiento de la tecnología de la información, han establecido nuevos parámetros de calidad, de innovación, de valores por parte de los consumidores, y niveles de productividad. Consecuentemente, las empresas están siendo presionadas por esta situación y no queda mayor alternativa que cambiar, con todos los riesgos que eso supone. Y cambiar significa, en este caso, orientar la calidad de los productos y servicios al consumidor, producir minimizando los costes y maximizando los índices de rendimiento, y acceder a mayores mercados para aumentar cualitativa y cuantitativamente la demanda.

Las distintas formas de cooperación entre empresas de diferentes mercados otorgan la posibilidad de dar una solución multimodal a los problemas que actualmente enfrentan muchas empresas con mayor intensidad.

En este sentido, las alianzas entre empresas pueden ser una herramienta efectiva para lograr los objetivos de crecimiento que la empresa necesita para resultar eficiente y pueden ser un medio ágil para que una pequeña empresa alcance las dimensiones necesarias para sobrevivir en el gran mercado global, gracias a la complementariedad y la acción de las sinergias que se crean en los emprendimientos conjuntos. Estas alianzas pueden considerarse estratégicas cuando buscan mejorar la posición competitiva de la empresa. Y casualmente el incremento de la utilización de alianzas estratégicas, particularmente, aquellas que implican compartir tecnologías entre las partes, es lo que mejor caracteriza a la actual globalización de los mercados (Medina, 1996).

A través de acuerdos estratégicos es posible que la empresa desarrolle nuevos productos, reduzca costes de explotación, acceda a nuevas tecnologías, acceda a nuevos mercados o canales de distribución y enfrente comercialmente a la competencia, dondequiera que esté, en mejores condiciones empresariales. Al mismo tiempo, la compañía ganará acceso a economías de escala en materias primas, disponibilidad de capacidad industrial y mejores recursos en gestión. A través de las alianzas cada una de las compañías individuales puede beneficiarse de un sinnúmero de prestaciones y recursos, algo que operando en solitario podría resultar muy dificultoso o prácticamente imposible.

Los rápidos avances de la tecnología de las comunicaciones han agregado un incentivo más para las empresas que necesitan expandir sus negocios hacia otros mercados para ganar competitividad a través de la cooperación empresarial y de alianzas estratégicas. Internet, las Redes de Valor Agregado (VANs) e Intranet, son algunos de los principales medios que hoy puede utilizar una empresa para buscar a sus aliados y potenciales socios en el mundo.

Este libro tiene por principal objetivo ofrecer al lector una explicación práctica de la forma de llevar a cabo uno de los principales medios de cooperación empresarial, las Joint Ventures; los medios más importantes de financiación internacional para la creación de Joint

Introducción 15

Ventures; y la forma de buscar socios o *partners* en el mundo a través de los recursos de Internet. Como cuestión complementaria, se analiza una figura comercial que muchas veces va unida a la formación de Joint Ventures, que es la transferencia de tecnología y know-how, y junto con esto se revisan los principales apoyos que la cooperación internacional y las universidades ofrecen a las empresas privadas para la promoción de investigación y desarrollo, y la explotación de los resultados de estas investigaciones científicas. Asimismo, se presenta una selección de recursos de Internet que enlazan directamente con las principales fuentes de información global sobre la materia. Y por último, se presenta una cuidadosa relación de los mejores medios de que se dispone en Internet respecto a los recursos directos y masivos para la presentación de oportunidades de formación de Joint Ventures Internacionales, transferencia de tecnología y know-how.

Este trabajo se edita en idioma español esperando poder contribuir a aumentar el interés en el tema por parte del público de habla hispana, de España, México, Estados Unidos, Argentina, Bolivia, Brasil, Chile, Colombia, Costa Rica, Cuba, Ecuador, Guatemala, Honduras, Nicaragua, Panamá, Paraguay, Perú, Filipinas, Puerto Rico, República Domicana, El Salvador, Uruguay y Venezuela.

El autor estará encantado de recibir todo tipo de opiniones y comentarios de esta obra, así como novedades sobre nuevos Sitios Web dedicados al comercio exterior, Joint Ventures, transferencia de tecnología, y en general, a los distintos aspectos del comercio electrónico de tipo «empresa-empresa» en la dirección de Correo Electrónico: eduardopaz@technologist.com.

Capítulo 1
Formación de Joint Ventures Internacionales

1.1. Razones y etapas para la formación de una Joint Venture Internacional

En términos generales, se entiende por cooperación entre empresas, el desarrollo de negocios empresariales de carácter productivo, comercial, tecnológico o financiero, entre dos o más empresas económica o jurídicamente independientes; que movidas por la reciprocidad de ventajas y la búsqueda de sinergias que puedan contribuir a incrementar su competitividad, convienen en colaborar estrechamente, para de esta forma reducir riesgos y compartir costes y beneficios.

Existen muchas formas de cooperación empresarial o alianzas estratégicas, las cuales ofrecen distintos niveles de oportunidades de crecimiento dentro de un mercado internacional, por ejemplo: alianza para la importación o exportación, acuerdo de marketing, alianza para la distribución, agencia de ventas, licencia de comercialización, leasing de tecnología, licencias cruzadas de tecnología (intercambio de licencias), transferencia de tecnología o licencia de tecnología, licencia de know-how, licencia de fabricación, acuerdo de investigación y desarrollo (I+D) conjunto, acuerdo de producción, Inversión Capital-riesgo y Joint Venture Internacional (JVI), entre otras. El esquema general de la internacionalización de las empresas responde también a un orden jerárquico que relaciona en grado la variable nivel de compromiso con la variable nivel de requerimientos de inversión. En este sentido, las acciones de exportación-importación presentan una relación compromiso/inversión pequeño; las políticas de cooperación empresarial (Joint Ventures, transferencia de tecnología, etc.) responden a una relación compromiso/inversión media; mientras que la inversión directa o el establecimiento de empresas subsidiarias y filiales en destino responde a una relación compromiso/inversión muy elevado.

La Joint Venture Internacional es una forma de cooperación empresarial mediante la cual dos o más partes independientes (personas físicas o jurídicas), establecidas en distintos países del mundo, acuerdan en participar en una sociedad conjunta de negocios, y contribuir con aportes tangibles o intangibles a crear una comunidad de intereses orientados al cumplimiento de unos propósitos mutuamente compartidos.

Los principales motivos que impulsan la creación de Joint Ventures, alguno de los cuales son analizados en profundidad por Valdés (1996), pueden ser:

- Razones estratégicas: Hacer frente a la competencia con mayores ventajas competitivas. Política de desarrollo y crecimiento con pocos recursos. Control de recursos o materias primas.
- Reducción de costes de transacción: Penetración en nuevos mercados salvando costes de logística, derechos de exportación e importación y distribución.
- Colusión: Ordenar la competencia en el mercado, eliminar la competencia actual entre los socios y excluir mercados.
- Factores Políticos: Por restricciones a la inversión directa, por incentivos especiales, etc.
- Mejora de la eficiencia: Diversificación de productos, reducción de costes por economías de escala, compartir y dispersar riesgos, aumento de personal, nuevas sinergias derivadas de la complementariedad, etc.
- Posibilidad y/o aceleración del aprendizaje: Permite el acceso a conocimientos tecnológicos, conocimientos del mercado, canales de distribución, etc. Se reduce el tiempo necesario de puesta en marcha de un producto o proceso.
- Ganar en imagen.

1.2. Etapa de Diagnóstico y Selección

El primer paso a dar para la formación de una Joint Venture Internacional es la elaboración de un programa de actividades en donde la propia empresa enunciará la táctica y estrategia a seguir basándose en un análisis interno de situación.

1.2.1. Elaboración del Plan Estratégico de Internacionalización

El Plan Estratégico será la herramienta esencial para la adopción de las decisiones más relevantes del inicio de la actividad de búsqueda del socio potencial, ya que otorgará elementos concretos para la definición de su perfil y las bases para la constitución de la alianza.

1.2.1.1. Diagnóstico de la Empresa y Determinación del Perfil del Socio Potencial

Se trata de un análisis interno de la empresa y de sus necesidades de cooperación empresarial. Los elementos a tener en cuenta son:

- Tamaño óptimo y eficiente de la empresa.
- Posibilidades de reducción de costes.
- Relación crecimiento/expansión comercial, etc.
- Conocimiento de la situación competitiva de la empresa.
- Análisis de la capacidad técnica de adaptación de las tecnologías empleadas a otros mercados o por emplear en el propio mercado.
- Tipo de cooperación necesaria.
- Disponibilidad de inversión.
- Perfil del cooperante.
- Previsión de cómo le afectará o se beneficiará de la cooperación empresarial buscada.

La empresa deberá analizar su propio negocio teniendo en cuenta los objetivos y su situación competitiva en cuanto a fortaleza y debilidades. Esto ayudará a la compañía a tener un panorama más realista en cuanto a los negocios que se propone llevar a cabo a través de la nueva asociación. El diagnóstico inicial debe también aclarar el tipo de cooperación empresarial que se quiere obtener y el perfil del socio idóneo para la alianza estratégica, o Joint Venture.

1.2.1.2. Plan de Actuación

El Plan de Actuación describe las pautas, líneas y consideraciones para el desarrollo de la búsqueda del socio ideal. Esta planificación preliminar permitirá definir la estrategia operativa de la cooperación.

- Forma de selección y determinación del país-objetivo
- Forma de búsqueda del/de los socios potenciales
- Medios idóneos para la exposición global del proyecto
- Principales pautas de negociación y elementos (inicialmente) no-negociables
- Principales puntos del futuro acuerdo contractual

1.2.2. Estudio del Mercado del País de Destino y de Implantación

Es preciso llevar a cabo una acción de recogida de información que permita contrastar la hipótesis de trabajo con la realidad. Sin información fiable no se pueden tomar decisiones adecuadas. En Internet se dispone de muchas herramientas muy interesantes para una prospección inicial de mercados exteriores. Un método de análisis de mercados internacionales simple que da muy buenos resultados por la posibilidad de una pronta comparación gráfica de las principales variables de un mercado, podría ser el que describe el Cuadro 1.

A fin de recabar información respecto a los factores generales de los mercados internacionales preseleccionados, se puede consultar los siguientes Sitios Web:

CIA Factbook - Análisis por Países de la CIA
http://www.odci.gov/cia/publications/nsolo/wfb-all.htm

Información sobre Negocios Internacionales de MIS-CIBER
http://ciber.bus.msu.edu/busres.htm

Factores de interés para la empresa	PAÍSES				
	A	B	C	D	n
1. Factores Generales					
1.1. Factores Políticos - Sistema Político - Sistema Económico - Estabilidad Interna - Estabilidad Externa - Riesgo Político Específico					
1.2. Factores Económicos - Desarrollo de la Economía del País - Desarrollo del Sector Industrial - Riesgo Económico					
1.3. Factores Tecnológicos - Progresos en Tecnología del Producto - Progresos en Tecnología de Producción					
1.4. Factores Socio-culturales - Conflictos Sociales - Relación de las Tendencias de los Conflictos Sociales con las Tendencias del Consumo - Riesgos Socio-culturales					
1.5. Factores Naturales - Factores Demográficos - Recursos Naturales - Infraestructuras					
2. Oportunidades del Mercado					
2.1. Tamaño Mínimo del Mercado - ¿El producto o servicio existe? - ¿Se desarrollará dentro de 3 años? - ¿Se desarrollará dentro de más de 3 años? 2.3. Crecimiento del Mercado Alto/Medio/Bajo 2.3. Intensidad de la Competencia Fuerte/media/baja					
Resultados					
Evaluación de Oportunidades Usar: + Muy Buenas ++ Buenas # Media 0 Bajas 00 Muy Bajas Evaluación de Riesgos Usar: ** Muy Bajo * Bajo x Medio - Alto -- Muy Alto					

Cuadro 1. Método de análisis de preselección de un mercado extranjero

Centro de Información Electrónica de Comercio Internacional (Tradebase)
http://www.ita.doc.gov/industry/oepc/

Grupo de Usuarios de Datos de Comercio Internacional
http://www.itdu.org/itdu

Biblioteca Telemática sobre Comercio Exterior / Automated Trade Library Service (ATLS)
http://caticsuf.csufresno.edu:70/1/atls

Servicios de Información de Dun & Bradstreet
http://www.dbisna.com/

Análisis de Mercado del Sector Industrial Mundial (Universidad de Michigan)
gopher://una.hh.lib.umich.edu:70/11/ebb/isa

Geopolítica, Geoestrategia, Política Internacional, Organizaciones Internacionales (Mercosur)
http://geocities.com/CapitolHill/6121

Organización Mundial del Comercio / World Trade Organization (WTO), Ginebra
http://www.unicc.org/wto/

Export-Import Bank of the United States
http://www.exim.gov/

Banco Mundial / World Bank, Washington, D.C.
http://www.worldbank.org

Información sobre la Población Mundial y Regional
http://www.census.gov/ipc/www/world.html

1.2.3. Identificación del Socio Potencial

La empresa podría tener en vista alguna empresa susceptible de ser su socio potencial comercial dentro del conjunto de sus clientes, competidores, o compañías relacionadas de cualquier otra forma. El hallazgo de una empresa con la afinidad suficiente para el desarrollo de la asociación puede ser producto de una búsqueda voluntaria a través de varias fuentes como ferias comerciales, información de instituciones públicas, foros de negocios, redes telemáticas de comercio electrónico, conferencias, redes profesionales especializadas en contactos, expertos industriales, literatura especializada, bases de datos, etc.

Las búsquedas deben orientarse a mercados exteriores, y obviamente, es necesario que los candidatos estén inmersos en el mismo ambiente de negocios que la empresa, con las mismas capacidades industriales y comerciales; que exista una similitud o compatibilidad entre los socios en cuanto a estilo y procedimiento de gestión, tamaño y culturas empresariales; y recursos, productos o servicios complementarios.

Las diferencias entre las características de la empresa, como dimensión y formas de administración, podrían resultar negativas para el futuro de la relación, ya que estas asimetrías pueden ser susceptibles de generar un sentimiento constante de incapacidad para trabajar juntos. Geringer (1988) afirma que una Joint Venture formada por socios de tamaños muy dispares, necesita la creación de un ambiente especial con el fin de fomentar con éxito el desarrollo de la cooperación. Así, por ejemplo, los efectos negativos derivados de tamaños diferentes pueden ser reducidos proporcionando a la nueva entidad la libertad para el desarrollo de un producto u otras actividades, o minimizando la burocracia administrativa en los procesos donde ésta sea parte. Este interés en la autonomía es particularmente apropiado para Joint Ventures que se enfrentan a entornos altamente cambiantes. Asimismo, la negativa de alguno de los posibles socios a conceder esta autonomía podría ser un aspecto crítico a la hora de decidir su selección.

El factor clave para la estabilidad de la Joint Venture es hacer bien las cosas desde un principio. La decisión de crear una alianza se debe siempre a una necesidad actual y una identidad de objetivos, compartida por dos o más partes. Pese a la inmediatez coyuntural que eso supone, es muy importante considerar las implicaciones a largo plazo que esa relación ha de originar. El acuerdo de asociación es, en definitiva, un contrato que debe ser examinado cuidadosamente antes de ser formalizado, especialmente, porque las «necesidades actuales» pueden fluctuar con el tiempo y, sin duda, es eso lo que la mantendrá a través del tiempo (estabilidad) o será óbice para disolverla (inestabilidad).

La «química» o «*afectio societatis*» entre los socios es muy importante y hasta el último detalle subjetivo del futuro *partner* puede ser relevante. ¿Se siente usted a gusto con esa gente? ¿Ellos son sinceros y están abiertos respecto al negocio y reconocen sus limitaciones? ¿Qué importancia le han dado a la futura relación y cuanto tiempo le ha demandado contestar a nuestras consultas y requerimientos de información? En los negocios en general es posible captar las señales de la gente e intuir los significados; en la negociación de alianzas estratégicas es una práctica ineludible.

Cuando se considera la formación de una alianza de negocios es fundamental entender que el éxito o fracaso depende del entendimiento mutuo, confianza e interés en llevar a cabo el negocio. Los principales valores a considerar son la honestidad, el *fair-play* (juego limpio), la disposición positiva, la eficacia y la excelencia.

Asimismo, resulta conveniente analizar la potencial efectividad del cliente, basándose en su estabilidad financiera, esquema de organización, situación y posicionamiento en el mercado, forma y factores de producción, contactos institucionales y posibles actitudes de negociación (Cuadro 2).

1.2.4. Aproximación al Socio Potencial

Una vez identificado el socio potencial, que responde perfectamente al perfil diseñado en el diagnóstico inicial de la empresa, es esencial que los primeros contactos con éste se realicen al más alto nivel entre ambas organizaciones. Un error muy común es dejar en manos de gente no experimentada o contactar con empleados sin capacidad de decisión dentro de la empresa-objetivo. Esto generalmente provoca errores, demoras o rechazo del emprendimiento antes de que el

1. Factores Financieros
   - Historia financiera de la empresa y situación financiera general. Análisis de los índices clásicos.
   - Posibles razones del éxito en las diferentes áreas de negocio.
   - Posibles razones del fracaso en las diferentes áreas de negocio.
2. Factores de la Organización
   - Estructura de la organización
   - Calidad y sueldo/beneficios de los gerentes
   - Condiciones de los trabajadores / relaciones laborales
   - Sistemas de información interna y métodos de planificación
3. Factores del Mercado
   - Reputación en el mercado y entre los competidores
   - Grado de investigación/interés en el servicio y la calidad
   - Método de ventas, calidad de la fuerza de ventas
   - Evidencias de debilidad de las condiciones del mercado
   - Resultados de nuevos negocios iniciados
4. Factores de Producción
   - Premisas para el trabajo
   - Eficiencia en la producción/esquemas
   - Inversiones de capital y mejoras
   - Procesos de control de calidad
   - Grado de Investigación (interna / externa) / introducción de nuevas tecnologías
   - Relaciones con los principales proveedores
5. Factores Institucionales
   - Contactos con el gobierno y empresarios (influencias)
   - Negociaciones exitosas con bancos, autoridades oficiales, etc.
   - Principales contactos con organizaciones y compañías extranjeras
   - Influencia regional
6. Posibles Actitudes de Negociación
   - Flexible / Línea Dura
   - Razonablemente abierto / cerrado y secreto
   - Orientado a corto plazo o largo plazo
   - Negociador «envolvente» o negociador objetivo
   - Tomador de decisiones prontas y positivas o aventurado
   - Negociador experimentado y con equipo de apoyo

Fuente: Walmsley (1982)

Cuadro 2. Síntesis de los principales factores para el Análisis de Efectividad asunto llegue a manos de quienes verdaderamente tienen la capacidad de resolver la suerte de una oportunidad como la planteada.

Es importante detectar dentro de la otra empresa a la persona «clave», con capacidad de decisión, que revele entusiasmo en el acuerdo y que actúe como un canal abierto entre las comunicaciones de las dos compañías.

1.3. Etapa de Pre-Venture

1.3.1. Plan de Viabilidad y Fijación de Objetivos Comunes

Una vez que el socio potencial ha expresado interés en la alianza es necesario fijar los objetivos, recursos y expectativas de cada una de las partes y determinar el nivel e importancia de la complementariedad entre ambas compañías. A tal fin se puede llevar a cabo un Plan de Viabilidad *Ad Hoc* en el que ambas partes aporten toda la información posible:

- Evaluación comercial
- Objetivos de producción
- Objetivos de ventas
- Análisis de costes de materias primas
- Necesidades de infraestructuras, personal, etc.
- Información del mercado nacional e internacional
- Análisis de la estructura de precios del mercado
- Análisis de los canales de distribución
- El cambio tecnológico
- Impacto ambiental
- Evaluación técnica del proyecto
- Evaluación financiera del proyecto

Desde un punto de vista técnico, el Plan de Viabilidad es importante para analizar y garantizar las posibilidades reales del proyecto, e imprescindible para la obtención de apoyos financieros por parte de instituciones privadas, instituciones de comercio exterior o instituciones internacionales especializadas en cooperación empresarial.

Desde un punto de vista más subjetivo, teniendo en cuenta el futu-

Formación de Joint Ventures Internacionales 27

ro de la relación de cooperación empresarial, es muy importante porque si se pone de manifiesto el significado estratégico de la relación entre ambos, será más fácil que los individuos involucrados en el tema asuman un compromiso que permita finalizar con éxito la alianza.

1.3.2. Análisis de la Financiación y de la Posible Ayuda por parte de Organizaciones de Cooperación Financiera y Técnica

Desde el principio se debe tener en cuenta que para la formación de una Joint Venture es necesario realizar una inversión, que dependerá del tipo de aporte y control de la sociedad que la empresa quiera asegurar. Por ese motivo, es fundamental la valoración de la inversión a realizar y la forma de obtener los recursos necesarios para llevar a cabo el proyecto.

Hay varias instituciones nacionales e internacionales que desarrollan una activa política de cooperación financiera y técnica, algunas de las cuales son específicas para la formación de Joint Ventures, alianzas estratégicas y otras formas de cooperación empresarial. En esta etapa es conveniente tomar contacto con las organizaciones especializadas en cooperación de ambos países y/o regiones a fin de intentar beneficiar el proyecto con una contribución adicional que alivie de alguna forma los costes de la operación.

Entidades como el Instituto de Crédito Oficial (ICO), la Compañía Española de Financiación del Desarrollo (COFIDES), Centro de Desarrollo Tecnológico e Industrial (CDTI), así como diversos fondos multilaterales derivados de acuerdos específicos, entre otros, tienen líneas abiertas para cofinanciar proyectos de Joint Venture con empresas de países de América Latina, Este y Centro de Europa, Asia y África. Para la fase inicial la Unión Europea dispone de programas ágiles y efectivos como el ECIP, JOPP y otros, que conceden ayudas y subvenciones para financiar gastos del proyecto (estudio de viabilidad; viajes de prospección y encuentros; e incluso, los honorarios de los consultores que colaboran en los estudios y los aspectos técnicos de la presentación y gestión del proyecto ante la Comisión Europea).

De todas formas, es importante considerar la posibilidad de que tales organizaciones no aprueben las solicitudes presentadas por las partes, o la efectiva realización de las subvenciones, créditos o montantes aprobados sufra una excesiva demora. Es decir, se debe pedir todo lo que se pueda, pero es mejor actuar como si no se hubiera pedido nada. Estas cuestiones se desarrollan en profundidad en el Capítulo 2.

1.3.3. Negociación de la Alianza o Cooperación Empresarial

La etapa del Pre-Venture se cierra con la negociación de la alianza que es la fase operacional en donde se evalúan cada uno de los detalles de la relación, y como consecuencia necesaria se abrirán las opciones de arribar al acuerdo final, o abandonar la idea de la formación de la Joint Venture.

La negociación es una interacción deliberativa de dos o más unidades sociales complejas (individuos, empresas, familia, etc.) que intentan definir o redefinir los términos y medidas de su interdependencia. Cada una de las partes, con su propia lógica interna y con su propia información o tácticas, tratan de (i) hallar soluciones para resolver un conflicto de intereses; (ii) encontrar los intereses comunes o complementarios; (iii) influenciar las actitudes de cada uno del resto de los participantes; o (iv) encontrar un punto de consenso entre los grupos que interactúan. Lo mismo ocurre en el contexto de las Joint Ventures.

La negociación es un verdadero arte, especialmente aquellas en que se suma a las condiciones normales el componente internacional, intercultural, la multilateralidad o en las que se debe afrontar procesos de negociación muy extendidos en el tiempo.

Durante las negociaciones, la empresa debe ser consciente de los riesgos implícitos en la formación de la futura asociación. Lo fundamental para la compañía es analizar profundamente cómo obtener los mejores resultados manteniendo en todo momento el control de sus ventajas, las consecuencias de la alianza a largo plazo, así como los beneficios inmediatos para ambas partes que puede aportar la relación.

Es imprescindible continuar el análisis profundo del candidato, sus motivaciones y capacidades, y mantener un alto grado de sensibilidad respecto a las prácticas culturales y comerciales de los empresarios de las partes implicadas. El decálogo del Cuadro 3 establece pautas razonables y prácticas para el desenvolvimiento de los actores de la negociación de la alianza.

Antes de entregar información reservada o valiosa, la empresa debe asegurarse la firma de un Acuerdo de Confidencialidad Recíproca que comprometa a las partes intervinientes en la negociación a la no difusión de lo negociado y, especialmente, que establezca la prohibición de dar a conocer a terceros cualquier aspecto relacionado con la producción, tecnologías, know-how, canales de distribución, precios, composición del capital de las sociedades, y cualquier otra información relacionada con las empresas, sus políticas y su gente.

Asimismo, teniendo en cuenta que al principio se genera un alto grado de entusiasmo en la posibilidad de que el nuevo emprendimiento otorgue a ambas empresas beneficios económicos adicionales, es importante dejar constancia de las pautas generales y posturas compartidas respecto al futuro negocio mediante una Carta de Intenciones formal.

Durante los encuentros se debe discutir profundamente la forma en que la alianza culmine como una batalla con dos grandes ganadores: cada una de las partes (lo que los anglosajones denominan *integración win-win* y *distribución zero-sum*). Si cada una de las partes mantiene una posición dominante durante la negociación, se corre el riesgo de que la relación se dañe o que queden pequeños beneficios para la otra parte, lo que provocará la pérdida de interés en la formación de la asociación.

Las cuestiones a tener en cuenta en la negociación (dejamos por ahora de lado los aspectos jurídicos) son, según Lewicki y Litterer (1985), las siguientes:

- La forma de interdependencia
- Detección de posibles ocultamientos o dimensionamiento de la apertura de las partes
- Las utilidades subjetivas (consideraciones culturales)
- La representatividad de los negociadores (autoridad)
- La dinámica en las relaciones de negociación
- La influencia de los observadores externos (analistas del mercado, y la discreción respecto a la información)
- El intercambio de información y las definiciones comunes

- El protocolo en el intercambio de propuestas
- Los bienes tangibles e intangibles (softwares, I+D, marcas, ingeniería, etc.).

Se podría complementar con lo siguiente:

- Aportes: Forma y momento de los aportes de cada uno de los futuros socios a la nueva sociedad y su efectiva valoración: dinero, edificios, instalaciones, materiales, propiedad industrial, know-how, derecho de utilización de un predio, herramientas y utillajes, etc.
- Coeficiente de Equidad: Forma en que se dividirá la estructura o mecanismos de poder o influencia en las decisiones de la Joint Venture (50/50 - 49/51 - 30/70 - etc.).
- Lugar de establecimiento de la empresa.
- Funciones de la Dirección: Aportes de cada parte en la integración de la dirección (marketing, personal, finanzas, contabilidad, etc.).

Si es oportuno, en virtud de la forma en que se esté llevando a cabo la negociación y si no ha de generar conflictos entre las partes, sería aconsejable desarrollar, en esta etapa, las principales líneas de la estrategia general de la futura empresa, que englobará en un único plan los principales objetivos, políticas y acciones a desarrollar en el momento de la conformación de la Joint Venture. Este plan podría comprender:

- Propósito de la Joint Venture: Detallada descripción de la misión corporativa o propósito/razón de la existencia de la empresa.
- Objetivos: Detallada descripción de qué es lo que quiere lograr la empresa y cuándo se obtendrán los resultados de esos objetivos.
- Estrategia: Detallada descripción de las secuencias y etapas que la empresa desarrollará a fin de lograr su Misión y Objetivos. Cómo se maximizarán las ventajas competitivas y cómo se minimizarán las desventajas competitivas.
- Políticas: Desarrollo de una guía de las principales decisiones a tomar, expresando los límites dentro de los cuales cada acción debe ser llevada a cabo.

Formación de Joint Ventures Internacionales   31

> 1. Identifique a la parte negociadora. En algunos países, en la negociación participan diversas personas, no todas ellas con el mismo poder de negociación.
> 2. Seleccione el intérprete cuidadosamente. El intérprete debería entender de qué se está hablando para poder transmitir e interpretar adecuadamente los términos de la negociación.
> 3. No deje nada por negociar. Todos los riesgos y temores deben quedar razonablemente cubiertos y disipados.
> 4. Nunca es demasiado tarde para romper. Sólo cuando se firma el acuerdo de Joint Venture es demasiado tarde.
> 5. Valore las consecuencias de la ruptura. En ocasiones, hay riesgos que son intrínsecos al país. O se aceptan o mejor no empezar. Una ruptura a tiempo puede suponer volver a empezar con otro socio.
> 6. Tome el tiempo que necesite. Aunque en ocasiones las decisiones tengan que tomarse bajo presión.
> 7. Tenga paciencia ante los retrasos. En algunos países, la negociación de contratos es un proceso especialmente lento.
> 8. Respete las formas y los aspectos culturales de la otra parte.
> 9. Permanezca atento. Conocer las necesidades de la otra parte es un activo muy poderoso.
> 10. Enfatice las ventajas para la otra parte y cree un ambiente de mutua confianza y respeto. De esta manera, se establecen los cimientos para una Joint Venture duradero.
>
> Fuente: Collado (1997)

Cuadro 3. Decálogo de la Negociación de una Joint Venture

1.4. Etapa de Joint Venture

1.4.1. Definición Contractual de la Joint Venture

En la formación de una Joint Venture Internacional la definición contractual presenta una extraordinaria importancia. Es un tema que ha de ser desarrollado por especialistas jurídicos y consultores especializados en la materia en virtud de las diferentes características, objetivos y términos que las partes en proceso de alianza y el derecho nacional de cada país impone al respecto. En general, las Joint Ventures tienen una dificultad adicional, en relación a otros tipos de contratos, porque se trata de acuerdos contractuales simultáneos entre dos o más empresas y separadamente, la creación de una nueva entidad legal o sociedad con sus propios propósitos. Por ese motivo, no es posible determinar un modelo único de contrato. Aquí se brindan algunos de los aspectos más relevantes de la definición contractual de este tipo de alianzas.

Desde un punto de vista jurídico, los pasos principales para la constitución de una Joint Venture son:

1.4.1.1. Confección y Firma del Contrato Principal y Accesorios

En algunos casos, los acuerdos desarrollan extensas descripciones de las voluntades, obligaciones y disposiciones de las partes; en otros, se realizan con escasas prescripciones formales o sólo con la constitución de una sociedad conjunta.

Cada alianza es un caso diferente. En términos generales, el contrato de Joint Venture debe reflejar de la manera más clara y detallada posible los propósitos y conclusiones a las que las partes llegaron en la negociación, teniendo en cuenta la línea particular del negocio de que se trata, las circunstancias, los preceptos legales que las legislaciones de derecho público y privado establecen, así como los posibles beneficios que las administraciones ofrecen para la radicación de inversiones, capitales y emprendimientos. Usualmente las partes negocian y establecen más de un contrato para definir con precisión e independencia el alcance de sus voluntades:

A. Contrato Principal o Contrato Marco

- Identificación de las partes
- Objetivos de la Joint Venture
- Capital de la sociedad
- Objetivos del negocio
- Limitaciones a la transferencia de acciones
- Quórums en la Junta o en el Consejo de la sociedad
- Responsabilidad en la gestión y nombramiento de los cargos
- Forma de reparto de beneficios y pérdidas

- Forma de resolución de disputas o conflictos
- Determinación del Idioma (y qué idioma prevalecerá)

B. Contratos Complementarios

Como Anexo del Contrato de Joint Venture se pueden establecer distintos tipos de acuerdos con fuerza contractual con el objeto de reforzar y hacer operativo el contrato principal, así como especificar los términos de las conclusiones alcanzadas en la etapa de negociación:

- Acuerdos de Confidencialidad
- Acuerdos de transferencia de tecnología/know-how
- Acuerdos de inversiones
- Acuerdos de producción
- Acuerdos de aprovisionamiento
- Acuerdos de exclusividad comercial
- Acuerdos sobre el tipo de cambio
- Acuerdos de delimitación de zonas comerciales
- Acuerdos de servicios (entrenamiento, capacitación, supervisión, puesta en marcha de planta, etc.)
- Acuerdos financieros
- Garantía de veracidad de determinadas afirmaciones o datos facilitados por las partes, etc.
- Acuerdo o Pacto sobre la Estrategia a largo plazo de la empresa (principales objetivos comerciales, políticas específicas y acciones).

De todos modos, los acuerdos de Joint Venture tienen como característica general su constante revisión durante el transcurso del tiempo. Tienden a ser extremadamente dinámicos y abiertos. Esto es razonable porque se trata de relaciones nuevas en donde la experiencia y el tiempo va marcando nuevos horizontes y nuevos objetivos conjuntos.

1.4.1.2. Constitución de Sociedad Mercantil

Constituir en el país anfitrión una sociedad mercantil con personería jurídica autónoma, con los requerimientos de registro y responsabilidad que se establezca (sociedad anónima, sociedad comanditaria, sociedad de responsabilidad limitada, sociedad de capital variable, etc.), y que responda a las normas vigentes de derecho comercial del mismo.

1.4.1.3. Permisos Administrativos para Funcionar

El país y región de la parte anfitriona determina las modalidades administrativas a cumplir, a fin de que los actos jurídicos y mercantiles de la organización creada tengan plena validez y la Joint Venture pueda gozar, en su caso, de los privilegios que las políticas de promoción nacionales o regionales pudieren otorgar.

1.4.2. Principales Disposiciones Legales para la Formación de Joint Ventures en la Región de Shenzhen (China). Caso Práctico

Por tratarse de una Zona de Economía Especial (ZEZ), las empresas que se establecen en la región gozan de una serie de beneficios especiales: reducciones fiscales, utilización de terrenos públicos, incentivos en derechos de importación, etc.

Según sus disposiciones legales, el contrato de Joint Venture es un acuerdo jurídico mediante el cual ambas partes invierten y dividen beneficios o pérdidas en proporción a las inversiones realizadas. Los contratos deben contener los siguientes elementos:

1. Nombre de las partes, domicilio comercial, domicilio legal y nombre del representante legal, nacionalidad.
2. Nombre de la empresa conjunta, domicilio, objetivos de las actividades y dimensiones de la empresa, dimensiones del terreno a utilizar.
3. Monto total de la inversión, capital registrado, contribución de capital por cada una de las partes, y provisiones de capital por períodos.
4. Equipos importantes y tecnología que se utilizará y su origen.
5. Forma de compra de materias primas y forma de venta de los productos.

6. Responsabilidad de cada parte en los trabajos preparatorios, construcción, producción, operaciones, etc.
7. Tiempo límite de la Joint Venture, procederes para el cómputo, finalización, división del capital ante la terminación de la Joint Venture.
8. Principios de la contabilidad, auditoría y finanzas.
9. Provisiones respecto a la gerencia de la empresa, salarios, beneficios sociales, protección de los trabajadores, seguros, etc.
10. Organización, duración de los mandatos y responsabilidades de la Junta de Dirección.
11. Forma de seleccionar al Director General y sus asistentes, personal de la organización y sus responsabilidades.
12. Limitaciones de responsabilidades y formas de división de los beneficios y pérdidas.
13. Garantías y responsabilidades por la ruptura del contrato.
14. Acuerdo de arbitraje u otras formas de resolución de conflictos.
15. Tiempo y lugar de ejecución del contrato.
16. Otras provisiones que las partes consideren necesarias.

Como se ha afirmado anteriormente, cada país o grupo regional establece los procedimientos y formalidades para la presentación de una Joint Venture, a fin de que ésta tenga pleno reconocimiento dentro de su estructura legal y administrativa en la nación y región donde operará empresarialmente. Algunos países prescinden de todo tipo de trabas burocráticas, a fin de facilitar la radicación de nuevos emprendimientos, pero otros, como China, mantienen exigencias estrictas para su registro. No atenerse a dichos preceptos es un impedimento para desarrollar actividades absolutamente necesarias para la vida de la empresa como: empleo de trabajadores del país, apertura de cuentas bancarias, importación de materiales libre de derechos aduaneros, obtención de líneas telefónicas, realizar publicidad, obtención de visado de múltiples entradas, alquilar una oficina o nave comercial, etc. En este caso, para obtener un Registro de Joint Venture en China se debe enviar al Ministerio de Cooperación Internacional y Comercio Exterior Ministry of Foreign Trade and Economic Co-operation (MOFTEC) un *dossier* completo de las aspiraciones empresariales en ese país, que incluya:

- Presentación de la propuesta
- Estudio de viabilidad comercial
- Estudio de viabilidad financiero o técnico (certificado por las autoridades competentes en China y que demuestre que el proyecto se enmarca dentro de las prioridades de esta nación)
- Referencias bancarias o de instituciones financieras
- Lista de candidatos a la Junta de Dirección de la empresa
- Contrato de Joint Venture o acuerdos comerciales. El contrato debe incluir la siguiente información:

  – Particularidades de la entidad y de los representantes que participan en el contrato.
  – Nombre de la Joint Venture, domicilio legal, propósitos y objetivos empresariales.
  – Inversiones, proporciones de las contribuciones de cada participante, forma de contribución, lista de contribuciones, estipulaciones relacionadas a las contribuciones, distribución de las acciones entre las partes de la sociedad.
  – Lista de la Junta de Dirección de la Joint Venture y las responsabilidades asignadas a cada miembro.
  – Capitales y tecnologías que se utilizarán.
  – Forma de aprovisionamientos y de distribución de productos.
  – Acuerdos de tipo de cambio.
  – Principios que se utilizarán en las finanzas, contabilidad y auditoría.
  – Políticas laborales.
  – Duración del emprendimiento.
  – Responsabilidades por ruptura del contrato.
  – Métodos de resolución de disputas.
  – Condiciones establecidas para la ratificación del contrato e inicio de las operaciones.

1.5. Etapa Operacional de la Joint Venture

Una vez que el contrato se ha firmado, la nueva sociedad se ha establecido y se ha puesto en marcha el negocio conjunto, comienza la etapa más dinámica de la Joint Venture, y es cuando se comprobará si todos los pasos anteriores han sido los correctos. El proyecto se ha convertido en una empresa operativa.

1.5.1. Organización y Seguimiento de la Relación

Uno de los aspectos principales de esta etapa es la implementación de la estrategia, analizada en las negociaciones preliminares e incorporada como acuerdo complementario al contrato marco o principal de la Joint Venture. El proceso mediante el cual se implementan las estrategias y las políticas se activa mediante el desarrollo de los programas específicos, presupuestos y procedimientos:

- Programas: Especifican paso a paso las secuencias de las acciones necesarias para obtener los principales objetivos de la empresa.
- Presupuestos: Detallan los costes de cada uno de los programas.
- Procedimientos: Especifican paso a paso y detalladamente los trabajos específicos que se han de realizar para lograr los resultados estratégicos acordados.

Es necesario mantener una comunicación constante y honesta entre las partes a fin de asegurar la continuidad del éxito inicial. En lo posible, establecer encuentros regulares de evaluación de los progresos así como una planificación de acciones inherentes a las relaciones entre los niveles gerenciales de ambas compañías. De la misma forma que la relación crecerá habrá mayores oportunidades para mejorar la alianza con el objeto de encontrar una eficiente convergencia de recursos, capacidades y objetivos comerciales.

Esta comunicación, que puede complementarse por medios tecnológicos, también es importante para el desarrollo conjunto de nuevos proyectos industriales. En este sentido, Pallot (1997) afirma que actualmente existe en WWW una serie de herramientas muy interesantes de apoyo a empresas unidas por relaciones de cooperación empresarial o alianzas estratégicas situadas en sitios geográficamente lejanos, como por ejemplo: Prototipos Virtuales (basados en VRML) para evaluación remota de productos existentes o futuros; Sistemas Flujos de Trabajo Distribuidos que permiten mejorar la coordinación entre socios; Sistema de Gestión de Configuración

Distribuida y otros sistemas de gestión de información distribuida para compartir productos y procesos de información, coanálisis, co-simulación, codiseño o cualquier otro tipo de herramientas *groupwhere* que permiten la exploración y la aplicación de alternativas, y más comúnmente, compartir conocimientos basados en métodos que brindan la oportunidad de reutilizar experiencias de proyectos previos.

Las tecnologías de la información que facilitan trabajos cooperativos tienen una importancia estratégica para las empresas. Uno de los más sofisticados sistemas de comercio electrónico que actualmente existe es el denominado Sala Virtual de Ventas (*Virtual Salesroom*) que da la posibilidad a los consumidores de configurar los productos a su gusto. Los conceptos de Producto Modular, Sistemas de Gestión de Información Distribuida y Modelos de Productos Digitales hacen posible esta tecnología. A través de Internet será posible desarrollar prototipos virtuales utilizando estas técnicas que otorgarán elevados niveles de realidad y permitirán también un mejor análisis visual de los productos (imágenes tridimensionales), de las conductas, actitudes y auditoría de las características de los mismos.

1.5.2. Rol de la Gestión de la Joint Venture

Uno de los problemas que se presenta cuando se crea una nueva estructura de acción empresarial (como las que se crean dentro de una Joint Venture) es el nuevo rol que asume la gestión o dirección de la empresa. Generalmente, la gerencia de una empresa está acostumbrada a trabajar en términos jerárquicos, es decir, respondiendo a una estructura vertical o con aliados «pasivos» como sus clientes, administración pública, competencia, cámaras de comercio, etc, es decir que sus decisiones no afectan mayormente las relaciones cotidianas de la organización.

El ambiente de una Joint Venture es completamente diferente y los recursos humanos de dirección necesitan una destreza especial para desempeñarse con éxito dentro de la nueva estructura. Por tal motivo, generalmente las empresas tienden a establecer una estructura de decisiones de forma vertical o red y los gerentes deben desarrollar nuevos conceptos de trabajo:

- Aceptar que se trabajará con un menor control directo sobre las decisiones e información
- Brindar mayores servicios personales
- Establecer decisiones que pueden cambiar en cualquier momento por políticas corporativas de la alianza
- Convertirse en fuente de información
- Construir nuevos recursos
- Desarrollar la gestión a través de la confianza y las relaciones

El cambio de la gestión de estructura jerárquica por la estructura en red de la alianza hace que las competencias centrales se concentren internamente, y se orienten al exterior aquellas funciones que otros puedan gestionar o llevar a cabo con mayor eficiencia. Es preciso por lo tanto tener en cuenta esta nueva concepción de las funciones de los recursos humanos de la empresa, en donde debe destacar por su importancia específica el factor cooperación.

Otra de las grandes problemáticas en la gestión de una Joint Venture Internacional es el «factor cultural entrecruzado», es decir, si se trata de una empresa donde una de las partes es originaria de un país escandinavo y la otra de un país oriental asiático, seguramente, se presentarán en sus actividades de interrelación numerosos conflictos originados, precisamente, por la disparidad cultural que existe entre ambos. Por ejemplo, existen diferencias entre los valores individualistas occidentales en relación a los sacrificados valores del Confucionismo chino (como la armonía con la familia y con el grupo de trabajo). Las empresas occidentales tienen mayores posibilidades de éxito en las relaciones con las empresas de las ciudades de la costa de China porque allí los valores son más occidentales. Una forma de solucionar estos conflictos es mediante la implementación de cursos para los recursos humanos implicados en la gestión y dirección de la empresa, en donde se trabaje profundamente en las diferencias de tipo cultural, empresarial, lingüístico, etc., a fin de que ambas partes puedan interpretar los valores y comportamientos de su socio comercial.

Capítulo 2

Fuentes de Apoyo Financiero y Jurídico para la Formación de Joint Ventures Internacionales

2.1. Fuentes de Cooperación de la Unión Europea para la Formación de Joint Ventures

La Unión Europea es la organización internacional que más recursos económicos y financieros destina al mundo en concepto de cooperación internacional. En este sentido, tanto las empresas europeas como las de varias regiones y países del mundo tienen la oportunidad de beneficiarse de programas específicos que cubren diferentes tipos de necesidades relacionadas con los aspectos financieros, técnicos, promocionales y de consolidación de empresas de carácter multilateral.

La Unión Europea ha desarrollado políticas específicas para regiones prioritarias como los países de América Latina y Caribe; de la Región Mediterránea; con Europa del Este, Central y Oriental; con Países de Asia; África, etc. Una de las formas de implementar esa cooperación es facilitando la creación de negocios conjuntos y alianzas estratégicas, mediante apoyos financieros y técnicos. Otra, es la financiación de encuentros y misiones comerciales con el fin exclusivo de promover el intercambio de cooperación empresarial entre los participantes. Se puede decir que los medios de apoyo son múltiples, y en esta sección se analizarán algunos de los más importantes y las formas de acceso mediante Internet a la información necesaria para las empresas que deseen participar en estos tipos de programas.

2.1.1. Euro Info Centres (EICs)

http://europa.eu.int/en/comm/dg23/eoleweb/en/e-compo.htm
http://europa.eu.int/en/ comm/dg23/eoleweb/en/e-eole.htm
Información: eichdt@belgium.eu.net
Información: carmelo.calamia@dg23.cec.be

La Unión Europea ha establecido más de 259 Centros de Información que informan y asesoran a las empresas en todos los temas relacionados con las actividades comunitarias. Estos centros forman una red que funciona mediante un sofisticado sistema electrónico de comunicaciones, que une a los EICs entre sí y a todos ellos con la Comisión Europea en Bruselas, de esta forma los centros disponen de la información más actualizada y completa, y se cubren todas las áreas de interés para las empresas.

Los EICs se encuentran en todas las regiones de Europa, en el seno de las estructuras económicas existentes (cámaras de comercio, agencias de desarrollo regional, organizaciones socioprofesionales, entidades bancarias, etc.).

Están preparados también para asesorar a las empresas sobre facilidades existentes para la formación de Joint Ventures, contactos con socios potenciales, e incluso respecto a iniciativas relacionadas con programas de investigación y desarrollo tecnológico, y transferencia de tecnología. Estos son un excelente punto de partida para acceder a la información que necesita una empresa (de cualquier lugar del mundo) para acceder a programas específicos de cooperación empresarial europeos.

2.1.2. Oficina de Cooperación Empresarial / Bureau de Rapprochements des Entreprises (BRE)

http://europa.eu.int/en/comm/dg23/eoleweb/en/e-eole.com
Información: carmelo.calamia@dg23.cec.be

El BRE es un sistema que permite dar a conocer sus ofertas y demandas a las empresas de todo el mundo que buscan contactos en la Unión Europea, y/o empresas de la Unión que buscan contactos en el mundo.

Funciona con carácter no confidencial. Las empresas completan un perfil con los datos referidos a su actividad junto con el tipo de cooperación que desean obtener y lo envían a su BRE local o a la oficina central de Bruselas. A su vez estas ofertas y demandas son retransmitidas al resto de los corresponsales BRE, establecidos en todos los países de la Unión y en algunos países de Asia, América Latina y África.

Los corresponsales BRE de los países destinatarios difunden las peticiones a la prensa local, revistas especializadas, boletines, sus propias bases de datos, o en el sistema que juzguen más eficaz; una vez que se obtienen las contestaciones, éstas o bien son enviadas a la empresa peticionaria a través de su corresponsal local, o bien las empresas son puestas directamente en contacto entre sí.

Para enviar su propuesta, petición u oportunidad de negocio conjunto o cooperación empresarial puede contactar con los centros de información de la Unión Europea, delegaciones de la Unión Europea, o directamente remitir por fax el formulario del Anexo 1. Las peticiones permanecen en el sistema durante seis meses, una vez pasados los cuales la empresa es notificada de la finalización, ofreciéndosele la opción de renovar su demanda por el mismo período.

BRE es un programa de la Dirección General XXIII (DG XXIII) de la Comisión Europea y geográficamente abarca los siguientes países y regiones: Alemania, Francia (Reunión, Guadalupe, Martinica, Nueva Caledonia), Italia, Holanda, Bélgica, Luxemburgo, Reino Unido, Irlanda, Dinamarca, Grecia, España, Portugal, Suecia, Finlandia, Austria, Mónaco, Noruega, Suiza, Malta, Eslovenia, Turquía, Latvia, Lituania, Polonia, República Checa, República Eslovaca, Hungría, Rumania, Bulgaria, Ucrania, Bielorrusia, Moldavia, Federación Rusa, Georgia, Azerbaijan, Kazakhstan, Uzbekistan, Marruecos, Túnez, Egipto, Estados Unidos de América, Canadá, México, El Salvador, Costa Rica, Colombia, Venezuela, Ecuador, Perú, Brasil, Chile, Bolivia, Paraguay, Uruguay, Argentina, Chipre, Líbano, Israel, Territorios Ocupados, Jordania, Pakistán, India, Sri Lanka, Filipinas, China, República de Corea, Japón y Hong Kong.

2.1.3. Red de Cooperación Empresarial / Business Cooperation Network (BC-NET)

http://europa.eu.int/en/comm/dg23/eoleweb/en/e-eole.com
Información: carmelo.calamia@dg23.cec.be
Información en América Latina: postmast@eurocent.org.pe

BC-NET, red de consejeros y de intermediarios creada por la Unión Europea para la búsqueda de socios comerciales a nivel regional, nacional, comunitario e internacional.

La red BC-NET permite identificar en forma gratuita a futuros socios, como resultado de una propuesta específica de cooperación que puede desarrollarse en todos los sectores de actividad y sobre cualquier tipo de cooperación (financiera, comercial, industrial y tecnológica). Las búsquedas se realizan en forma confidencial a través de un sistema de codificación.

El proceso de identificación de socios se inicia con una etapa de diagnóstico de la empresa y de su potencial desarrollo, elaborando un perfil de cooperación con las principales características del socio potencial. Este perfil se envía a Bruselas, donde se coteja con miles de demandas de cooperación, basándose en tres criterios: el tipo de cooperación, el sector y el área geográfica deseada. Una vez identificada una oportunidad comercial, que se ajusta a las necesidades del demandante, el consultor y el socio potencial son informados y pueden reunirse para tratar directamente las posibilidades de negocio detectadas. Por último, el consultor BC-NET también puede prestar asistencia en todas aquellas cuestiones jurídicas, fiscales o técnicas que se presenten al concluir el acuerdo.

Actividades de interés para BC-NET:

- Joint Ventures de distribución comercial
- Joint Ventures para infraestructuras logísticas con el fin de disminuir costes de aprovisionamientos mediante compras compartidas
- Cesiones o adquisiciones de licencias de utilización de marcas
- Creación, ampliación o formación de franquicias comerciales
- Introducción en nuevos mercados
- Adquisición de imagen de marca
- Adopción o transferencia de tecnologías

- Participación financiera en otra empresa
- Asociaciones interempresariales para la participación conjunta en licitaciones públicas
- Búsquedas de socios para participación en programas de la Unión Europea

BC-NET es un programa de la Dirección General XXIII (DG XXIII) de la Comisión Europea.

2.1.4. Europartenariat

http://europa.eu.int/es/comm/dg23/news23.htm
Información: carmelo.calamia@dg23.cec.be

Los Europartenariats son encuentros empresariales bianuales entre empresas de la Unión, que han sido diseñados por la Comisión Europea para potenciar el desarrollo de las regiones menos favorecidas. Estos encuentros tienen como principal objetivo estimular a las empresas de la Unión Europea, de la AELC, de Europa Central y Oriental, del Mediterráneo y del Mercosur a establecer relaciones de todo tipo, sobre todo tecnológicas, comerciales y financieras con sus homólogas en estas regiones. Los encuentros se realizan dos veces al año y su duración es de dos días. A los mismos concurren las empresas de la región anfitriona seleccionadas por la Comisión Europea y los empresarios de todas partes del mundo que estén interesados en el desarrollo de actividades de cooperación empresarial con compañías de la región anfitriona.

La iniciativa Europartenariat es un proyecto conjunto de la Dirección General de Políticas Regionales (DG XVI) y la Dirección General de Política de la Empresa, Comercio, Turismo y Economía Social (DG XXIII) de la Comisión Europea.

2.1.5. Iniciativa de Fomento de la Cooperación entre Empresas y Servicios en Europa (INTERPRISE)

http://europa.eu.int/es/comm/dg23/news23.htm
Información: carmelo.calamia@dg23.cec.be

El principal objetivo de Programa Interprise es apoyar las acciones locales, regionales y nacionales de la Unión Europea con el propósito de estimular la cooperación y la asociación entre empresas situadas en cualquier lugar de Europa.

Los encuentros, a efectos de permitir un mejor conocimiento y una negociación adecuada, se realizan de forma personalizada y previamente convenida, centrando la atención en un aspecto determinado de la industria. Los proyectos deben incluir de quince a veinte empresas procedentes de al menos tres regiones de los estados miembros, y en algunos casos pueden ampliarse a otras regiones de países extra-comunitarios de Asia, África o América Latina.

El apoyo que ofrece la UE para la organización de tales encuentros se limita a un 50% del presupuesto, hasta el límite de 50.000 ECUs.

Cada proyecto se presenta como resultado de la iniciativa local de un organismo, que puede ser cámara de comercio e industria, agencia de desarrollo local, regional o nacional, centro europeo de innovación, centro europeo de información empresarial, BC-NET, BRE, centro de investigación y desarrollo tecnológico o consejeros privados. Estos organismos locales son los encargados de sacar adelante los proyectos, que tienen que ser presentados ante la Comisión Europea con una antelación de nueve meses antes de la fecha fijada para la celebración del encuentro.

INTERPRISE es una iniciativa de la Comisión Europea (DG XXIII/B2).

2.1.6. *Programa Europeo para la Financiación de Joint Ventures / European Community Investment Partners (ECIP)*

http://europa.eu.int/en/comm/dg1b/programmes.hml
http://europa.eu.int/en/comm/dg23/guide_en/ecip.htm

El ECIP es un instrumento de la Comisión de la Unión Europea, diseñado especialmente para financiar la creación de Joint Ventures entre empresas de la Unión Europea y empresas de América Latina, Región Mediterránea, Medio Oriente, Asia y Sudáfrica. Asimismo, sirve para el apoyo de programas de infraestructura privada y privatizaciones en las regiones indicadas.

El Programa ECIP financia cinco etapas del proceso de gestación y realización de la inversión a través de las denominadas «Facilidades». La financiación del proyecto puede tomar diferentes formas, dependiendo de la fase de que se trate:

- Subvenciones para la identificación de socios potenciales y proyectos.
- Anticipos sin intereses para la realización de estudios de viabilidad y otras acciones de preparación de la Joint Venture.
- Préstamos sin intereses para la capacitación de los recursos humanos de la Joint Venture.
- Participación en el capital de la empresas o préstamos participativos para la inversión en la Joint Venture.

La Financiación ECIP cubre hasta un máximo del 50% de los costes relativos a los estudios de viabilidad o programas de formación de personal, y puede significar hasta un 20% del capital de la empresa. El total de la ayuda acumulada por proyecto puede llegar hasta 1 millón de ECUs.

Las empresas interesadas en obtener información completa respecto a las subvenciones o posibilidades de financiación deben dirigirse a cualquier Centro Europeo de Información, delegaciones de la UE, a las instituciones financieras aprobadas por la Comisión Europea para el Programa ECIP, o enviando por fax el formulario del Anexo 2 a la Unidad de Asistencia Técnica del Programa, o en el Sitio Web cuyo URL figura arriba.

El Programa ECIP fue creado en el año 1988 por la Dirección General de Relaciones Exteriores (DG IB/D3) de la Comisión Europea y abarca geográficamente los siguientes países y regiones: Argentina, Argelia, Bangladesh, Bolivia, Chipre, Brunei, Brasil, Egipto, Bhutan, Chile, Consejo de Cooperación de los Países del Golfo, Camboya, Colombia, Irán, China, Costa Rica, Israel, India, Cuba, Jordania, Indonesia, Ecuador, Líbano, Laos, El Salvador, Malta, Macao, Guatemala, Marruecos, Malasia, Honduras, Territorios Autónomos de Palestina, Maldivas, México, Territorios Ocupados, Mongolia, Nicaragua, Siria, Nepal, Panamá, Túnez, Pakistán, Paraguay, Turquía, Filipinas, Perú, Yemen, Singapur, Uruguay, Sri Lanka, Venezuela, Tailandia, Vietnam y República de Sudáfrica.

2.1.7. Iniciativa ADAPT

http://europa.eu.int/en/comm/dg23/eoleweb/en/e-eole.com
Información: sigloxxi@arrakis.es

El propósito de la iniciativa ADAPT es facilitar la adaptación de los trabajadores al cambio y a las transformaciones industriales, mejorar la competitividad mediante la formación práctica, prevenir el desempleo a través del aumento de la profesionalidad de la mano de obra y posibilitar la creación de nuevos puestos de trabajo.

La iniciativa ADAPT se ha creado como complemento de la Iniciativa PYME de la UE, mediante la potenciación de los recursos humanos, obteniendo de ellos su máximo rendimiento y mejorando la calidad de la gestión de la empresa.

Las medidas elegibles de las que pueden beneficiarse las empresas son las siguientes:

- Identificación de los cambios en el entorno industrial.
- Elaboración de planes de modernización de las empresas.
- Creación de redes y Joint Ventures y sistemas de producción.
- Cooperación en nuevas áreas económicas.
- Asistencia para el desarrollo de nuevas iniciativas de empleo.
- Estudios referidos a la dirección y gestión de las empresas.

Todos los proyectos deben ser innovadores y disponer de una dimensión transnacional dentro del territorio de la Unión Europea.

2.1.8. Programa Phare de Joint Ventures / Joint Venture Phare Programme (JOPP)

http://europa.eu.int/en/comm/dg1b/programmes.hml
Información: jean-marie.magnett@dg18.cec.be

JOPP es un programa específico dentro de la Iniciativa de la Unión Europea PHARE (Polonia, Hungría: Ayuda a las Economías en Reestructuración) cuyo objetivo es desarrollar acciones de apoyo a la creación de Joint Ventures en los países del Centro y Este de Europa

Fuentes de Apoyo para la Formación de Joint Ventures Internacionales 49

(CEECs o PECOs) y de la Confederación de Estados Independientes (CEI) entre empresas de la Unión Europea y de la región CEEC. Otro de los objetivos buscados es la promoción de las inversiones de empresas europeas en el exterior.

A través de este programa la Comisión Europea apoya económicamente la realización de estudios de viabilidad, participa en la integración del capital de la Joint Venture, en acciones de capacitación de los miembros de la empresa, y brinda la información necesaria para su creación.

Los estados participantes en este programa son Albania, Bosnia-Herzegovina, Bulgaria, Eslovenia, Estonia, Hungría, Letonia, Lituania, Macedonia, Polonia, República Checa, Rumania y la Federación Rusa. Los principales beneficiarios del Programa JOPP han sido Polonia, Hungría y la República Checa, y los principales sectores implicados en la cooperación económica han sido: la producción industrial, bienes de consumo, servicios y sector agroalimentario. Casi el 70% de los proyectos aprobados han sido presentados por empresas con menos de 100 trabajadores, esto indica que la prioridad de la Comisión es apoyar a las empresas más pequeñas.

2.1.9. EU-USA Transatlantic Business Dialogue (TADB)

http://www.tabd.com
Información: sj2@skynet.be

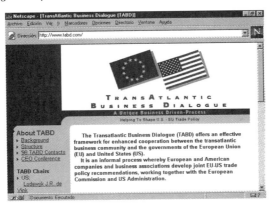

La Unión Europea y los Estados Unidos de América han encontrado una fórmula de cooperación recíproca dentro del marco de las políticas denominadas «Diálogo Trasatlántico de Negocios». Esta política tiene como finalidad ofrecer un entorno efectivo para el fortalecimiento de la cooperación empresarial y gubernamental entre las dos regiones. Se trata de un proceso informal que promueve, por un lado, el desarrollo de empresas y asociaciones de negocios conjuntas entre la Unión Europea y Estados Unidos (mediante actividades concretas como Europartenariats), y por otro, la cooperación en materia de políticas comerciales que afectan a los intercambios mediante el diálogo directo entre la Comisión Europea y la Administración de los Estados Unidos.

2.2. Programa para la Cooperación y Acciones Conjuntas entre Empresas de la Unión Europea y América Latina (AL-INVEST)

http://www.al-invest.org/
Información: al-invest@dg1b.cec.be

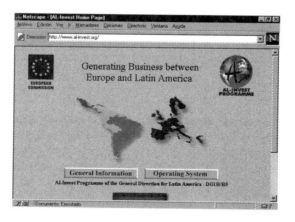

El objetivo general de AL-INVEST es favorecer el acercamiento y las transferencias de tecnología, pericia profesional y financiación, y generar negocios entre empresas europeas y latinoamericanas, de modo que ambas partes resulten beneficiadas.

A fin de posibilitar los flujos de apoyo financiero, técnico y comer-

Fuentes de Apoyo para la Formación de Joint Ventures Internacionales

cial, las regiones han establecido un conjunto de poderosas redes de operadores económicos europeos y latinoamericanos. Las redes europeas son la Red de Cooperación Económica (Coopeco), BC-NET, BRE y RIOST. Las redes latinoamericanas están integradas por la Red de Eurocentros (ECE), la Red BC-NET, la Red BRE, el Programa TIPS y el Programa ALABSUD.

Las empresas de ambas regiones pueden participar en actividades específicas de cooperación empresarial, formación de Joint Ventures, transferencia de tecnología, descubrimiento de socios comerciales, actividades de capacitación, etc. Las herramientas específicas de cooperación más importantes que este programa ofrece son: organización de encuentros sectoriales entre empresas de Europa y de América Latina y los encuentros de tipo Partenariat que desarrolla entre ambas regiones, como por ejemplo el Mercopartenariat dedicado a la formación de Joint Ventures y transferencia de tecnologías entre la UE y el Mercosur.

AL-INVEST es un Programa de la Comisión Europea, la Dirección General de Relaciones Económicas Externas y la Dirección para América Latina (DG1/B).

2.2.1. Red de Cooperación Económica con América Latina (Coopeco)

http://www.al-invest.org/
Información: alinvest@brusl.com

Es una red abierta especializada en la cooperación industrial con América Latina, que reúne a cientos de operadores (cámaras de comercio e industria, organizaciones patronales y profesionales, entidades financieras, agencias regionales, instituciones que actúan en el ámbito de la cooperación internacional, asesores especializados, etc.). En su mayoría, afiliados a las redes europeas de cooperación empresarial BRE y BC-NET y con representación en todos los países de la Unión.

Las empresas europeas pueden dirigirse a las organizaciones miembros de la Red a fin de solicitar información sobre el programa AL-INVEST y acciones de cooperación empresarial de la Unión Europea con América Latina. Las listas de los miembros y sus direcciones de correo electrónico están en el URL arriba indicada.

2.2.2. Red de Eurocentros (ECE) en América Latina

http://www.al-invest.org/pagece.htm
Información: al-invest@dg1b.cec.be

Bajo el auspicio de la Unión Europea se han constituido 30 centros de servicios empresariales repartidos por toda América Latina, con el objetivo de promover acciones de cooperación empresarial con empresas europeas. Estos operadores, denominados Eurocentros, ofrecen una amplia gama de servicios con la garantía de la experiencia y el conocimiento del tejido económico local.

Sus funciones son:

- Informar y sensibilizar a las empresas de las dos regiones acerca de las posibilidades de cooperación en el marco del programa AL-INVEST.
- Identificar operadores europeos interesados en la cooperación con empresas latinoamericanas.
- Proponer encuentros empresariales con financiación compartida con la Comisión Europea.
- Identificar las necesidades particulares empresariales y colaborar en la presentación de proyectos de cooperación industrial, búsqueda de oportunidades y contactos de negocios.
- Fomentar la creación de subredes locales con otros organismos de cooperación industrial.

Algunos miembros de la Red de Eurocentros son los siguientes:

- Fundación de Empresas (Córdoba - Argentina)
  Información: fundem@nt.com.ar
- Fundación Bolsa de Comercio de Mar del Plata (Argentina)
  http: www.argenet.com.ar/eurocentro
  Información: ricpol@argenet.com.ar
  Información: eurocen@argenet.com.ar

- Cámara de Comercio de Guayaquil (Ecuador)
  Información: camcomg@g.camcom.arg.ec

Fuentes de Apoyo para la Formación de Joint Ventures Internacionales 53

- Fundación para el desarrollo de Guatemala
  Información: fundesa@guare.net

- Fundación Empresarial Comunidad Europea - Chile (Euro-chile)
  Información: garenas@chilepac.net

- Fundación para la Inversión y Desarrollo de Exportaciones (Honduras)
  Información: eurohon@simon.intertel.hn

- Cámara Nacional Industria de Transformación (México)
  http: www.caligrafia.com/caligraf/eurocentro
  Información: ecmex@planet.com.mx
  Bancomext (México)
  Información: 74173.132@compuserve.com

- Bolsa de Subcontratación del Paraguay
  Información: bsp@bsubind.una.py

- Cámara de Comercio de Lima (Perú)
  Información: postmaster@eurocen.org.pe

- Conapri (Venezuela)
  http://lanic.utexas.edu/la/venezuela/conapri/venezuelanow.html
  http://reac.net.ve/conapri/venezuelanow.html
  Información: conapri@dino.conicit.ve

- Cámara de Industrias del Uruguay
  Información: eurocen@ciu.com.uy

- Instituto Nicaragüense de Desarrollo (INDE)
  Información: euronica@ns.tmx.com.ni

2.2.3. Red de la Asociación Latinoamericana de Bolsas de Subcontratación (ALASUB)

http://www.al-invest.org/

Información: alinvest@brusl.com

La Red ALASUB es una red de operadores especializados que integra a 13 bolsas de subcontratación latinoamericanas especializadas en la promoción de la cooperación industrial sectorial con una estructura similar a la Red Internacional de Organismos de Subcontratación (RIOST).

Estas instituciones propician el contacto entre las empresas europeas y latinoamericanas, a través de la participación en ferias especializadas y encuentros de empresarios, en materia de subcontratación de procesos y servicios industriales, tanto en Europa como en América Latina. Las bolsas también se encargan de las actividades de formación necesarias.

Su ubicación en asociaciones y cámaras industriales facilita la relación fluida con los empresarios locales, mediante el continuo intercambio de ofertas y demandas.

Los encuentros empresariales de subcontratación se celebran durante ferias sectoriales y las empresas interesadas en participar en el programa deberán ponerse en contacto con cualquiera de las bolsas asociadas a la Red ALABSUB, y deben proceder, como mínimo, de tres países distintos en Europa y uno en América Latina.

2.2.4. Sistema de Promoción de Informaciones Tecnológicas (Programa TIPS)

http://tips.org.uy
Información: tips@chasque.apc.org

Es una red de centros especializados repartidos por todo el mundo y, en particular, en América Latina. Sus objetivos generales son:

- Promover un crecimiento de las capacidades nacionales y colectivas de los países interesados en los intercambios comerciales y tecnológicos.
- Suscitar la cooperación técnica y económica entre los países en desarrollo, por un lado, y entre éstos y los países industrializados por otro.
- Incrementar las exportaciones en el sentido Sur-Norte.

Fuentes de Apoyo para la Formación de Joint Ventures Internacionales 55

Tips es una de las mayores redes de información comercial, tecnológica, financiera y de negocios que actualmente existe en América Latina. Posee varias herramientas de búsqueda en extensas bases de datos de esta región y de casi todo el mundo, y un servicio de difusión de oportunidades comerciales de tipo «empresa a empresa» a través de medios telemáticos e impresos muy eficientes.

2.3. Instituciones Financieras de Países Europeos para el Desarrollo e Inversiones de Cooperación con Mercados Emergentes

http://www.edfi.com/INDEX0.htm

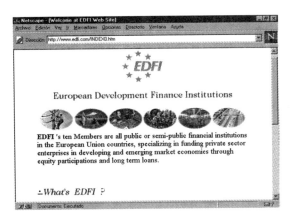

En muchos países de Europa existen instituciones nacionales y multilaterales que proveen recursos económicos, financieros y préstamos para empresas y Joint Ventures en mercados de países en vías de desarrollo. La asociación denominada Institución Europea para el Desarrollo Financiero (EDFI) está formada por 10 organizaciones financieras nacionales, entre ellas COFIDES de España, que en las páginas siguientes se detalla.

Los miembros de EDFI son:

- Austria: Finanzierungsgarantie-Gesellschaft mit Beschränkter Haftung (FGG) es una empresa y consultora estatal que provee garantías para proyectos de inversión nacionales e internacionales.
http://www.edfi.com/ch5/ch5-4.HTM
http://www.fgg.at/ - en construcción -

- Bélgica: La Corporación Belga para las Inversiones Internacionales (SBI/BMI) participa a través de préstamos en proyectos con África, Asia, América Latina y países del Centro y Este de Europa.
http://www.edfi.com/ch5/ch5-8.HTM

- Dinamarca: El Fondo para la Industrialización de los Países en Desarrollo (IFU) promueve inversiones y actividades económicas en países en vías de desarrollo a través de préstamos, garantías y participación en inversiones, en colaboración con la Agencia de Comercio e Industria de este país.
http://www.ifu.dk/

- Francia: La Compañía Francesa para la Promoción e Inversiones para la Cooperación Económica (PROPARCO) promueve y apoya la creación y expansión de empresas privadas en países en vías de desarrollo mediante participación en inversiones, créditos a medio y largo plazo, garantías financieras y servicios de consultoría.
http://www.cfd.fr/international/pres/proparco1.html

- Alemania: La Compañía Alemana para la Inversión y el Desarrollo (DEG) es una institución financiera y consultora cuyo objeto es promover las actividades del sector privado en África, Asia, América Latina y Europa Central y Oriental. DEG provee muchos servicios diferentes, como créditos, garantías, participación en inversiones, etc. En los últimos 35 años ha intervenido en más de 740 proyectos de 110 países.
http://www.deginvest.de/

- Italia: La Corporación Italiana para las Joint Ventures Internacionales (SIMEST) provee asistencia técnica a pequeñas y medianas empresas que invierten en países extranjeros.
http://www.edfi.com/ch5/ch5-9.HTM
http://www.simest.it/

- Holanda: La Compañía Holandesa de Desarrollo Financiero (FMO) es el banco de desarrollo de este país especializado en créditos y participación en capitales de empresas privadas de economías en transición y países en desarrollo. Son muy activos en África, Asia, América Latina y Europa del Este. En los últimos años han trabajado con 450 empresas de más de 65 países.
http://www.edfi.com/ch5/ch5-5.HTM

- Suecia: Swedfund International AB es una compañía de capital-riesgo estatal que, junto con empresas de este país, invierte en Joint Ventures industriales en África, Asia, América Latina y Centro y Este de Europa. En los últimos años ha participado en más de 80 Joint Ventures de 38 países.
http://www.swedfund.se/

- Reino Unido: Commonwealth Development Corporation (CDC) apoya a la inversión privada de muchos sectores británicos, mediante préstamos y participación minoritaria de capital. En 1996 ha participado en 393 negocios conjuntos de 54 países.
http://www.cdc.co.uk/

- Finlandia: El Fondo Finés para la Corporación Industrial (FINN-FUND) es una empresa de inversiones financieras que provee préstamos, garantías e inversión financiera compartida para empresas de mercados emergentes. Trabaja en conjunto con empresas finesas y extranjeras.
http://www.finnfund.fi/

- Suiza: La Organización Suiza para la Facilitación de Inversiones (SOFI) es una organización de promoción de inversiones en el exterior que ayuda a las empresas suizas a identificar oportunidades de negocio en países extranjeros y, a su vez, ayuda a empresas de países en desarrollo que buscan socios comerciales o financiación. SOFI provee servicios de promoción de inversiones e información, también brinda asistencia para encontrar *partners*, desarrollo de proyectos, identificación de fuentes de recursos e ingeniería financiera.
http://www.sofi.ch/

2.4. Fuentes de Cooperación Española para la Formación de Joint Ventures

2.4.1. *Dirección General de Política de las PYMEs (DGPYME)*

http://www.mcx.es/pyme/pyme
Información: infocx@ipyme.org

Este Sitio Web provee información sobre las diferentes políticas de cooperación empresarial exclusivas para empresas pequeñas y medianas dentro del marco de programas españoles y de la Unión Europea.

2.4.2. *Instituto Español de Comercio Exterior (ICEX)*

http://www.icex.es/
Información: icex@icex.es

El Sitio Web del Instituto Español de Comercio Exterior (ICEX) provee información sobre las exposiciones bienales de promoción de comercio y cooperación internacional entre empresas (Expotecnias), bases de datos (CD-EXPORT), SIBILA, repertorio de fabricantes españoles, etc.

2.4.3. *Agencia Española de Cooperación Internacional (AECI)*

http://www.rau.edu.uy/aeci/
Información: aeci@netgate.comintur.com.uy

Este Sitio Web de la Agencia Española de Cooperación Internacional (AECI), que está ubicado geográficamente en Uruguay, provee información sobre las diferentes políticas de cooperación de la AECI. Algunos programas están directamente relacionados con la creación de empresas conjuntas entre países iberoamericanos.

2.4.4. Red de Fundaciones Universidad-Empresa de España

http://www.mcx.es/redfue/inst.html

Las fundaciones Universidad-Empresa de España llevan a cabo la importante actividad de interrelacionar el mundo universitario y académico con la realidad de las empresas de productos y servicios. Estas fundaciones están unidas en red y desarrollan proyectos propios o participan como gestores o intermediarios en proyectos de la Unión Europea o de importantes instituciones españolas. En el Sitio Web que arriba se indica, se puede acceder a las direcciones de contacto de los miembros de la red: Asociación Universitaria Universidad-Empresa de Salamanca (Auesa); Centro Universidad-Empresa de la Cámara Oficial de Comercio, Industria y Navegación de Cantabria; Fundación Bosch i Gimpera de la Universidad de Barcelona; Fundación Empresa-Universidad de Alicante (Fundeum); Fundación Empresa-Universidad de Granada; Fundación Empresa-Universidad de la Laguna; Fundación Empresa-Universidad de Zaragoza (Feuz); Fundación Empresa-Universidad Gallega (Feuga); Fundación Empresa y Ciencia; Fundación Euskoiker; Fundación para el Fomento en Asturias de I.A. Investigación Científica Aplicada y la Tecnología (Ficyt); Fundación Universidad-Empresa de Madrid; Fundación Universidad-Empresa de Valladolid (Fueva); Fundación Universitaria de las Palmas.

2.4.5. Compañía Española de Financiación del Desarrollo (COFIDES)

http://www.cofides.es/ - en construcción -
Fax: +34 915610015

COFIDES es una sociedad anónima española de capital mixto que presta apoyo financiero a proyectos de inversión de empresas españolas en países menos desarrollados de América Latina, África, Asia y Europa Central y Oriental.

Esta organización facilita contactos entre inversores españoles y socios potenciales. Asesora a las empresas interesadas en realizar proyectos de inversión en otras regiones del mundo. Financia parcial, directa y/o indirectamente los proyectos de inversión que las empresas realicen en otras regiones del mundo. Proporciona apoyo institucional a las empresas españolas en los proyectos en que participan. Moviliza cofinanciación a largo plazo de la Unión Europea, de Instituciones Multilaterales de Desarrollo, de sus accionistas o de instituciones financieras locales para proyectos en los que intervienen. Colabora con el resto de las Instituciones Financieras de Desarrollo de países de la Unión Europea, agrupadas en European Development Finance Institutions (EDFI), en la ejecución conjunta de programas de promoción y en la cofinanciación de proyectos.

Gestiona programas de la Unión Europea como:

- European Community Investment Partners (ECIP)
- Joint Venture Phare Programme (JOPP)
- Banco Europeo de Inversiones (BEI)
- Centro para el Desarrollo Tecnológico Industrial (CDTI)

Asimismo, concede con fondos del Instituto de Crédito Oficial, tanto a los inversores españoles como a las empresas participadas por ellos, préstamos a medio y largo plazo que pueden cubrir una parte sustancial de las necesidades financieras del proyecto.

2.5. Fuentes Internacionales de Cooperación Empresarial, Financiera y Técnica

2.5.1. Instrumentos de Cooperación del Banco Mundial

El Banco Mundial tiene varias líneas de financiación y apoyo a la cooperación empresarial, pero generalmente actúa a través de los gobiernos y agencias gubernamentales. Actualmente, las más relevantes para las empresas que acuden por sus propios medios a este tipo de herramientas, son las siguientes:

a) Private Sector Development Department (PSD) - Banco Mundial

http://www.worldbank.org/html/fpd/psd/psd.html
Información: okarasapan@worldbank.org

El Departamento para el Desarrollo del Sector Privado (PSD) provee servicios de consultoría especializada a otras entidades del Grupo del Banco Mundial en una amplia gama de sectores relacionados con el sector privado, como impuestos administrativos, legislación laboral, políticas de competencia, exportaciones y políticas de comercio exterior, refuerzo de sistemas contractuales, normalización/patentes/derechos de propiedad intelectual e industrial, sistemas de regulaciones industriales, financiación de comercio exterior, programas de productividad, apoyo a empresas de pequeña escala, políticas tecnológicas, e infraestructuras para las privatizaciones y emprendimientos privados.

Este departamento posee cuatro unidades, denominadas: Grupo del Ambiente Comercial, Grupo de Servicios a las Privatizaciones, Grupo de Privatización y Reestructuración y Grupo para la Participación Privada en Infraestructuras. A través de sus páginas Web, las empresas e instituciones que lo deseen, pueden obtener valiosa información sobre los proyectos y políticas que este Departamento está desarrollando en todo el mundo.

Asimismo, ha establecido una estrategia específica para los países de la Ex Unión Soviética y los Países de Europa Central y Oriental (PECOs) denominada FundLine, que se describe a continuación.

b) FundLine - Banco Mundial

http:/www.worldbank.org/html/fpd/psd/fundline/fundline.htm?
Información: mroth@worldbank.org

FundLine es un recurso basado en Internet, creado por el Banco Mundial, su principal objetivo es ayudar a establecer vínculos recíprocos entre las empresas e instituciones que buscan socios y capital para invertir en Europa Central y Oriental o en la Ex Unión Soviética, y empresas de la región que buscan inversores y/o socios para proyectos conjuntos.

Se trata de una base de datos *on line* donde se describen las organizaciones que proveen fondos o créditos para inversiones en la región. FundLine está gestionada por el Departamento para el Desarrollo del Sector Privado del Banco Mundial.

c) International Finance Corporation - Banco Mundial

http://www.ifc.org

La Corporación Financiera Internacional (IFC) es uno de los miembros del Grupo del Banco Mundial y su objetivo principal es la mejora de la calidad de vida de la gente de países en vías de desarrollo. Actualmente, IFC es una de las más importantes fuentes del mundo en lo que respecta a préstamos y de financiación para proyectos del sector privado para países en desarrollo.

Esta institución financia y provee asesoramiento para Joint Ventures y proyectos de países en desarrollo en asociación con inversores privados; asimismo, ayuda a los gobernantes a crear las condiciones necesarias para estimular los flujos de inversiones. Particularmente, promueve el desarrollo económico mediante el crecimiento de empresas productivas y mercados eficientes de capital.

IFC coordina sus actividades con otras instituciones del Banco Mundial como IBRD, IDA y MIGA. Todas las empresas de países miembros del Grupo del Banco Mundial pueden recurrir a esta institución para solicitar información específica y en relación a los proyectos empresariales que quieran llevar a cabo en países en desarrollo.

d) *Agencia Multilateral de Garantía de Inversiones (MIGA) - Banco Mundial*

http://www.miga.org

La Agencia Multilateral de Garantía de Inversiones fue creada en el año 1988 como una respuesta inicial a la crisis de los años 80, y ante la convicción de los países acreedores de que las deudas de los países en vías de desarrollo podrían solucionarse a través de facilidades en las inversiones privadas. En la mayoría de los casos, los flujos de inversiones son posibles si ante una solicitud de crédito para un proyecto determinado existe una institución que garantice su devolución. MIGA tiene como principal función apoyar y aumentar la capacidad aseguradora de estas instituciones garantes mediante coseguros o reaseguros. Otras de las funciones son asegurar las inversiones en países en que por políticas se restringen o excluyen otros seguros, y dar servicio a inversores que no tienen acceso a seguros oficiales.

Pero sus funciones no sólo se limitan a esto, sino también a llevar a cabo investigaciones y actividades para promover los flujos de inversiones, diseminar información sobre oportunidades de inversión en países en vías de desarrollo, con el objetivo de mejorar las condiciones para atraer inversiones en estos países, y brindar asistencia técnica tanto al sector público como privado con relación a las formalidades de los proyectos de inversión y los seguros a estas actividades.

Las empresas que buscan oportunidades de inversión en países en desarrollo pueden solicitar información y contactos a través de este Sitio Web.

2.5.2. *Instrumentos de Cooperación Empresarial en Estados Unidos y Canadá*

2.5.2.1 Overseas Private Investment Corporation (OPIC)

http://www.opic.gov
Información: info@opic.gov

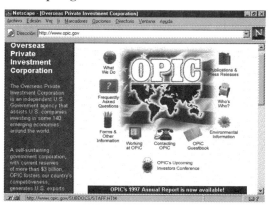

La corporación norteamericana de inversiones en el extranjero contribuye sustancialmente al crecimiento y fortalecimiento de la economía de este país, mediante la mejora de la competitividad de las empresas en los mercados internacionales. También, colabora con las naciones en desarrollo a expandir sus economías y encontrar mercados para productos y servicios en los Estados Unidos.

Desde su creación, en el año 1971, OPIC ha sido la agencia gubernamental americana que se ha encargado de la promoción de inversiones del sector privado en países en desarrollo y nuevas democracias emergentes. Actualmente, OPIC presenta programas para nuevas empresas y expansión de negocios en 140 países y regiones de todo el mundo.

Las actividades diseñadas para ayudar a los inversores americanos en el marco de las políticas de cooperación de OPIC, centradas en promover las inversiones y reducir los riesgos asociados a las mismas, son cuatro:
1. Financiación de negocios a través de créditos y garantías crediticias.
2. Apoyo a fondos de inversión privados para proyectos en el exterior.
3. Seguros de inversiones contra riesgos políticos.
4. Provisión de informaciones sobre oportunidades de negocio en el extranjero.

Los resultados de sus actividades han sido muy positivos tanto para la economía americana como para los países receptores de las inversiones. Desde su creación, OPIC ha apoyado inversiones por un total de 84 billones de dólares, y ha generado más de 43 billones de dólares en exportaciones, creando aproximadamente 200.000 puestos de trabajo en los Estados Unidos.

2.5.2.2. The Bulgarian American Enterprise Fund (BAEF)

http://www.baefinvest.com/
Información: baefsofia@aol.com

El Fondo para Empresas de Estados Unidos y Bulgaria (BAEF), es una corporación privada establecida por el Congreso americano en el

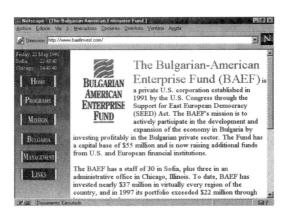

año 1991, a fin de apoyar la expansión del desarrollo y la economía húngara mediante inversiones en su sector privado.

A tal fin se han establecido dos instrumentos de cooperación empresarial:

1) Programa de Inversiones Directas: es una facilidad crediticia para financiación de deuda e inversiones participativas cuyo montante puede ir desde los 100.000 USD a los 7 millones de USD.

Entre 1996 y 1997 BAEF ha realizado el 83% de las acciones del programa, apoyando un total de 41 inversiones americanas en este país, principalmente, en el sector de negocios agrarios, manufacturas, construcción, viviendas y empresas financieras.

2) Programa de Pequeños Créditos: es un instrumento de apoyo a pequeñas inversiones. Dentro de este programa se han establecido tres subprogramas. Uno para inversiones en el sector hotelero de Bulgaria y que facilita préstamos de entre 30.000 USD a 800.000 USD. Hasta el momento se han realizado 45 inversiones en hoteles para turistas y empresarios en Bansko, Smolyan, Costa del Mar Negro y Sofía. Los otros dos programas incluyen los programas Nachala y Kompass, que proveen micro y pequeños préstamos para pequeños negocios.

Fuentes de Apoyo para la Formación de Joint Ventures Internacionales 67

2.5.2.3. Central Asian - American Enterprise Fund (CAEF)

http://www.caaef.com/
Información: us@caaef.com

El Fondo para la Empresa entre Asia Central y América (CAEF) promueve el desarrollo de la empresa privada norteamericana en Kazakstan, la República de Kyrgyz, Tadzikistán, Turkmenistán y Uzbekistán mediante operaciones de capital-riesgo por parte de firmas que quieren establecerse en la región.

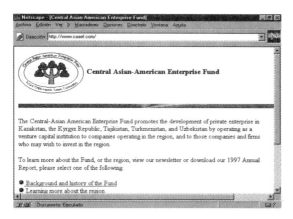

2.5.2.4. Export Development Corporation (EDC) Canadá

http://www.edc.ca/english_frame/risk/insurance_product/99-26.html
Información: export@edc4.edc.ca

La Corporación Canadiense de Desarrollo de las Exportaciones (EDC), a través de sus Instituciones de Desarrollo Financiero promueve las inversiones en países en desarrollo y las protege mediante seguros especiales para las inversiones. Estas facilidades, que se traducen principalmente en servicios de gestión financiera y de riesgo como seguros de crédito, financiación de ventas y garantías, son ofrecidas a las compañías canadienses que quieran establecer nuevas operaciones en el exterior.

2.5.2.5. The Canadian International Development Agency (ACDI-CIDA)

http://www.acdi-cida.gc.ca/
info@acdi-cida.gc.ca

La Agencia de Desarrollo Internacional de Canadá (ACDI-CIDA) es la principal institución de cooperación internacional de este país. Sus áreas prioritarias de acción son la mejora de las necesidades básicas de los países en desarrollo (salud, educación, planificación familiar, nutrición, asistencia sanitaria y agua); desarrollo de la mujer en el mundo; desarrollo de servicios de infraestructuras (electricidad y comunicaciones rurales); derechos humanos, democracia y mejora de la administración pública en el mundo; desarrollo del sector privado (promoción del desarrollo sostenible, micro empresas y pequeños negocios), protección del medio ambiente en los países en vías de desarrollo.

La Agencia CIDA ha establecido un programa específico para la cooperación empresarial [The Industrial Cooperation Program (INC)], que funciona con la participación del sector privado canadiense. Todos los proyectos financiados por el Programa INC se centran en los seis ámbitos prioritarios arriba descritos. Las empresas participantes deben tener una facturación anual de al menos 1 millón de USD.

En general el Programa INC apoya todo tipo de emprendimientos y Joint Ventures con empresas de países en desarrollo, con excepción de

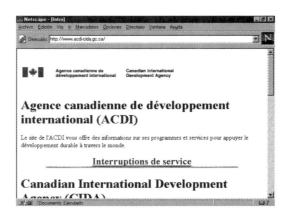

proyectos que tengan como único objetivo la apertura de nuevos mercados sin creación de riqueza en el país de destino (demostración de productos y servicios, actividades que se limitan al marketing, venta o exportaciones, establecimiento de agencias de servicios, proyectos preliminares de identificación de actividades, actividades especulativas (como exploración de minas o desarrollo inmobiliario), proyectos cuyo resultado no podría incluir la incorporación de mano de obra en el país de destino, proyectos relacionados con la energía nuclear, entre otros.

2.5.3. Agencia Alemana de Cooperación (GTZ)

http://www.gtz.de/home/english/index.html

La Agencia Alemana de Cooperación (GTZ) posee una extraordinaria capacidad de acción en todo el mundo y mediante múltiples herramientas. Uno de sus principales objetivos es promover la cooperación empresarial con los países en desarrollo, especialmente a través de capacitación y la formación de Joint Ventures. Según la asociación Alemana de Comercio Exterior, el 50% de las compras que realiza comercio minorista de este país, proceden de países o regiones donde GTZ coopera. Esto representa una gran oportunidad para fabricantes de América Latina, Asia, África y el Este de Europa para aumentar su posición en el mercado alemán y, a través de éste, de otros países europeos.

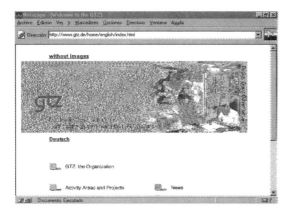

En el Sitio Web de GTZ se puede encontrar una ingente cantidad de información sobre programas y contactos relacionados con la cooperación internacional alemana en los diferentes sectores empresariales.

2.5.4. Instrumento de Cooperación del Banco Interamericano de Desarrollo - Programa Bolivar

http://netrunner.net/~uspboliv/
http://www.iadb.org/IDB/Texto/Xbusi.html
Información: uspboliv@netrunner.net

El Programa Bolivar (Red de Integración Tecnológica Regional) es una ambiciosa iniciativa que reúne a los países de América Latina y Caribe, América del Norte, Europa y Asia a través de proyectos directamente relacionados a la cooperación para integración tecnológica regional, y la innovación y competitividad industrial. Uno de los principales impulsores de este programa es el Banco Interamericano de Desarrollo (BID). Los interesados en promocionar sus propuestas de formación de Joint Ventures, y transferencia de tecnología o know-how pueden hacerlo a través de la Oficina Central del Programa, o de las 96 Oficinas Nacionales de Enlace, o de sus oficinas satélites (ubicadas estratégicamente en organizaciones empresariales y de fomento industrial). Asimismo, esta red ofrece apoyo jurídico, financiero y técnico para la definición de los proyectos.

2.6. Cuestiones Legales Relacionadas con Joint Ventures y Transferencia de Tecnología y Know-how. Fuentes de Información en Internet

A continuación el lector podrá encontrar una completa serie de puntos de información editados en Internet en donde se ofrece el acceso, mediante motores de búsqueda, a legislación local, nacional e internacional. La importancia de estas fuentes para la formación de Joint Ventures y transferencia de tecnología y know-how, está dada en la simplicidad de localización de los marcos jurídicos vigentes en los distintos países del mundo.

Federal Statutes, Codes and Regulations
http://www.ljx.com/Government/Test07.html

Government Resources
http://www.ljextra.com/Government/index.html

Federal Agencies
http://www.ljx.com/Government/Test03.html

Library of Congress
http://www.loc.gov/

Legislative Resources on the Internet (Thomas)
http://thomas.loc.gov

U.S. House of Representatives
http://www.ljextra.com/Government/Test05.html

International Law and Foreign Government Resources
http://www.ljextra.com/practice/internat/index.html

State Law Resources
http://www.ljx.com/Government/Test11.html

Fedworld
http://www.ljx.com/Government/Test10.html

SEC: Edgar Database
http://www.sec.gov/edgarhp.htm

The Law Library
http://library.ljextra.com

European Union Internet Resources
http://www.lib.berkeley.edu/GSSI/eu.html

The Federal Web Locator
http://www.law.vill.edu/Fed-Agency/

Find Law
http://www.findlaw.com

The Law Engine!
http://member.gnn.com/PeterC/laweng.htm

The Seamless Website (Law Related Resources)
http://seamless.com/

The Virtual Law Library Reference Desk
http://law.wuacc.edu/washlaw/reflaw/reflaw.html

The World Wide Web Virtual Law Library
http://www.charm.net/~web/Vlib/Users/Search.html

Comisión de Naciones Unidas sobre Legislación de Comercio Internacional / United Nations Commission on International Trade Law (UNCITRAL)
http://www.un.or.at/uncitral/

Law Resources on the Internet
gopher://marvel.loc.gov:70/11/global/law

Research Guides to Law Resources on the Internet
gopher://marvel.loc.gov:70/11/global/law/guides

Law-Related Discussion Group Archives
gopher://marvel.loc.gov:70/11/global/law/lists

Trade Law Home Page
http://ananse.irv.uit.no/trade_law/nav/trade.html

Franklin Pierce Law Center Home Page
http://www.fplc.edu/

Capítulo 3
Transferencia de Tecnología y Know-how

3.1. La Licencia como Forma de Explotación Comercial de un Patrimonio Tecnológico

La transferencia de tecnología es la «innovación» que una parte facilita a otra para que ésta la explote empresarialmente. Según Schumpeter (1961) la diferencia entre el concepto de «invento» e «innovación» está dada por una cuestión objetiva: mientras no se pone en práctica, un invento no tiene ninguna significación en el terreno económico.

La tecnología en su acepción más relacionada con las actividades de internacionalización de una empresa, es la aplicación de los conocimientos científicos a la técnica, a fin de obtener nuevos productos y servicios, o calidad superior, o precios más bajos, o menos tiempo de fabricación.

Por su parte, *know-how*, expresión inglesa que cuya traducción al español es «saber como» o «saber hacer», se refiere a las experiencias y conocimientos tecnológicos secretos, de tipo organizativo, financieros o de otra naturaleza, de que disponen determinadas personas físicas o jurídicas y que se hacen imprescindibles para el desarrollo de una cierta actividad o industria. Este concepto engloba la descripción de procedimientos de fabricación, recetas, fórmulas, modelos, diseños, planos, dibujos industriales, información y especificaciones técnicas, y servicios técnicos.

La transferencia de tecnología comprende, en forma genérica, la transferencia de innovaciones, el know-how, la franquicia y la consultoría. En términos jurídicos, la principal diferencia entre transferencia de tecnología (como innovación) y transferencia de know-how, radica en que la primera generalmente goza de un reconocimiento especial y protección de tipo administrativo (derecho intelectual o industrial en forma de patente), en cambio no siempre este reconocimiento recae sobre el know-how. Ambos pueden ser perfectamente transferibles a terceros mediante contrato de licencia, y el precio o compensación que paga el beneficiario de estos conocimientos se denomina royalty o regalía.

El contrato de licencia de tecnología hace posible que empresas poseedoras de una ventaja tecnológica ingresen con mayor rapidez y con menores riesgos financieros y legales a un mercado extranjero, que mediante la inversión directa de producción y operaciones en el exterior, o incluso, que la participación en una Joint Venture internacional. Asimismo, en muchos países del mundo la licencia de tecnología permite a las empresas obtener ventajas en derechos de importación y exportación, que no existirían si se exportase o importase el producto desarrollado con la aplicación industrial de esa misma tecnología.

Consecuentemente, las licencias son utilizadas para adquirir tecnología extranjera con el propósito de incrementar el activo tecnológico de una empresa, evitando o reduciendo los costes y el tiempo en investigación y desarrollo tecnológico necesarios para producir el producto o servicio en cuestión.

La licencia de tecnología no se limita al sector industrial. La franquicia es otra forma importante de licencia de tecnología utilizada por muchos sectores de servicios industriales. En las franquicias, el franquiciante (licenciante) permite al franquiciado (licenciado) el empleo de su marca o servicio bajo la condición de que sean utilizados de una manera específica. El franquiciante generalmente queda ligado al franquiciado en una relación en donde prevalece el apoyo en las actividades empresariales de promoción y publicidad institucional, contabilidad, capacitación permanente y en muchos casos, el aprovisionamiento de los productos que el franquiciado necesita para la explotación comercial de la empresa.

La licencia de tecnología como forma de exportación puede, en algunos aspectos, resultar negativa tanto para el licenciante como para el licenciado. Por ejemplo, el control sobre la forma de utilización de la tecnología y su eficacia es siempre menor y, en consecuencia, las licencias pueden producir menores beneficios que las exportaciones de los bienes o servicios. Asimismo, en ciertos países pueden existir problemas de copia, imitación o plagio a causa de inadecuadas o inexistentes políticas de protección de los derechos intelectuales e industriales.

Por esta razón, las legislaciones de muchos países acogen con mayor interés la transferencia de tecnología en el contexto de inversión directa más que a través de acuerdos de licencias puros y simples. Para la empresa que transfiere la tecnología como un aporte o inversión (en una Joint Venture, por ejemplo), esto ofrece un mayor control sobre la calidad y comercialización del producto final. También, una mejor posición para prevenir el uso no autorizado de la tecnología.

Para la empresa receptora de la tecnología (y para la legislación de muchos países anfitriones, adoptantes o receptores de tecnologías), la transferencia en este tipo de contexto, asegura que la empresa exterior tendrá un incentivo mayor para el control de la aplicación correcta de la tecnología adoptada y su utilización eficiente. Este tema está directamente relacionado con la gestión de las innovaciones, ya que muchas veces la introducción de nuevas tecnologías afecta a las estructuras de la organización de las empresas y a sus estrategias. El éxito de la transferencia de tecnología suele depender más de su correcta utilización que de las características propias de la misma. Es decir, que una buena tecnología puede ser inútil si no es empleada correctamente. A este respecto se refiere Archibugi y Michie (1994) afirmando que los conocimientos no son sólo específicos de cada empresa, sino también de cada país, y los costes derivados de su transmisión son muy altos aun cuando se trate de partes de una misma empresa. Los intentos de las empresas de explotar a escala mundial su potencial innovador sólo pueden resultar fructíferos si llevan aparejada una actividad directa en los países objeto de sus intereses, bien en forma de inversiones directas o creando Joint Ventures con firmas locales.

En muchos de los países importadores de tecnología, sus regulaciones tienden a perpetuar los derechos del adquirente una vez que se ha realizado la transferencia, por ejemplo, pasado el término de siete o diez años. En ese sentido, la tecnología y el know-how quedan en poder del licenciado; por lo tanto, el licenciante no puede restringir el uso de la licencia al momento de la finalización del contrato. Otros países dejan al arbitrio de las partes tanto los términos como las consecuencias del decaimiento del contrato de licencia.

La forma en que se organizan las empresas transferentes y adoptantes de tecnología puede, a veces, ser un punto de cuidadoso análisis a la hora de arribar a acuerdos de esta naturaleza. Un estudio realizado por Tyre (1991) revela que el tiempo de introducción e iniciación de las operaciones, una vez acordada la transferencia de tecnología, es sustancialmente más corto cuando los transferentes son empresas americanas que cuando éstos son empresas de la Unión Europea. La diferencia está dada en que los americanos capacitan muy bien a los recursos humanos que integran sus equipos de trabajo, tanto para identificar problemas asociados a las nuevas tecnologías, como para resolverlos.

En cierto modo, las problemáticas que enfrentan las empresas que transfieren tecnología a nivel internacional son parecidas a las que aparecen en los casos de formación de Joint Ventures Internacionales, particularmente: las secuencias o etapas para constituir el proceso de transferencia, relación entre la asimilación extranjera y sus capacidades de desarrollo, opciones de organización para la transferencia de tecnología, factores externos que afectan el desarrollo de capacidades tecnológicas (Cosumano y Elenkov, 1992). En las Joint Ventures destaca el problema de la asimilación de la nueva gestión empresarial, mientras que en la transferencia de tecnología, el problema está en la asimilación de los nuevos procesos tecnológicos.

3.1.1. *Valoración del Precio de la Tecnología y Know-how*

Sin duda, el valor de la tecnología, especialmente en la forma de know-how, es muy difícil de definir y ésta es una de las principales cuestiones que enfrenta quien compra o vende tecnología. El problema para el transferente (cedente, licenciante, exportador) es poder establecer un precio justo que contemple los esfuerzos realizados por la empresa en I+D técnico y tecnológico, el coste de oportunidad de no poder operar comercialmente en el país del receptor (si la licencia es en exclusiva) o no poder operar en otros países (si se contempla la posibilidad de exportación por parte del cesionario), los riesgos implíci-

Transferencia de Tecnología y Know-how 77

tos en la operación, etc. Generalmente, más aún si se trata de una empresa pequeña, a esto se le suma la falta de experiencia para identificar y codificar su know-how.

El problema para el receptor (cesionario, licenciado, importador) se centra, especialmente, en las lógicas dudas de que si el precio a pagar garantizará o no el retorno de inversión esperado por la tecnología adquirida y en las reales posibilidades de su empresa de llevar a cabo una utilización eficiente de la misma. El precio de la tecnología es en definitiva una compensación por el privilegio por parte del receptor de utilizar la tecnología.

3.1.2. Royalties o Regalías

Los pagos del precio por la tecnología transferida (royalties o regalías) se llevan a cabo mediante:

- Porcentaje sobre las ventas del producto.
- Porcentaje sobre el volumen de producción.
- Sistema ecléctico (una combinación entre ambas).

U otras formas de compensación como:

- Compromiso de aprovisionamiento (se transfiere la tecnología y como compensación la receptora se compromete a adquirir partes, materia prima y servicios de posventa al transferente)
- Transferencia cruzada (cambio de tecnología por tecnología)

A su vez, el porcentaje sobre ventas puede ser expresado en mercancías, en dinero, a precios de producción, o a precios de venta al público, o en la forma que las partes establezcan al contratar.

Asimismo, conviene tener en cuenta que además del precio establecido, suelen existir otros pagos vinculados a la tecnología transferida como: asistencia técnica, formación, capacitación, muestras, embarques de las muestras, etc. En algunos casos, maquinarias de fabricación, herramientas, utillajes, repuestos, suministros, etc.

Dentro del marco del contrato de licencia puede convenirse el momento de la realización del pago:

- Anticipo de un pago ante la recepción de la información y planos por parte del importador (*down payment*). A su vez se puede establecer que este pago inicial se realice en partes porcentuales: entrega de la documentación, fabricación, lanzamiento de las primeras unidades, etc.
- Pago por envíos (*payment after shipment*) ante el envío de muestras de productos.
- Pago por aceptación (*payment after acceptance*) una vez que haya transcurrido un período de verificación y el importador haya aceptado la tecnología transferida.

Sidro Cazador (1988) afirma que la primera cuestión que la receptora de la tecnología debe plantearse es conocer el plan de negocio para un horizonte temporal determinado, en función al tipo de tecnología, mercado, novedad del producto a introducir, vida útil de las patentes, etc. Períodos de 5 a 10 años pueden ser referencias válidas que, en cada caso, se deberán definir, teniendo en cuenta que no es lo mismo adoptar tecnología para resolver un problema puntual, que adoptar tecnología para la estructuración de un nuevo negocio. Es muy importante profundizar en la forma y cantidades del pago, a fin de equilibrar los beneficios de las partes haciendo posible la rentabilidad del proyecto.

3.1.3. Valor Equitativo de la Regalía en Transferencia de Tecnología y Know-how. Caso Práctico

- La compañía C cede tecnología a la compañía R para la fabricación y venta de maquinaria agrícola durante un período de 10 años.
- Las ventas estimadas son de 100 unidades a 5 M ptas./u. (precio actual).
- La fabricación será en el país de la receptora, pero se incorporarán un 20% de componentes de la cedente.
- Se establece que R pague a C una cantidad inicial de 10 M ptas., además de una regalía del 5% sobre ventas, descontando de las mismas los suministros de C a R.
- La asistencia técnica de C a R se estima en 2 M ptas., necesaria para conseguir la fabricación del equipo.

Transferencia de Tecnología y Know-how

- Los repuestos, que se estiman en un 30% de las ventas de equipos, se gravan con una regalía del 7%.

Compañía	Valor de los Equipos	Valor de los Repuestos	Total en M ptas.
R	400	120	520
C	100	30	130
Total	500	150	650

Ante este planteamiento, la compañía R ha de evaluar los pagos que, directa o indirectamente, va a satisfacer a la compañía C. Pues, como se verá, no son sólo los derivados por la transferencia de tecnología, sino que, además, aparecen (casi siempre) otros vinculados, que conviene inferir, para utilizarlos como instrumento de negociación, ya que en definitiva se trata de un beneficio que, vía tecnología, se va a generar en C.

Pagos por tecnología	**40,4 M ptas.**
• Pago inicial (*down payment*)	10 M ptas.
• Pago por regalía del 5% sobre el 80% de las 100 unidades	20 M ptas.
• Pago por regalía del 7% sobre el 80% de repuestos	8,4 M ptas.
• Pago por asistencia técnica	2 M ptas.
Pagos por margen comercial de suministros de C a R	**26 M ptas.**
• Comisiones por suministros de equipos del 20% (margen estimado)	20 M ptas.
• Comisiones por suministros de repuestos del 20% (margen estimado)	6 M ptas.
Beneficio estimado para C	**66,4 M ptas.**

De acuerdo con estos datos, puede obtenerse el valor de la regalía media equivalente:

Regalía Media Equivalente $\text{Req.} = \dfrac{66,4}{650} = 10,2\%$

En este caso la Req es sensiblemente superior a la pactada del 5 y 7 % para equipos y repuestos, respectivamente.

- En el supuesto de que R fabricase el 100% de los equipos y repuestos, la Regalía Media Equivalente sería de:

Regalía Media Equivalente $\text{Req.} = \dfrac{40,4}{650} = 6,2\%$
(Req) = 40,4/650 = 6,2%

- Pero véase ahora la incidencia que estas regalías tienen sobre el beneficio de R y C.

$$\text{Req.} = \dfrac{\text{Pagos a C}}{\text{Importe de ventas}} = \dfrac{\text{B° de R}}{\text{Ventas}}$$

Esta expresión podría escribirse como:

$$\text{Req.} = \dfrac{\text{Beneficios de R}}{\text{Ventas}} = \dfrac{\text{Beneficios de C}}{\text{Beneficios de R}}$$

O lo que es lo mismo, denominando:

$$\dfrac{\text{Beneficios de R}}{\text{Ventas}} = a \qquad \dfrac{\text{Beneficios de C}}{\text{Beneficios de R}} = z$$

Req = a × z. Donde z: $z = \dfrac{\text{Req}}{a}$

En este caso, estimando en un 20% el beneficio de R sobre las ventas (a = 0,2) supone:

$$z = \dfrac{10,2}{0,2} = 51\% \qquad \text{(para el primer caso) y de}$$

$z = \dfrac{6,2}{0,2} = 31\%$ (en el caso de que R fabricase el 100% de los equipos y repuestos).

Es decir, en esta operación C participa en un 51% de los posibles beneficios de R y, en el caso de que R llegase al 100% de la fabricación, este porcentaje quedaría en un 31%.

Esto da la idea de cómo C puede obtener, sin riesgo, unos importantes beneficios adicionales que suponen, en este caso, entre un 30-50% del beneficio de R.

Según se pudo apreciar, la participación de C sobre el beneficio de R es mucho mayor cuanto menor es el beneficio de R. Por eso, es muy importante para R afinar sobre las regalías que puede soportar su negocio, sobre todo cuando se espera una baja rentabilidad, pues bien pudiera ocurrir que de todo el beneficio de R, recibiera C la mayor parte (80-90%). Como regla general, es tan importante analizar la distribución de los beneficios, como el valor absoluto de los mismos.

Distribución de Beneficios entre la Adquirente (R) y Exportador (E) según el Valor de la Regalía y el Margen de la Adquirente en el Negocio

Beneficio de R sobre Ventas (a %)	Participación de C en los Beneficios de R (z%)				
Margen	Regalía 1-2 (%)	Regalía 2-3 (%)	Regalía 3-4 (%)	Regalía 4-5 (%)	Regalía 5-6 (%)
10 - 20 (%)	3-10	10-30	15-40	20-50	25-60
20 - 30 (%)	5-20	7-15	10-20	13-25	17-30
30 - 40 (%)	2,5-7	5-10	7,5-13	10-17	12,5-20
40 - 50 (%)	2-5	4-7,5	6-10	8-12,5	10-15
50 - 60 (%)	1-4	3-6	5-8	6-10	8-12
60 - 70 (%)	1-3	2-5	4-6	5-8	7-10

Fuente: Sidro Cazador (1988)

3.2. Fuentes Internacionales y Universitarias de Cooperación para la Transferencia de Tecnología e Investigación y Desarrollo Tecnológico

3.2.1. Transferencia de Tecnología e Investigación y Desarrollo Tecnológico en el Marco de la Cooperación de la Unión Europea

En los últimos años la Unión Europea ha dedicado una especial atención a los diferentes aspectos que entraña el fomento de la investigación y el desarrollo tecnológico. Uno de los mayores retos, de cara al siglo XXI, es el revertir la escasa importancia que el grupo asigna a la explotación comercial (y aplicación industrial) de los resultados de las políticas de investigación y desarrollo tecnológico (Comisión Europea, 1994).

Dentro de los programas de la Unión Europea para la transferencia de tecnología e investigación y desarrollo destacan CORDIS, con toda una serie de programas y servicios alternativos, y los Programas Marco (FP4 y FP5).

A continuación se adjunta una relación de los principales programas de la Unión Europea, en muchos de los cuales es posible la participación directa o indirecta de empresarios e investigadores de países no europeos). Junto con la definición de las iniciativas, se incluyen las formas de contacto vía Internet. En muchos casos se puede acceder directamente, no sólo a la información pertinente, sino también a los formularios necesarios para la participación en dichos programas.

3.2.1.1. Servicio de Información de la Unión Europea para la Investigación y el Desarrollo / The Community Research and Development Information Service (CORDIS)

http://www.cordis.lu/
Información: helpdesk@cordis.lu

CORDIS provee un simple y ágil acceso a muy buena información sobre los sectores de I+D e Investigación Tecnológica de la Unión Europea. Edita un Sitio Web con acceso *on line* a varias bases de datos de excelente nivel y acceso gratuito:

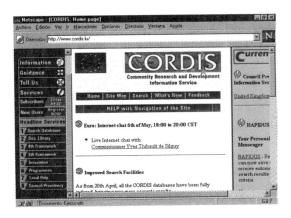

- **Base de Datos R&D-News:** Es un periódico de noticias sobre todas las actividades de la Unión Europea de I+D, ciencia y tecnología. Incluye invitaciones para presentación de proyectos, concursos, legislación y políticas, eventos, publicaciones, etc. Es de renovación diaria y se edita en inglés, alemán y francés.
- **Base de Datos R&D-Programmes:** Provee información detallada de aproximadamente 500 programas de la Unión Europea, en trámite y/o finalizados relacionados con I+D científico, técnico y tecnológico.
- **Base de Datos R&D-Partners:** Es un servicio de apoyo para la búsqueda de socios para la participación en proyectos de la Unión Europea relacionados con programas de todo tipo, especialmente de investigación y desarrollo tecnológico, explotación comercial de las tecnologías y nuevas tecnologías de la información.
- **Base de Datos R&D-Projects:** Información sobre proyectos individuales que se llevan a cabo bajo el marco de programas de I+D de la Unión Europea.
- **Base de Datos R&D-Results:** Provee acceso a información sobre resultado de investigaciones susceptibles de explotar comercialmente, así como oferta de tecnología obtenida mediante programas de la Unión Europea y otros programas no-comunitarios. Es un excelente recurso para la búsqueda de apoyos tanto públicos como privados para la explotación empresarial de una invención o resultado de una investigación científica.

- **Base de Datos R&D-Publications:** Contiene *abstracts* y detalles bibliográficos sobre aproximadamente 72.000 publicaciones, reportes y *papers* científicos.
- **Base de Datos R&D-Contacts:** Es un directorio de puntos de contactos oficiales que proveen información, asistencia o consejos respecto a programas de la Unión Europea y actividades nacionales de I+D.
- **Base de Datos R&D-Comdocuments:** Resúmenes de documentos clave de la Comisión Europea respecto a I+D.
- **Base de Datos R&D-Acronyms:** Es un diccionario de acrónimos y abreviaciones de la Unión Europea y de otros países no-comunitarios.
- **VIP - Scientific Press Service:** Es una base de datos dedicada a la diseminación de resultados de proyectos de I+D europeos.

3.2.1.2. Red de Centros de Transmisión de Innovación de la Unión Europea (IRCs) - Network of Innovation Relay Centres (IRCs)

http://www.cordis.lu/ irc/home.html
Información: p.cornelius@cordis.lu

La Red de Transmisión de Innovación de la UE es una red de cooperación técnica y tecnológica de 52 centros que se extiende a través de todo el territorio de la Unión, Noruega e Islandia. Los IRCs tienen como principal objetivo desarrollar proyectos de investigación y tecnología en estrecha relación con las empresas europeas, cooperando en la explotación comercial de los resultados de las investigaciones realizadas (mediante transferencia de tecnología) y apoyando la participación de empresas industriales en programas comunitarios y en los Programas Específicos de I+D.

Cada IRC es una oficina consultora independiente de negocios y tecnología, financiada parcialmente por el Programa de Innovación de la UE.

Sus principales líneas de servicios son:

- Servicios de Transferencia de Tecnología hacia la empresa: a través de los cuales los IRCs ayudan a empresas locales y centros de investigación a identificar sus necesidades de nuevas tecno-

logías, encontrar proveedores de nuevas tecnologías y brindar asistencia para la negociación de acuerdos y alianzas para la implementación de las transferencias de tecnología.
- Servicios de Transferencia de Tecnología hacia el mercado: a través de los cuales los IRCs ayudan a empresas locales y centros de investigación a identificar las tecnologías que pueden ser susceptibles de ser transferidas a otras regiones o industrias, promoviendo estas ideas novedosas o innovaciones a través de la UE mediante la Red de IRC. Proveen asistencia en las negociaciones y apoyo en la implementación de la transferencia de las tecnologías.
- Servicios de Búsqueda de Socios Comerciales y otros servicios: los miembros de la Red brindan el servicio de asesoramiento y formación para la transferencia de tecnología y explotación comercial de los resultados de las investigaciones que se desarrollan. Asimismo, promueven la participación en los Programas RTD, asisten a las empresas en la preparación de propuestas y proyectos, colaboran en la búsqueda de socios para los proyectos y asesoran a las mismas respecto a financiación de apoyo a las innovaciones dentro del marco de programas comunitarios y nacionales.

3.2.1.3. Cuarto Programa Marco / Fourth Framework Programme (FP4)

http://www.cordis.lu/info/frames/if006_en.htm
Información: helpdesk@cordis.lu

La Unión Europea provee apoyo financiero para la Investigación y el Desarrollo Tecnológico (IDT) a través de una herramienta denominada Cuarto Programa Marco. El ámbito temporal de aplicación se extiende desde 1994 hasta finales de 1998, y a continuación se aplican las políticas del Quinto Programa Marco.

El FP4 constituye el instrumento legal que engloba 18 Programas Específicos, que a su vez integran cuatro grupos de actividades (programas de I+D tecnológico y demostración, cooperación internacional, diseminación y explotación de los resultados, y capacitación y movilidad de investigadores). Cada uno de los programas específicos se orienta a la investigación de una problemática tecnológica particular. A pesar de que todos los programas tienen objetivos comunes, cada uno de los mismos posee un conjunto de reglas y procedimientos propios para la participación, y son publicados en diferentes directivas comunitarias.

Programas Específicos de IDT dentro del FP4

Programa de Aplicaciones Telemáticas / Telematics Applications
Información: telematics@dg13.cec.be

Programa de Tecnologías Avanzadas de las Comunicaciones y Servicios / Advanced Communications Technologies and Services (ACTS)
Información: aco@postman.dg13.cec.be

Programa de Tecnologías de la Información / Information Technologies (ESPRIT)
Information Desk: esprit@dg13.cec.be

Programa de Tecnologías Industriales y de Materiales / Industrial and Materials Technologies (IMT- Brite-Euram 3)
Información: imt-helpdesk@dg12.cec.be

Normalización, Medidas y Comprobaciones / Standards, Measurements and Testing (SMT)
smt-helpdesk@dg12.cec.be

Programa de Medioambiente y Clima / Environment and Climate
environ-infodesk@dg12.cec.be

Programa de Ciencias Marinas y Tecnología / Marine Science and Technology (MAST)
Información: mast-info@dg12.cec.be

Programa de Biotecnología / Biotechnology
Información: life-biotech@dg12.cec.be

Programa de Biomedicina y Salud / Biomedicine and Health
Información: alain.van-vossel@dg12.cec.be

Programa de Agricultura y Pesca
Información: helpdesk@cordis.lu

Programa de Energías No Nucleares
Información: helpdesk@cordis.lu

Programa de Fusión Termonuclear Controlada / Controlled Thermonuclear Fusion
Información: helpdesk@cordis.lu

Programa de Transporte
Información: helpdesk@cordis.lu

Programa de Investigación Socioeconómica / Targeted Socio-Economic Research (TSER)
Información: tser-secr@dg12.cec.be

Programa de Cooperación Internacional con Países y Organizaciones Internacionales No Europeas / International Cooperation With Third Countries and International Organisations (INCO)
Información: inco-desk@dg12.cec.be

Programa PYME / SME Program
Información: marc.van-achter@dg12.cec.be

Programa de Capacitación y Movilidad de Investigadores / Training and Mobility of Researchers (TMR)
Información: tmr-info@dg12.cec.be

Generalmente, la financiación de los proyectos por parte de la Unión Europea se realiza teniendo en cuenta el sistema de Costes de Acción Compartida, es decir, la Comisión provee el 50% de la financiación de los proyectos de investigación transnacionales y compartidos.

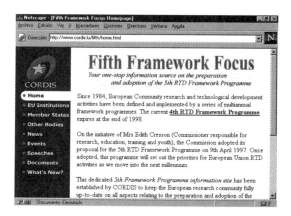

3.2.1.4. Quinto Programa Marco / Fifth Framework Programme (FP5)

http://www.cordis.lu/fifth/home.html

Como continuación del Cuarto Programa Marco, la Comisión Europea ha diseñado la estructura de su política de IDT para el período 1999-2002. Las temáticas de los programas son las siguientes:

1. Apertura de los recursos del mundo en que vivimos y del ecosistema
   - Salud y alimentación
   - Control de virus y otras enfermedades infecciosas
   - Las «fábricas prisión»
   - La gestión y calidad del agua
   - Medioambiente y salud
   - Desarrollo integrado de las áreas rurales y costeras

2. Creación de una Sociedad de la Información de simple acceso
   - Sistemas y servicios para los ciudadanos
   - Nuevos métodos de trabajo y comercio electrónico
   - Contenido multimedia
   - Tecnologías esenciales e infraestructuras

3. Promover el crecimiento competitivo y sostenible

- Productos, procesos y organización
- Movilidad sostenible e intermodal
- Nuevas perspectivas en aeronáutica
- Tecnologías marinas
- Sistemas energéticos avanzados y servicios
- La ciudad del futuro

Asimismo el Quinto Programa Marco se ha fijado como objetivo llevar a cabo una política de estructura horizontal, con el fin de confirmar el rol internacional de la Unión Europea en los diferentes campos de la investigación y el desarrollo tecnológico. En ese contexto desarrollará políticas para aumentar la cooperación científica y tecnológica internacional con organizaciones e investigadores de países no europeos, facilitando el acceso de investigadores extranjeros a los centros de investigación y de negocios establecidos en la Unión, y otras medidas orientadas a la profundización de las relaciones internacionales en el campo de ITD.

En cuanto a los objetivos relacionados con las empresas, se ha propuesto aumentar el impacto económico y social de las actividades de investigación de los programas, mediante el refuerzo de los mecanismos designados para asegurar una mejor explotación de los resultados y de las transferencias y diseminación de las tecnologías. Se facilitará el acceso a instrumentos financieros específicos a las empresas más pequeñas participantes de los programas que presenten ideas creativas e innovadoras.

En cuanto a los recursos humanos, los objetivos generales se centran en el apoyo y desarrollo de la calidad de los mismos en Europa, particularmente apoyando la capacitación y promoviendo la movilidad y la innovación.

3.2.1.5. Centro de Investigación Conjunta / Joint Research Centre (JRC)

http://www.jrc.org
Información: prp@jrc.it

El Centro de Investigación Conjunta es el centro de investigación científico y técnico de la Unión Europea. Está formado por cinco unidades de investigación ubicadas en Bélgica, Alemania, Italia, Holanda y España, en donde se integran institutos para el medio ambiente, materiales avanzados, materiales de referencia y medias, sistemas, informática y seguridad, aplicaciones espaciales, y estudios de prospección tecnológica.

Cada instituto se especializa en las investigaciones que puede llevar a cabo con mayor eficacia con los recursos que la Unión Europea les facilita. El Sitio Web arriba indicado presenta las acciones de cada instituto, describe sus actividades generales, unidades específicas de investigación, proyectos y herramientas, y las posibilidades de colaboración con la industria europea.

3.2.1.6. Fuentes de Información en Internet sobre la Cooperación de la Unión Europea en el Sector de IDT

Dirección General XII de la Comisión Europea (Ciencia, Investigación y Desarrollo)
http://europa.eu.int/en/ comm/dg12/dg12tst2.html
Información: michel.claessens@dg12.cec.be;stephen.gosden@dg12.cec.be

La DG XII es la unidad administrativa de la Comisión Europea que lleva adelante la mayoría de los programas específicos de investigación. Su Unidad de Comunicación distribuye información general sobre los Programas Específicos de Investigación, incluso notas de prensa, catálogos, datos de contactos, información sobre iniciativas, un boletín electrónico y una revista denominada RTD Info.

Oficina del Proyecto de la Sociedad de la Información / Information Society Project Office (ISPO)
http://www.ispo.cec.be/
Información: ispo@ispo.cec.be

ISPO es el centro de la Comisión Europea que canaliza todo lo concerniente a la Sociedad de la Información en Europa. Ayuda a las empresas y usuarios a utilizar los instrumentos y recursos que existen en la Unión Europea. Actúa como broker de información e ideas, trabaja en el impacto de la Sociedad de la Información y ayu-

Transferencia de Tecnología y Know-how

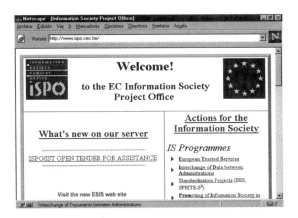

da al lanzamiento de acciones internacionales de gran envergadura. ISPO publica dos revistas: *IS Trends* e *IS News*, ambas proveen información actualizada sobre temas relacionados con la Sociedad de la Información.

En su Sitio Web publica un compendio de información sobre el desarrollo de la Sociedad de la Información tanto de la Unión Europea como de todo el mundo, informa sobre las políticas, iniciativas y programas (incluido los de I+D) y noticias de todo tipo.

Proyecto de Inventario Global (G7-GIP)
http://www.geocities.com/CapeCanaveral/Lab/9964/gippage.html
http://www.gip.int/es
Información: eduardopaz@technologist.com

Los Proyectos del G7 en relación a las nuevas tecnologías de la información tienen su origen en la Conferencia Interministerial del Grupo de los Siete (G7) sobre la Sociedad de la información, celebrada en Bruselas los días 25 y 26 de febrero de 1995. Con la participación de Rusia, pasaron a denominarse en 1998 «Proyectos G8». Los países miembros del G7 y la Comisión Europea se pusieron de acuerdo en designar una serie de diez proyectos piloto internacionales destinados a demostrar el potencial de la Sociedad de la Información y a estimular su desarrollo.

Uno de los diez proyectos, denominado Proyecto de Inventario Global (G7-GIP), tiene como principal objetivo crear un inventario de todos los proyectos nacionales o internacionales relacionados con la Sociedad de la Información, a fin de diseminar en todo el mundo su alcance y encontrar socios para un mejor desarrollo de los mismos.

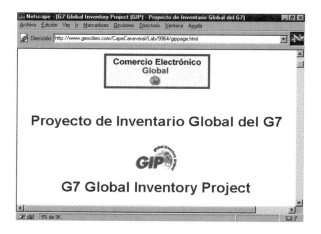

Los integrantes del G7-GIP son los principales centros de observación tecnológica del mundo, como el National Institute of Standards and Technology - (NIST USA), CINCH de Canadá, el Ministerio de Industria de Alemania, el INRIA de Francia, el Ministerio de Telecomunicaciones de Japón (MTA), el Ministerio de Comercio Exterior e Industrias de Japón (MITI), la Agencia Italiana para Nuevas Tecnologías, Energía y el Medioambiente, la Sociedad de la Información de Corea, el Ministerio de Comunicaciones del Reino Unido, la Sociedad de la Información de Suiza, la Comisión Europea a través del ISPO y de varias iniciativas como The Global Bengemann Challenge, Cordis, Esis, Ethos, Eurostat, I'm Europe, Infowin, Prosoma, y Comercio Electrónico Global de España.

El GIP es un inventario de todos los proyectos, estudios nacionales e internacionales y otras iniciativas que tengan que ver con la Sociedad de Información. Los proyectos y estudios susceptibles de ser incuidos en el GIP deben tener al menos una de las siguientes características:

- Tener relación con temas novedosos de la Sociedad de la Información.
- Que demuestren soluciones originales y transferibles.
- Que sean de interés y uso para las pequeñas y medianas empresas.
- Que promuevan la implementación de redes de soporte interactivo y los servicios multimedia.
- Que tengan importancia desde el punto de vista educacional y de la formación.

La información generada forma parte de una red para el libre intercambio de información sobre iniciativas nacionales e internacionales relacionadas con la Sociedad de la Información (mediante un foro electrónico), que sirve para promover las actividades de la Sociedad de Información y comprender su impacto sobre la economía, industria y sociedad, y potencia la creación de alianzas internacionales y proyectos e inversiones multinacionales.

EUROPA
http://europa.eu.int/

Es el Servidor Central de la Unión Europea y contiene información sobre los objetivos, políticas y actividades de la Unión. Muchos miembros de las Direcciones Generales de la Comisión tienen sus propias páginas Web, en donde comunican las novedades y proyectos. La DG XII (Ciencia, Investigación y Desarrollo), EUR-OP, y los Centros de Información Europea tienen también sus Sitios de exposición y contacto.

En este Servidor podrá acceder a importante información sobre proyectos de investigación europeos, por ejemplo, en Europa Feedback:
http://europa.eu.int/index-es.htm

I'M Europe
http://www.echo.lu/

Provee información detallada de varios programas, iniciativas y actividades llevados a cabo por la Comisión Europea a fin de estimular el mercado de servicios del sector información y las actividades industriales con contenido multimedia, como el Programa de Aplicaciones Telemáticas, INFO2000 y el Programa para la Sociedad de la Información Multilingüe.

European Commission Host Organisation (ECHO)
http://www.echo.lu/echo/en/menuecho.html
Información: echo@echo.lu

ECHO se incluye como Sitio Web en el mismo servidor de I'M Europe descrito arriba. A su vez ofrece acceso Telnet a aproximadamente 20 bases de datos que cubren temas relacionados con investigación y desarrollo, mercado electrónico de la información, industria y economía, tecnologías del lenguaje, y otros temas de gran importancia.

3.2.2. Transferencia de Tecnología e Investigación y Desarrollo Tecnológico en el Marco de la Cooperación de España y América Latina

España, a través de la Agencia Española de Cooperación Internacional (AECI), de Programas Interministeriales de Investigación y Desarrollo, del Centro de Desarrollo Tecnológico Industrial (CDTI) y de otras instituciones públicas y privadas, participa activamente en planes y políticas específicas de I+D tecnológico y de transferencia de tecnología. Entre estas acciones, destaca la aplicación de los Programas Marco (programas europeos definidos anteriormente), los programas específicos para la innovación y el Programa Iberoamericano de Ciencia y Tecnología (CYTED), programa dedicado a la cooperación en el sector científico-tecnológico con los países de América Latina.

Según un estudio reciente, la transferencia de tecnología industrial española presenta un desarrollo muy pequeño debido al escaso esfuerzo innovador desarrollado por las empresas, y su distribución sectorial se concentra en sólo siete u ocho sectores (Cuadro 4). Este estudio también destaca que la industrialización de la economía española tiene peculiaridades importantes, como su nivel de dependencia de la tecnología importada, consecuencia de la insuficiencia cuantitativa y cualitativa de la creación de recursos tecnológicos propios. En términos generales, la exportación de tecnología española comenzó a tener un desarrollo más relevante en la década de los setenta, tras un proceso de liberalización exterior notable y asentado en la maduración de ciertos sectores productivos de nivel intermedio.

Principales Sectores	Sectores secundarios
Productos minerales no metálicos	Industrias del cuero
Alimentación, bebidas y tabaco	Energía eléctrica
Fabricación de productos metálicos	Construcción naval
Industria textil	Extracción de minerales radioactivos
Industrias del papel y artes gráficas	Refino de petróleos
Industrias de la madera, corcho y muebles	Construcción de automóviles y recambios
Transformación del caucho y plásticos	Construcción de maquinaria y equipo mecánico
Industrias del calzado y confección	
Minerales no metálicos	Instrumentos de precisión
Construcción de maquinarias y material eléctrico	Minería, carbón y extracción de petróleo y gas
Otras industrias manufactureras	Minería metálica
Fabricación material electrónico	Maquinaria de oficina y ordenadores
Construcción de otro material de transporte	
Productos de transformación de metales	
Industria química	

Fuente: Molero (1996)

Cuadro 4. Exportaciones de Tecnología de España
(según Sectores Industriales).

3.2.2.1. Puntos de Contacto en España de los Programas Específicos del IV Programa Marco de IDT

- **Programa de Aplicaciones Telemáticas de Interés Común**
  Información: jpm@cdti.es (CDTI)
  Información: escanciano@dgt.es (D. G. Tel. del Ministerio de Fomento)

- **Programa de Tecnologías de la Información (ESPRIT)**
  Información: jlff@cdti.es (CDTI)

- **Programa de Tecnologías Industriales y de los Materiales (BRITE-EURAM)**
  Información: chr@cdti.es (CDTI)

- **Programa de Normalización, Medidas y Ensayos (SMT)**
  Información: sancho@cicyt.es (Secretaría Gral. del Plan Nacional de I+D

- **Programa de Medio Ambiente y Clima**
  Información: mdelgado@cicyt.es (Sec. Gral. Plan Nac. de I+D)

- **Programa de Ciencias y Tecnologías Marinas (MAST)**
  Información: mdelgado@cicyt.es (Sec. Gral. Plan Nac. de I+D)

- **Programa de Biotecnología (BIOTECH)**
  Información: abge@cdti.es (CDTI)

- **Programa de Agricultura y Pesca (FAIR)**
  Información: abge@cdti.es (CDTI)

- **Programa de Energías no nucleares (JOULE-THERMIE)**
  Información: mimi@cicyt.es (Sec. Gral. Plan Nac. de I+D)

- **Programa de Investigación Socioeconómica con Fines Propios (TSER)**
  Información: mimi@cicyt.es (Sec. Gral. Plan Nac. de I+D)

Transferencia de Tecnología y Know-how

- **Programa de Cooperación con Terceros Países y Organizaciones Internacionales (INCO)**
  Información: mdelgado@cicyt.es (Sec. Gral. Plan Nac. de I+D)

- **Programa de Difusión y Explotación de los Resultados de la I+D (INNOVACION)**
  Información: jcfd@cdti.es (CDTI)
  Información: mzan@cicyt.es (Sec. Gral. Plan Nac. de I+D)

- **Programa de Formación y Movilidad de los Investigadores (TMR)**
  Información: mimi@cicyt.es (Sec. Gral. Plan Nac. de I+D)

- **Becas Marie Curie (I+D)**
  Información: eloy.monje@seuix.seui.mec.es (Sec. de Edo. de Universidades, Investigación y Desarrollo)

3.2.2.2. Red Española de Centros de Enlace para la Innovación y Unidad Coordinadora Española de Centros de Enlace. Contactos en Internet

CETEMA / CENEO (Madrid, Castilla-La Mancha, Extremadura, Aragón, Navarra, La Rioja y Canarias)
http://www.cetema.es/cetema/
Información: cetema@fi.upm.es

CESEAND (Andalucía)
http://www.ceseand.cica.es
Información: aramirez@ceseand.cica.es
Información: fumanal@ceseand.cica.es

CENEMES (Comunidad Valenciana, Baleares y Murcia)
http://www.cenemes.ua.es/cenemes.html

CIDEM (Cataluña)
http://www.upc.es/irc
Información: cidem@servicom.es

Unidad Coordinadora Española de Centros de Enlace
Secretaría General del Plan Nacional de I+D
Información: mimi@cicyt.es

Centro para el Desarrollo Tecnológico Industrial (CDTI)
Información: jcfd@cdti.es

3.2.2.3. IBEROEKA Instrumento para la Cooperación Tecnológica y Empresarial en Iberoamérica

http://www.cicyt.es/
http://www.rau.edu.uy/aeci/
Información: aeci@netgate.comintur.com.uy

Los Proyectos de Innovación IBEROEKA, puestos en marcha en 1991, son un instrumento dirigido al sector industrial para fomentar la cooperación entre empresas en el campo de la investigación y el desarrollo tecnológico.

El objetivo principal del programa es aumentar la productividad y competitividad de las industrias y economías nacionales a fin de consolidar la prosperidad económica dentro de la comunidad Iberoamericana mediante el apoyo técnico, logístico y financiero. A tal fin, el programa promociona la cooperación industrial, tecnológica y científica entre los participantes (empresas y centros de investigación), orientada al desarrollo de productos, procesos y servicios dirigidos a un mercado potencial.

Los requisitos que deben reunir los proyectos son los siguientes:

1. Proyecto con participación de empresas de al menos dos países miembros de la Red Iberoamericana
2. Proyecto innovador en un área tecnológica
3. El resultado sea un producto, proceso o servicio próximo al mercado
4. Sólo aplicaciones con fines civiles
5. Intercambio tecnológico abierto entre los participantes
6. Desarrollo del proyecto en los países participantes y en su beneficio

7. Suficiente cualificación técnica y organizativa de los participantes
8. Participantes con los medios financieros adecuados para realizar el proyecto y su explotación

Para participar en un proyecto IBEROEKA existen cuatro situaciones de partida:

- Búsqueda de socios iberoamericanos para iniciar un proyecto
- Iniciación de un proyecto para el que ya tiene socios
- Búsqueda de nuevos socios para un proyecto que ya está en marcha
- Ingreso a un proyecto ya existente

La gestión de IBEROEKA corresponde a la Red Iberoamericana de Organismos Gestores designados en cada uno de los países Iberoamericanos participantes en el programa.

La red Iberoamericana de Organismos Gestores de IBEROEKA está formada por: la Secretaría de Ciencia y Tecnología (Argentina); el Concsejo Nacional de Ciencia y Tecnología (Bolivia); la Financiadora de Estudos e Projetos - FINEP (Brasil); la Corporación de Fomento de la Producción - CORFO (Chile); el Instituto Colombiano para el Desarrollo de la Ciencia y la Tecnología - COLCIENCIAS (Colombia); el Fondo Privado de Desarrollo Tecnológico - FODETEC - CONICIT (Costa Rica); el Ministerio para la Inversión Extranjera y la Colaboración Económica (Cuba); la Secretaría Nacional de Ciencia y Tecnología (Ecuador); el Consejo Nacional de Ciencia y Tecnología - CONACYT (El Salvador); el Centro para el Desarrollo Tecnológico Industrial - CDTI (España); el Consejo Nacional de Ciencia y Tecnología - CONCYT (Guatemala); el Consejo Hondureño de Ciencia y Tecnología (Honduras); Consejo Nacional de Ciencia y Tecnología - CONACYT (México); Universidad Tecnológica de Panamá (Panamá); Instituto Nacional de Tecnología y Normalización (Paraguay); Consejo Nacional de Ciencia y Tecnología - CONCYTEC (Perú); Junta Nacional de Investigaçao Científica e Tecnológica - JNICT (Portugal); Asociación de Industrias de la República Dominicana (República Dominicana); Unidad Asesora de Promoción Industrial del Ministerio de Industria y Energía (Uruguay); y el Consejo Nacional de Investigaciones Científicas y Tecnológicas - CONICIT (Venezuela).

Existe un compromiso entre los países participantes mediante el cual la financiación de cada uno de los proyectos es descentralizada y cada país asume la financiación de sus empresas. Una vez que el proyecto sea certificado, cada socio solicitará en su país ayuda pública para su participación. El tipo de ayudas, así como los mecanismos y esquemas de financiación, serán los utilizados internamente en cada país para la promoción de la investigación científica y el desarrollo tecnológico.

IBEROEKA es un programa de la Secretaría General del Programa Iberoamericano de Ciencia y Tecnología para el Desarrollo (CYTED) del Instituto de Cooperación Iberoamericana (IECI).

3.2.3. *Transferencia de Tecnología e Investigación y Desarrollo Tecnológico en el Marco de los Países de la APEC*

Dentro del marco del grupo de los países de la APEC, las empresas pequeñas y medianas juegan un rol muy importante para su integración y cooperación regional. Como consecuencia de ello, la APEC se ha propuesto generar una mayor competencia comercial entre las dieciocho naciones integrantes del grupo y apoyarlas mediante la creación de un centro específico para el intercambio de tecnología y capacitación.

Centro del Grupo APEC de Intercambio de Tecnología y Formación para la Pequeña y Mediana Empresa / APEC Centre for Technology Exchange and Training for Small and Medium Enterprises (ACTETSME)
http://www.actetsme.org/
Información: webmaster@actetsme.org

A través de este Sitio Web, se puede tomar contacto con este centro y formular las consultas que los empresarios del mundo quieran realizar respecto a las posibilidades de integrar proyectos relacionados con la transferencia de tecnología dentro de este grupo regional. Los contactos se realizan a través de puntos de contacto o Focal Points, que son organizaciones privadas, departamentos gubernamentales, asociaciones de negocios, y agencias de promoción comercial que conjuntamente con instituciones de formación e investigación trabajan para incrementar la competitividad de las pequeñas y medianas empresas por medio de la cooperación empresarial. Los Focal Points están ubicados geográficamente en: Australia, Indonesia, Nueva Guinea, Brunei, Japón, Filipinas, Canadá, Corea, Singapur, Chile, Malasia, Taipei, República de China, México, Tailandia, Hong Kong, Nueva Zelanda y Estados Unidos de América.

3.3. El Rol de las Universidades en la Transferencia de Tecnología e Investigación y Desarrollo Tecnológico. Principales Sitios Web

Las universidades de los Estados Unidos y de Europa están llevando a cabo interesantes acciones tendentes a acercar los conocimientos tecnológicos formales que se desarrollan en los Campus hacia los sectores privados empresariales. El beneficio de esta actividad es inobjetable ya que permite la creación de nuevos negocios en el sector de ciencia y tecnología, la creación de nuevos empleos, la apertura de nuevos mercados y la elevación del nivel de vida de los usuarios de estas aplicaciones tecnológicas.

Dos interesantes puntos de contacto españoles relacionados a IDT de tipo universitario son el Consejo Superior de Investigaciones Científicas (http://www.csic.es) y la Secretaría de Estado de Universidades, Investigación y Desarrollo (http://www.seui.mec.es).

Según la Asociación de Gerentes de Tecnología Universitaria de Estados Unidos (1997), que desarrolla anualmente encuestas y sondeos sobre los resultados de las transferencias de licencias de nuevas tecnologías desde las universidades e instituciones académicas de Estados Unidos y Canadá hacia los sectores privados, las transferencias por parte de estas instituciones añaden a la economía de estos países aproximadamente 21 billones de USD y apoyan la creación de 180.000 nuevos puestos de trabajo. Sólo en 1995, las licencias académicas permitieron la formación de 223 compañías nuevas.

Cabe destacar que, en estos momentos, la mayoría de las universidades norteamericanas que se presentan a continuación, desarrollan actividades de explotación comercial de inventos e innovaciones proporcionadas por particulares. Los recursos que la universidad obtiene por la intermediación, son utilizados en la mejora de sus infraestructuras universitarias. El proceso de comercialización se inicia con la presentación, por parte del creador o inventor, de un *dossier* que contiene el desarrollo del concepto y la descripción de la innovación, en algunos casos se adjunta también un prototipo. La universidad lleva a cabo un análisis tecnológico, un análisis de marketing y un análisis de patentabilidad. Cumplidas estas etapas y aceptado el proyecto, se realiza la difusión de las innovaciones a través de redes de contactos con empresas privadas.

3.3.1. Transferencia de Tecnología en Universidades Norteamericanas. Contactos en Internet

Baylor College of Medicine's Office of Research
http://johnson.bcm.tmc.edu/

Brown University Research Foundation
http://www.brown.edu/Research/Research_Foundation/BURF.html

California Polytechnic at Pomona - Research Office
http://www.csupomona.edu/research/title2.htm

Colorado State University - Technology Transfer
Correo Electrónico: jbrown@vines.colostate.edu

Colorado State University - CSU Research Foundation
Correo Electrónico: kbyington@vines.colostate.edu

Colorado State University - Industrial Assessment Center
http://www.lance.colostate.edu/depts/me/iac

Florida State University - Office of Research
Correo Electrónico: bsouth@res.fsu.edu

Indiana University Technology Transfer
http://www.indiana.edu/~rugs/tto/tto.html

Israel Institute of Technology - Technion R&D Foundation Ltd
http://www.technion.ac.il/technion/trdf/

Iowa State - New Instrumentation and Technology Transfer
http://www.cnde.iastate.edu/catd.html

Johns Hopkins University School of Medicine - Office of Technology Licensing
http://www.jhu.edu/

Loyola College (Maryland) - JTEC/WTEC
http://itri.loyola.edu

Massachussets Institute of Technology (MIT)
http://web.mit.edu

Michigan State University - Office of Intellectual Property
http://web.miep.org/oip/

Mississippi State University - Office of Sponsored Programs
http://www.msstate.edu/Dept/SPA/spa.html

North Carolina State University College of Engineering Industrial Extension Service
http://www.ies.ncsu.edu:80/

Ohio University Technology Transfer Office (TTO)
http://ra.cs.ohiou.edu/gopher/non-academic/tto/tto.html

Penn State Research and Tech Transfer Organization (RTTO)
http://infoserv.rttonet.psu.edu/index.htm

Rutgers University - Office of Corporate Liaison and Technology Transfer (OCLTT)
http://info.rutgers.edu/Services/Corporate/corporate/

Texas A&M University System: Technology Licensing Office
http://engineer.tamu.edu/tlo/

University of Arkansas - Office of Research
http://www.uark.edu/admin/rsspinfo/

University of Colorado - Office of Intellectual Property and Technology Transfer
http://spot.colorado.edu/~techtran/Home.html

University of Colorado at Boulder - Technology Transfer & Industry Outreach
http://txfr35.colorado.edu/home.html

University of Colorado at Boulder - Health Sciences
http://txfr35.colorado.edu/UCHSCref.html

University of Colorado at Colorado Springs - Colorado Institute for Technology Transfer
http://txfr35.colorado.edu/UCCSref.html

University of Colorado at Boulder - Office of IR & Technology Transfer (OIRTT)
http://txfr35.colorado.edu/Centralref.html
Coopera en la comercialización de tecnologías

University of Connecticut Health Center - Cooperative Research
http://cortex.uchc.edu: 80/~coopres/index.html

University of Georgia - Technology Transfer Office
http://www.ovpr.uga.edu/ugarf/rf-index.html

University of Hawaii Office of Technology Transfer and Economic Development
http://www.mic.hawaii.edu/otted/otted.html

University of Illinois at Urbana-Champaign - Research and Technology Management Office (RTMO)
http://www.oc.uiuc.edu/rtmo

University of Illinois at Urbana-Champaign - Institute for Competitive Manufacturing
http://128.174.125.91/vmc/icm/icmintro.html

University of Kaiserslautern Software Technology Transfer
http://uomo.informatik.uni-kl.de: 2080/STTI/stti.html

University of Maryland at College Park
http://www.umd.edu/

University of Maryland at College Park Office of Technology Liaison
http://www.inform.umd.edu: 8080/EdRes/GradInfo/.WWW/OTLTechnologies.html

University of Michigan - Office of Technology Transfer Engineering
http://ott-outreach.engin.umich.edu/ott/

University of Michigan Technology Management Office
http://www.tmo.umich.edu

University of Pennsylvania
http://www.upenn.edu/VPR/CTT.html

University of Texas Intellectual Property
http://gold.utsystem.edu/OGC/IntellectualProperty/INDEX.HTM

University of Rochester
http://www.cc.rochester.edu: 80/ORPA//tto/

University of Washington - Office of Technology Transfer
http://cary.u.washington.edu/ott/ott.html

University of Wisconsin Biotechnology Center
http://www.biotech.wisc.edu/Pages/tektran.html

University of Wisconsin-Madison, University-Industry Relations
http://www.wisc.edu/uir

Washington University en St. Louis - Corporate Research Collaboration
http://ibc.wustl.edu:80/res_collab/

3.3.2. Transferencia de Tecnología en Universidades de Canadá. Contactos en Internet

British Columbia Institute of Technology - BCIT Technology Centre
http://www.arcs.bcit.bc.ca/tc/home.html

Carleton University Development Corporation
gopher://ernest.carleton.ca:406/11/cudc

Lambton College - Centre for Advanced Process Technology (CAPT)
http://www.lambton.on.ca/capt/capt.html

McMaster University - Innovation Research Centre
http://www.mcmaster.ca/busdocs/irc.html

McMaster University - Office of Research Contracts & Intellectual Property
Correo Electrónico: mcdermot@fhs.csu.McMaster.CA

Memorial University of Newfoundland - Seabright Corporation Ltd.
http://www.ucs.mun.ca/~stephenm/seabright.html

Queen's University (Kingston, Ontario) - PARTEQ Innovations
http://www.queensu.ca/parteq/

Simon Fraser University - Industry Liaison Office (U/ILO)
http://www.sfu.ca/uilo

Technology Based Learning Network Canada TBL.CA
http://www.humanities.mcmaster.ca/~misc2/tblca1.htm

University of Alberta - Industry Liaison Office
http://pansy.rgo.ualberta.ca/index.html

University of BC - Office of Research Services and Administration
http://www.orsil.ubc.ca

University of Calgary - University Technologies International - UTI
http://janus.arc.ab.ca: 8000/CTN/UTI/

University of Guelph - Office of Research
http://www.uoguelph.ca/Research/

University of Lethbridge - Centre for Technology Studies
http://www.mngt.uleth.ca/deprtmnt/tech/tech.htm

University of New Brunswick Manufacturing Technology Centre
http://music2.unb.ca/~mtcunb/http/mtc.html

University of Victoria - Innovation and Development Corporation
http://web.uvic.ca/idc

University of Waterloo - Office of Research
http://www.adm.uwaterloo.ca/infoor/

University of Western Ontario - Office of Research Services
http://www.uwo.ca/research/

Wilfrid Laurier University - Research Centres and Consulting Services
gopher: //schoolnet.carleton.ca: 418/11/Trans-Forum/english/can-tech-sites.dir/wilfred-laurier

3.3.3. Transferencia de Tecnología en otras Universidades del Mundo. Contactos en Internet

University of Glasgow - Industrial and Commercial Development Service
gopher: //info.gla.ac.uk/1/Otherdepts/ICDS/
C&C Technology Exchange, Estocolmo

http://www.it.kth.se/Electrum/CC/TT.html

Chalmers University of Technology, Gothenburg - Industrial Liaison and Development Office
http://www.chalmers.se

City University of Hong Kong - Industrial and Business Development Office
http://www.cuug.ab.ca:8001/~fortuned/://www.cityu.edu.hk/ibdo/

Kingston University Enterprises Ltd
gopher://gopher.king.ac.uk:7777/1Mou%3DKingston%20Universit
y%20Enterprises%20Ltd%2C%20o%3DKingston%20University%2C
%20c%3DGB

Brno Technical University - Technopark
Correo Electrónico: holec@ro.vutbr.cz

Lappeenranta University of Technology - Centre for Training and Development
http://www.lut.fi/english.html

Ljubljana Technology Park (Eslovenia)
http://www.arnes.si/doc/tp-ijs.html

Nara Institute of Science & Technology (NAIST) - Japón
http://www.aist-nara.ac.jp/RCAST/rsc.html

National University of Singapore - Industry & Technology Relations Office
http://irdu.nus.sg/INTRO/welcome.html

Open University (Reino Unido) - Office of Technology Development
http://www.open.ac.uk/OU/Admin/OTD/OTDHome.html

Open University (Reino Unido) - Knowledge Media Institute
http://kmi.open.ac.uk/

Technical University of Liberec - Faculty of Mechanical Engineering
Correo Electrónico: jaroslav.exner@vslib.cz

University of Munich - Technology Transfer Office (en alemán)
http://www.uni-muenchen.de/lmu/kft/

Humboldt-University, Berlín (Alemania)
http://www.hu-berlin.de/forschung/fotransf.html

University of Magdeburg - Technology Transfer Center (en alemán)
http://www.uni-magdeburg.de/~ttz/ttz.html

Proyecto WorlTech (base de datos en español sobre I+D)
http://www.worldtech.net/default.htm

3.4. Propiedad Intelectual, Marcas, Patentes y Modelos Industriales. Principales Sitios Web

La patente es el título legal que garantiza la posesión exclusiva de un derecho a utilizar una invención por un tiempo y en un área limitada, y entre otras cosas, impide la utilización o comercialización del mismo sin la oportuna autorización del inventor.

Todas las patentes son publicadas. Esto proporciona un indicador muy útil para hacer un seguimiento de las tendencias del mercado y al mismo tiempo sirve de fuente de información sobre los desarrollos de la innovación en todas las áreas de la tecnología, y se evita la duplicación de gastos en investigación.

Los sistemas de patentes juegan un rol muy importante en el estímulo de las transferencias de tecnología, ya que otorgan una garantía jurídica sobre el riesgo de la imitación o copia. Asimismo, el derecho exclusivo de la explotación comercial estimula también a las compañías a financiar procesos de investigación y desarrollo tecnológico. En síntesis, las licencias de patentes promueven la diseminación de las nuevas tecnologías.

Se ha incluido en este capítulo una selección de fuentes directas de información respecto a propiedad intelectual, marcas, patentes y modelos industriales, a fin de que aquellas empresas que necesiten información respecto a los costes de registros, tratamiento técnico o jurídico, e incluso sobre registros existentes similares al que se pretende patentar, puedan dirigir sus consultas a través de Internet.

IBM Patent Server - Poderoso Motor de Búsqueda de Patentes de Invención que incluye una extraordinaria información respecto a más de 2.000.000 de patentes, en donde se pueden observar, incluso, los gráficos de los diseños registrados.
http://patent.womplex.ibm.com/

Organización Mundial de la Propiedad Intelectual / World Intellectual Property Organization (WIPO)
http://www.wipo.org

Oficina Nacional de Propiedad Intelectual de Oficina Europea de Patentes (EPO)
http://www.epo.co.at/epo/

Oficina Nacional de Propiedad Intelectual de Australia
http://www.aipo.gov.au

Oficina Nacional de Propiedad Intelectual de Austria
http://www.ping.at/patent/index.htm

Oficina Nacional de Propiedad Intelectual de Brasil
http://www.bdt.org.br/bdt/inpi

Oficina Nacional de Propiedad Intelectual de Canadá
http://info.ic.gc.ca/opengov/cipo/

Oficina Nacional de Propiedad Intelectual de la República Popular China
http://www.cpo.cn.net/

Oficina Nacional de Propiedad Intelectual de Croacia
http://pubwww.srce.hr/patent

Oficina Nacional de Propiedad Intelectual de Dinamarca
http://www.dkpto.dk/

Oficina Nacional de Propiedad Intelectual de Estados Unidos (USPTO)
http://www.uspto.gov

Oficina Nacional de Propiedad Intelectual de Finlandia
http://www.prh.fi/

Oficina Nacional de Propiedad Intelectual de Francia
http://www.evariste.anvar.fr/inpi/

Oficina Nacional de Propiedad Intelectual de Alemania
http://www.deutsches-Patentamt.de/

Oficina Nacional de Propiedad Intelectual de Grecia
http://www.epo.co.at/epo/patlib/country/greece/

Oficina Nacional de Propiedad Intelectual de Hong Kong
http://www.houston.com.hk/hkgipd

Oficina Nacional de Propiedad Intelectual de Hungría (HPO)
http://www.hpo.hu

Oficina Nacional de Propiedad Intelectual de Italia
http://www.epo.co.at/epo/patlib/country/um_noit.htm

Oficina Nacional de Propiedad Intelectual de Japón (JPO-MITI)
http://www.jpo-miti.go.jp

Oficina Nacional de Propiedad Intelectual de Corea
http://www.ik.co.kr/kopatent/work.htm

Oficina Nacional de Propiedad Intelectual de Lituania
http://vytautas.is.lt/vpb/engl/

Oficina Nacional de Propiedad Intelectual de Luxemburgo
http://http://www.etat.lu/EC/

Oficina Nacional de Propiedad Intelectual de Malasia
http://kpdnhq.gov.my/ip/

Oficina Nacional de Propiedad Intelectual de Mónaco
http://www.epo.co.at/epo/patlib/country/monaco/

Oficina Nacional de Propiedad Intelectual de Nueva Zelanda
http://www.govt.nz/ps/min/com/patent/

Oficina Nacional de Propiedad Intelectual de Perú
http://www.rcp.net.pe/INDECOPI/indecopi.htm

Oficina Nacional de Propiedad Intelectual de Polonia
http://www.ibspan.waw.pl/

Oficina Nacional de Propiedad Intelectual de Portugal (INPI)
http://www.inpi.pt/

Oficina Nacional de Propiedad Intelectual de Rumania
http://www.osim.ro/

Oficina Nacional de Propiedad Intelectual de Eslovenia
http://www.mzt.si/mzt.html

Oficina Nacional de Propiedad Intelectual de España
http://www.eunet.es/InterStand/patentes/index.html

Oficina Nacional de Propiedad Intelectual de Suecia
http://www.prv.se

Oficina Nacional de Propiedad Intelectual del Reino Unido
http://www.patent.gov.uk/

Información General sobre Marcas y Patentes
http://www.naming.com/trademark2.htm

Capítulo 4

Promoción Internacional de Ofertas y Demandas para la Formación de Joint Ventures, Transferencia de Tecnología y Know-how Técnico y Tecnológico

4.1. Selección de las Mejores Fuentes de Información y Sitios Web para la Promoción de Propuestas de Joint Ventures, Transferencia de Tecnología y Know-how

El presente capítulo recoge una selección de los mejores recursos de Internet dedicados al intercambio global de ofertas y demandas de oportunidades comerciales de tipo «empresa-empresa», haciendo hincapié en los recursos que Internet ofrece para la promoción internacional de oportunidades de cooperación empresarial. En ese sentido, a través de medios aquí enunciados es posible exponer las necesidades de la empresa en relación a búsquedas de:

- Socios inversores para la formación de una Joint Venture Internacional, u otra forma de cooperación interempresarial.
- Socios que aporten nuevas tecnologías o know-how técnico o tecnológico
- Socios para compartir actividades de Investigación y Desarrollo
- Empresas transferentes de patentes o licencias
- Empresas adquirentes de patentes o licencias
- Socios que aporten medios de producción
- Socios que aporten sistemas de almacenamiento

- Socios para compartir presentaciones en licitaciones internacionales
- Empresas para relaciones de subcontratación
- Socios que aporten nuevos productos a la línea
- Socios que aporten sistemas logísticos y distribución
- Socios que aporten el conocimiento de un nuevo mercado
- Socios que aporten nuevos sistemas de dirección o gestión
- Empresas internacionales para compartir proyectos de publicidad compartida (Joint Venture en comunicación)

En general, a través de estos medios se toma contacto simultáneo con varios miles de empresarios de diversos países del mundo. Cada uno de ellos recurre a estas fuentes por razones o motivaciones diferentes y evalúan el interés de las oportunidades que reciben de acuerdo a criterios muy selectivos. Por ese motivo aconsejamos diseñar las ofertas y demandas de cooperación empresarial de forma tal que resulte fácil comprender las dimensiones del proyecto para el cual se está buscando un «*partner*». Es decir, que el mensaje debe ser claro y sintético, y muy orientado al perfil del socio potencial. Asimismo, no se extralimite nunca en el empleo de estos medios, ya que la falta de moderación en su utilización puede ser perjudicial para sus propios objetivos.

Si usted no está muy acostumbrado al uso de Newsgroups, Mailing Lists o páginas Web, consulte al personal técnico de su proveedor de Internet y con breves explicaciones podrá comenzar a trabajar en Red sin ninguna dificultad.

4.1.1. *Recursos de Internet Específicos para el Intercambio de Información para la Creación de Joint Ventures, Alianzas Estratégicas, Transferencia de Tecnología y Know-how*

IndiaOnline Joint Ventures
Correo Electrónico: joint-venture@IndiaOnline.com

La empresa ISOL Inc. de los Estados Unidos ofrece el servicio de unir ofertas y demandas relacionadas con la formación de Joint Ventures, alianzas estratégicas, transferencias de tecnologías y otras formas de cooperación empresarial con el mercado de la India.

Tradewinds
http://www.scbbs.com/~tradewinds
Gopher: gopher.scbbs.com
Información: Trade@Telalink.Net
Información: wgray@telalink.net

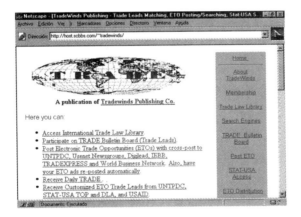

TRADE, Mailing List publicada por Tradewinds es una herramienta muy útil para la promoción gratuita de ofertas de formación de Joint Ventures, transferencia de tecnología, know-how, patentes y licencias a través de Internet. Es una Lista en donde participan miles de empresarios interesados en negocios internacionales.

Las cinco primeras líneas de los mensajes son también distribuidas automáticamente por Tradewinds a la Red Electrónica de Oportunidades Comerciales de las Naciones Unidas (UNTPDC-ETO).

- Para suscribirse a la Lista, envíe un mensaje respetando la siguiente estructura:
  A (To): Trade-L-Request@Intl-Trade.Com

Tema o Asunto (Subject): SUBSCRIBE
Cuerpo: SUBSCRIBE

- Para abandonar la Lista, envíe un mensaje que diga lo siguiente:
A (To): Trade-L-Request@Intl-Trade.Com
Tema o Asunto (Subject): UNSUBSCRIBE
Cuerpo: UNSUBSCRIBE

- Una vez que se ha agregado a la Lista, recibirá un formulario especial y todos los anuncios de los otros participantes directamente en su buzón de correo electrónico. Si usted quiere hacer un anuncio o consulta, envíe un mensaje como el siguiente, y éste será distribuido entre todos los participantes:
A (To): Trade@Intl-Trade.Com
Tema o Asunto (Subject): Seek Partner for International Joint Venture
Cuerpo: Definir la oportunidad, preferentemente en inglés, de acuerdo al formulario.

Hay que respetar todos los espacios originales del formulario, e incluso deberán ser incluidas las frases «START FORM» y «END FORM» en las líneas de inicio y finalización de la oportunidad. Sólo hay que incorporar la información que el formulario solicita en los espacios apropiados; es importante no excederse en la descripción de los objetivos, que no debe ser superior a 35 caracteres por línea y no más de 5 líneas (ver modelo en Anexo 3). La misma oferta puede ser enviada sólo una vez cada 7 días.

Tradewinds ha establecido *Opp Types* o códigos especiales para cada tipo de oportunidad comercial, que permiten simplificar el mecanismo de promoción y búsqueda (Cuadro 5).

Código	Tipo de Oportunidad Comercial
T101	Oferta - general
T102	**Oferta - tecnología**
T103	**Oferta - know-how**
T104	**Oferta - patente/licencia**
T105	Oferta - manufacturas
T106	Oferta - subcontratación
T107	**Oferta - licencia de manufacturas**
T108	Oferta - producto
T109	Oferta - producto usado
T110	Oferta - representación
T111	**Oferta - cooperación**
T112	Oferta - servicio
T113	Oferta - misceláneas
T114	**Oferta - adquisición/fusión**
T115	Oferta - inmuebles
T116	Oferta - agencia
T117	**Oferta - licencia**
T201	**Demanda - tecnología**
T202	**Demanda - know-how**
T203	**Demanda - patente/licencia**
T204	*Demanda - manufacturas*

Cuadro 5. Códigos de Oportunidades Comerciales de Tradewinds

TradeNet World Service
http://www.TradeNet.org
Información: info@TradeNet.org

TradeNet World Service es una organización privada de exportadores e importadores donde sus miembros pueden acceder en forma muy simple a una cantidad muy importante de información comercial actualizada y clasificada.

Su arquitectura permite la doble posibilidad de enviar o recibir ofertas y demandas a través de listas de correo electrónico o ingresando en su Sitio Web.

La suscripción es gratuita y actualmente posee más de 18.000 miembros permanentes, en su mayoría, comerciantes internacionales, agentes, representantes y consultores de comercio exterior de todos

los países del mundo. Asimismo, el Sitio Web es visitado por más de 3.000 no-miembros al día.

Para recibir y enviar oportunidades comerciales hay que ser miembro por suscripción. Hay dos formas para hacerlo:

- Una, es completando el formulario electrónico que existe en el Sitio Web de TradeNet cuyo URL es
http://www.TradeNet.org/join.html

- La otra, enviando un mensaje respetando la siguiente estructura:
A (To): join@TradeNet.org
Tema o Asunto (Subject): [dejar este espacio en blanco]
Cuerpo: SUBSCRIBE

Una vez realizada la suscripción, recibirá usted las instrucciones para el envío correcto de sus oportunidades comerciales o cooperación empresarial y quedará habilitado para enviar sus ofertas.

Los pasos a seguir para la formulación de una oferta comercial o cooperación empresarial en TradeNet son los siguientes:

1. Redactar el mensaje explicativo de la oportunidad empresarial, indicando sus datos contacto y sin exceder nunca las 20 líneas.

2. Indicación de Tipo de Oportunidad y breve descripción del pro-

ducto: En el Tema o Asunto del mensaje hay que establecer el Tipo de oportunidad de que se trata, seguido de una breve descripción del producto o servicio. Los Tipos de Oportunidades son cinco:

SELL	BUY	SEEK	NEWS	HELP
(Vendo)	(Compro)	(Busco)	(Noticias)	(Ayuda)

Ejemplos:
SELL License
BUY Know-how of Marketing Course
SEEK Partner for International Joint Venture
NEWS Book About Joint Ventures
HELP Technology Transfer

3. Enviar la oportunidad a la Lista correcta: El tercer paso es seleccionar correctamente la categoría del producto o servicio que queremos publicar, dentro de las catorce posibilidades que TradeNet ha establecido. Cada categoría tiene una dirección de correo electrónico diferente (ver Cuadro 6).

Categoría de Producto	Dirección E-Mail
Lista de Bienes de Consumo Pesado	con-hard@tradenet.org
Lista de Bienes de Consumo Ligero	con-soft@tradenet.org
Lista de Monedas y Metales Preciosos	currency@tradenet.org
Alimentos Sin Procesar y Commodities	food-com@tradenet.org
Lista de Alimentos Envasados	food-pack@tradenet.org
Lista de Textiles y Confecciones	garments@tradenet.org
Lista de Maquinaria Industrial	ind-machine@tradenet.org
Lista de Materia Prima Industrial	ind-raw@tradenet.org
Lista de Manufacturas Industriales	ind-supply@tradenet.org
Lista de Equipos y Proveedores Médicos	medical@tradenet.org
Lista de Servicios Profesionales	service@tradenet.org
Lista de Transporte y Flete Disponibles	shipping@tradenet.org
Lista de Tecnología	**technology@tradenet.org**
Lista de Vehículos de Transporte	vehicles@tradenet.org

Cuadro 6. Categorías de TradeNet y sus direcciones

United Nations Transaction Development Centre (UNTPDC)
http://www.untpdc.org/untpdc/welcome.html
Información: cmoreira@eto.geis.com

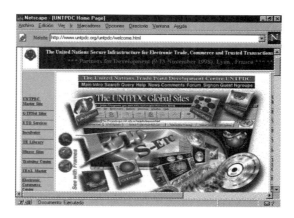

La Conferencia para el Comercio y el Desarrollo de las Naciones Unidas (UNCTAD) es el órgano permanente de la ONU encargado de la promoción del comercio internacional y del incremento del comercio entre países en vías de desarrollo con sistemas económicos y sociales muy diferenciados.

En el año 1992, UNCTAD lanzó un programa denominado Iniciativa para la Eficiencia del Comercio, por el cual se establecían en muchos países unas estructuras de información comercial en áreas estratégicas de la comercialización y de la capacitación denominadas Trade Points (TP) o Puntos Comerciales. En el Simposio Internacional para la Eficiencia del Comercio (UNISTE) del año 1994, la Secretaría General de las Naciones Unidas decidió enlazar todos los Trade Points dispersos en el mundo mediante redes telemáticas, creando de esta forma la Red Global de Trade Points (GTPNet) a cargo de una organización especializada denominada United Nations Trade Point Development Centre (UNTPDC). Actualmente, existen más de 131 Trade Points en más de 120 países, todos unidos mediante Internet y tecnología EDIFACT.

UNTPDC, que ahora se denomina «United Nations Transaction Development Centre», tiene su base operativa en Melbourne (Australia) y desde allí distribuye el tráfico de las ofertas y demandas comerciales que, mediante el sistema de Oportunidades Comerciales Electrónicas (ETO System), se canalizan a través de la Red de Trade Points. El Sistema ETO recurre a las herramientas más populares de la red como e-mail, newgroups y listas de distribución. Este es el principal recurso que tienen las empresas interesadas en promocionar internacionalmente sus oportunidades de cooperación empresarial, Joint Ventures, alianzas estratégicas, transferencia de tecnología, know-how, etc.

Desde el año 1993, UNTPDC ha retransmitido más de 2 billones de oportunidades comerciales electrónicas mediante el Sistema ETO y ha enviado aproximadamente 1,6 billones de e-mails a casi 8 millones de empresas en 148 países. Actualmente, cada día el Sistema ETO envía aproximadamente 2,6 millones de mensajes electrónicos. Por ejemplo, el Trade Point de Corea distribuye diariamente las ofertas o demandas del Sistema ETO a sus 67.000 clientes. La suscripción es gratuita y el sistema llega a cada rincón del planeta.

Hay dos formas de participar en el sistema ETO:

1. ETO Mailing List y Foros ETO

a) Suscripción en ETO Intelligent Agent: La suscripción es gratuita y constituye el primer paso para participar en ETO, recibir diariamente las ofertas, participar en los Foros, acceder a los programas para crear su propio sistema «off-line» de ofertas comerciales, etc. A tal fin hay que ingresar en el Sitio:
http://www.unicc.org/untpdc/eto/etoagent.html

Luego, completar la solicitud que allí se presenta con sus datos de contacto, los servicios que utilizará y las categorías de productos que se corresponden con su interés.

Es importante destacar que mediante esta suscripción usted podrá enviar y recibir ofertas y demandas en textos no codificados, lo cual constituye por un lado una ventaja porque no deberá tomarse la molestia de confeccionar el extenso formulario que UNTPDC impone, pero por otro lado sólo las ofertas y demandas realizadas en textos codificados son enviadas a los Servidores Centrales de UNTPDC y a todos los Trade Points para su archivo. La codificación ha sido realizada para permitir la utilización de un formato EDIFACT. Por lo tanto, enviando mensajes de texto libre o no codificados perderá usted la posibilidad de que su oferta sea incorporada junto con las más de 12.000.000 que se guardan en los archivos y son exploradas permanentemente.

b) Suscripción Completa: Para poder enviar ofertas a los Trade Point en texto codificado hay que contactar directamente con un Trade Point regional mediante WWW o correo electrónico (cuyas direcciones se indican abajo) o a UNTPDC y solicitar el formulario con codificación EDIFACT. El Programa ETO-Tagger, diseñado para facilitar el envío de mensajes codificados, puede ser una herramienta interesante para quienes envían asiduamente mensajes a este Foro. A fin de conocer la forma de utilización consultar en:
   http://www.esosoft.com/etotagger.html
   Una vez registrado, automáticamente será usted incluido en el Mailing List de ETO-IAgent y en los Foros pertinentes.
   http://www.unicc.org/untpdc/welcome.html
   Información: cmoreira@eto.geis.com

c) Abandono del Servicio: Enviar un mensaje solicitando la cancelación del servicio a la dirección: untpdc@urgento.gse.rmit.edu.au

2. Newsgroups de ETO

ETO distribuye oportunidades comerciales y empresariales a través de Newsgroups. Cada grupo tiene categorías y subcategorías diferentes que, a su vez, se clasifican por productos y países. Los usuarios de correo electrónico pueden suscribirse a los Newsgroups específicos y recibir directamente las oportunidades de las categorías que seleccione en su buzón.

Contacto directo con los Trade Points de las Naciones Unidas

1. Relación de Servidores Operativos de UNTPDC

Los Servidores de UNTPDC están ubicados en los siguientes Sitios de la Red:

Argentina - Buenos Aires y Córdoba http://www.untpdc.msite.ar
Australia 1 (Melbourne) http://urgento.gse.rmit.edu.au/untpdc/
Australia 2 (Melbourne) http://harmonic.gse.rmit.edu.au/untpdc/
Australia 3 (Sydney) http://w3.gsm.mq.edu.au/untpdc/
Australia 4 (Melbourne) http://heroic.gse.rmit.edu.au/untpdc/
Australia 5 (Melbourne) http://historic.gse.rmit.edu.au/untpdc
Australia 6 (Melbourne) http://hectic.gse.rmit.edu.au/untpdc/
Austria http://www.untpdc.msite.at
Bahrein http://www.untpdc.msite.bh
Bélgica http://untpdc.tradepoint.be/untpdc/
Bolivia http://www.untpdc.msite.bo
Brasil http://pucaix.rdc.puc-rio.br/untpdc/
Canadá http://www.globalcon.org/untpdc/
Chile http://www.untpdc.msite.cl
China - Pekín, Shanghai http://www.untpdc.msite.cn
Colombia http://www.untpdc.msite.co
Corea del Sur http://www.untpdc.msite.kr
Costa Rica http://www.cinde.or.cr/untpdc/
Costa Rica http://www.untpdc.msite.cr
Croacia http://www.untpdc.msite.hr
Dominica http://www.untpdc.msite.dm
Ecuador http://www.untpdc.msite.ec
Egipto http://sunsite.scu.eun.eg/untpdc/
Egipto http://www.untpdc.msite.eg
El Salvador http://www.untpdc.msite.sv
Emiratos Arabes Unidos http://www.untpdc.msite.ae
Eslovenia http://www.tradepoint.si/untpdc/
España http://www2.ulpgc.es/untpdc/
Estonia http://www.untpdc.msite.ee
Fiji http://www.untpdc.msite.fj
Filipinas http://www.untpdc.msite.ph
Finlandia http://tradepoint.cs.tut.fi/untpdc/
Francia http://www.untpdc.msite.fr
Grecia http://www.untpdc.msite.gr
Guatemala http://www.untpdc.msite.gt
Honduras http://www.untpdc.msite.hn
Hong Kong http://www.untpdc.msite.hk
Hong Kong http://sunsite.ust.hk/untpdc/

Hungría http://www.untpdc.msite.hu
India - Madrás, N. Delhi, Cochin, Calcuta
http://www.untpdc.msite.in
Indonesia (Jakarta) http://www.dprin.go.id/untpdc/
Indonesia (Subaya) http://untpdc.petra.ac.id/untpdc/
Irlanda http://www.untpdc.msite.ie
Islandia http://www.untpdc.msite.is
Israel http://www.tptelisr.org.il/untpdc/
Italia http://www.cineca.it/untpdc/
Jamaica http://www.untpdc.msite.jm
Japón http://sunsite.sut.ac.jp/untpdc/
Jordania http://www.untpdc.msite.jo
Kenia http://www.untpdc.msite.ke
Kuwait http://www.untpdc.msite.kw
Latvia http://www.untpdc.msite.lv
Líbano http://www.untpdc.msite.lb
Lituania http://www.untpdc.msite.lt
Luxemburgo http://www.untpdc.msite.lu
Malasia http://www.untpdc.msite.my
Maldivas http://www.untpdc.msite.mv
Malta http://www.untpdc.msite.mt
Marruecos http://www.untpdc.msite.ma
Mauricio http://www.untpdc.msite.mu
México http://www.untpdc.msite.mx
Micronesia http://www.untpdc.msite.fm
Namibia http://www.untpdc.msite.na
Nepal http://www.untpdc.msite.np
Nicaragua http://www.untpdc.msite.ni
Noruega http://www.untpdc.msite.no
Nueva Zelanda http://www.untpdc.msite.nz
Pakistán http://www.untpdc.msite.pk
Panamá http://www.untpdc.msite.pa
Perú http://www.untpdc.msite.pe
Polonia http://sunsite.icm.edu.pl/untpdc/
Polonia http://www.untpdc.msite.pl
Portugal http://www.infos.pt/untpdc/
Reino Unido http://www.untpdc.msite.uk
República Checa http://sunsite.ms.mff.cuni.cz/untpdc/

Promoción Internacional de Ofertas y Demandas para la Formación   125

República Dominicana http://www.untpdc.msite.do
República Eslovaca http://www.untpdc.msite.sk
Rumania http://www.untpdc.msite.ro
Rusia http://www.sai.msu.su/untpdc/
Santa Lucía http://www.untpdc.msite.lc
Singapur http://www.tpsingapore.org/untpdc/
Singapur http://www.untpdc.msite.sg
Sudáfrica http://sunsite.wits.ac.za/untpdc/
Suecia http://www.untpdc.msite.se
Suiza (Servidor Central de UNTPDC) http://www.unicc.org/untpdc/
Swazilandia http://www.untpdc.msite.sz
Tailandia http://www.untpdc.msite.th
Ucrania http://www.untpdc.msite.ua
Uruguay http://www.untpdc.msite.uy
USA (Los Ángeles) http://www.tradepointla.org/untpdc/
USA (St. Paul/Minneapolis) http://sealus.umn.edu/untpdc/
USA, Tampa, N.Y., San Fco., Detroit, Miami
http://www.untpdc.msite.us
Venezuela http://www.untpdc.msite.ve
Zambia http://www.untpdc.msite.zm
Zimbabwe http://www.zimtrade.co.zw/untpdc/

2. Relación de las Direcciones de Correo Electrónico de los Principales Trade Points de UNTPDC en todo el Mundo

Trade Point de UNTPDC en Barranquilla, Colombia
tpbquill@colcig3.colciencias.gov.co
Trade Point de UNTPDC en Pekín, China
tpbj@www.tpbj.go.cn
Trade Point de UNTPDC en Belo Horizonte, Brasil
tradebhz@fumsoft.softex.br
Trade Point de UNTPDC en Bogotá, Colombia
tpbogota@colcig3.colciencias.gov.co
Trade Point de UNTPDC en Brasilia, Brasil
tpdcsame@guarany.unb.br
Trade Point de UNTPDC en Bucaramanga, Colombia
comexter@multicomputo.multinet.com.co

Trade Point de UNTPDC en Cairo, Egipto
itpegypt@frcu.eun.eg
Trade Point de UNTPDC en Cali, Colombia
camarcom@mafalda.univalle.edu.co
Trade Point de UNTPDC en Campinas, Brasil
tpcampin@mailhost.hq.rnp.br
Trade Point de UNTPDC en Cartagena, Colombia
tpcartag@ns.axisgate.com
Trade Point de UNTPDC en Cochabamba, Bolivia
mabec@dicyt.nrc.edu.bo
Trade Point de UNTPDC en Columbus, USA
info@tpusa.com
Trade Point de UNTPDC en Córdoba, Argentina
tpcba@nt.com.ar
Trade Point de UNTPDC en Curitiba, Brasil
tpcuritiba@lserver.cits.br
Trade Point de UNTPDC en Dakar, Senegal
tpdakar@sonatel.senet.net
Trade Point de UNTPDC en Detroit, USA
wtcdw@sprintmail.com
Trade Point de UNTPDC en Florianópolis, Brasil
tpfln@antares.ctai.rct-sc.br
Trade Point de UNTPDC en Fortaleza, Brasil
tpfort@fiec.sfiec.org.br
Trade Point de UNTPDC en Ginebra, Suiza
wtcgv@iprolink.ch
Trade Point de UNTPDC en Grenoble, Francia
grextp@esc-grenoble.fr
Trade Point de UNTPDC en Harare, Zimbabwe
tpharare@harare.iafrica.com
Trade Point de UNTPDC en Jakarta, Indonesia
putu@pusdata.dprin.go.id
Trade Point de UNTPDC en La Plata, Argentina
zfranca2@startel.com.ar
Trade Point de UNTPDC en Lisboa, Portugal
tplisbon@mail.telepac.pt
Trade Point de UNTPDC en Los Ángeles, USA
dross@tradepointla.org

Trade Point de UNTPDC en Mendoza, Argentina
tpmendoza@tpmnet.com.ar
Trade Point de UNTPDC en Ciudad de México, México
canaci1@ibm.net
Trade Point de UNTPDC en Montevideo, Uruguay
tpmonte@adinet.com.uy
Trade Point de UNTPDC en Moscú, Rusia
minves@dol.ru
Trade Point de UNTPDC en Namur, Bélgica
robin.stock@skynet.be
Trade Point de UNTPDC en Porto Alegre, Brasil
tradepoa@procempa.com.br
Trade Point de UNTPDC en San Cristóbal, Venezuela
tpscven@mai1.lat.net
Trade Point de UNTPDC en Santa Fe, Argentina
tpstafe@tpstafe.satlink.net
Trade Point de UNTPDC en Santiago, Chile
tp-stgo@bhif.cl
Trade Point de UNTPDC en Shanghai, China
tpsftcc@public.sta.net.cn
Trade Point de UNTPDC en Tampa, USA
untp_florida@msn.com
Trade Point de UNTPDC en Tampere, Finlandia
kari.haikkola@tradepoint.fi
Trade Point de UNTPDC en Tel Aviv, Israel
tptelisr@netvision.net.il
Trade Point de UNTPDC en Tunis, Túnez
tptunis@att.mail.com
Trade Point de UNTPDC en Vitoria, Brasil
tpvix@tpvix.com.br
Trade Point de UNTPDC en Yerevan, Armenia
vjh@tpa-gw1.amilink.net
Trade Point de UNTPDC en Argel, Argelia
cnide@ist.cerist.dz
Trade Point de UNTPDC en Ankara, Turquía
burhan@igeme.org.tr
Trade Point de UNTPDC en Bamaku, Mali
tpoint@usaid.gov

Trade Point de UNTPDC en Burdeos, Francia
wtcbx@wtca.geis.com
Trade Point de UNTPDC en Casablanca, Marruecos
tpcmepe@onpt.net.ma
Trade Point de UNTPDC en Genova, Italia
alps_ge@tn.village.it
Trade Point de UNTPDC en Ciudad de Guatemala, Guatemala
business@tradepoint.org.gt
Trade Point de UNTPDC en Helsinki, Finlandia
kari.raatikainen@ffta.mailnet.fi
Trade Point de UNTPDC en Kiev, Ucrania
olegk@mfer.freenet.kiev.ua
Trade Point de UNTPDC en Las Palmas, España
tpcanary@eto.geis.com
Trade Point de UNTPDC en Lausanne, Suiza
wtclausanne@ping.ch
Trade Point de UNTPDC en Le Havre, Francia
wtclh@wtca.geis.com
Trade Point de UNTPDC en Lille, Francia
wtcll@etnet.fr
Trade Point de UNTPDC en Lima, Perú
postmaster@tplima.org.pe
Trade Point de UNTPDC en Ljubljana, Eslovenia
peter.cerar@tradepoint.si
Trade Point de UNTPDC en Lusaka, Zambia
ebzint@zamnet.zm
Trade Point de UNTPDC en Lyon, Francia
wtcly@wtca.geis.com
Trade Point de UNTPDC en Malta, Malta
Santo@metco.u-net.com
Trade Point de UNTPDC en Manila, Filipinas
pcciintr@mozcom.com
Trade Point de UNTPDC en Montpellier, Francia
wtcmp@wtca.geis.com
Trade Point de UNTPDC en Nueva Delhi, India
ncti@x400.nicgw.nic.in
Trade Point de UNTPDC en Nouakchott, Mauritania
cimedt@pactec.org

Trade Point de UNTPDC en Porto Velho, Brasil
tppvh@pop-ro.rnp.br
Trade Point de UNTPDC en Oporto, Portugal
jpauloq@telepac.pt
Trade Point de UNTPDC en Praga, República Checa
tpprague@alef.mpo.cz
Trade Point de UNTPDC en Rostock, Alemania
tprostock@t-online.de
Trade Point de UNTPDC en Sao Paulo, Brasil
rparolin@fiesp.org.br
Trade Point de UNTPDC en Seúl, Corea
tpseoul@kotis.net
Trade Point de UNTPDC en Sevilla, España
wtcsv@wtca.geis.com
Trade Point de UNTPDC en Singapur, Singapur
benjamin@sns.com.sg
Trade Point de UNTPDC en Sofía, Bulgaria
tpwtcsofia@mail.wtcsofia.bg
Trade Point de UNTPDC en San Petersburgo, Rusia
tpspb@frinet.spb.su
Trade Point de UNTPDC en Tallinn, Estonia
tpest@tpest.etc.ee
Trade Point de UNTPDC en Venado Tuerto, Argentina
morema@openware.com.ar
Trade Point de UNTPDC en Yaoundé y Duala, Camerún
oumarou@cyberkoki.net
Trade Point de UNTPDC en Zoetermer, Holanda
ephendriks@knoware.nl

En el año 1998, UNTPDC lanzó la Infraestructura de Seguridad a través de Enlaces Autenticados (ISET-SEAL), que es un sistema diseñado por UNTPDC y cuya principal función es dotar a las transacciones electrónicas en redes abiertas, como Internet, de un marco de seguridad específico. Los SEALs se implantan sobre la extensa Red de Trade Points y UNTPDC emerge como la cúspide de la estructura y la máxima Autoridad de Certificación (CA). A su vez, transmite hacia SEALs nacionales o regionales la facultad de proveer varios servicios que permiten el comercio exterior electrónico, como servicios de pasarelas, reenvíos, funciones de certificación, mecanismos de encriptación y notaría digital que hasta ahora no existían en esta red. Toda esta *jerarquía de confianza* se transmite, a su vez, a la Red Global de Trade Points, y luego a las personas, empresas o instituciones, que

operan en el sistema.

Por ejemplo, una empresa puede solicitar que el Trade Point certifique el envío y recepción de una documentación importante transmitida por medios electrónicos hacia otra empresa suscrita a su Trade Point en el exterior. El Trade Point recurre al SEAL local, éste se pone en contacto con el SEAL del exterior y se certifica el documento. Toda la operación se realiza electrónicamente utilizando, si se quiere, navegadores de Internet como Microsoft Internet Explorer 4.01 o Netscape Communicator 4.01 y una tarjeta tipo *smart card* provista por el Trade Point.

The North American Association for Exports to Eastern Europe (N.A.A.F.E.T.E.E.)
http://www.cyberstreet.com/users/~naafetee
Información: naafetee@cyberstreet.com

La Asociación Norteamericana para la Exportación al Este de Europa (N.A.A.F.E.T.E.E.) es una institución cuya principal finalidad es potenciar las relaciones comerciales con los países del Este de Europa y la difusión de las oportunidades que la región ofrece. Esta especialización de tipo geográfico no impide que comerciantes de cualquier lugar del mundo que tengan interés en cualquier tipo de cooperación empresarial en la región puedan participar en sus Listas. N.A.A.F.E.T.E.E. publica tres Mailing Lists EEUROPE-BUSINESS, EEUROPE-CHANGES y EEUROPE-NEWS. La primera de éstas es específica para el intercambio de ofertas y demandas comerciales y de cooperación empresarial (Joint Ventures, transferencia de tecnología, know-how, etc.).

EEUROPE-BUSINESS es una Lista clásica, de acceso gratuito, donde miles de exportadores, importadores, operadores comerciales intermediarios, e incluso gobiernos envían sus anuncios promocionando las oportunidades de negocio del más diverso tipo. Es una lista intencionalmente «no moderada», es decir, nadie controla el contenido de los mensajes, no se puede incluir mensajes demasiado extensos (superiores a 40 líneas), ni poner mensajes idénticos dentro de un plazo de 7 días. Es posible, enviar hasta dos mensajes de diferente contenido por día siempre que se envíe uno cada doce horas.

- Para la suscripción hay dos formas:

  1. O enviando un mensaje que respete la siguiente estructura:
  A (To): LISTMANAGER@HOOKUP.NET
  Tema o Asunto (Subject): [deje esta línea en blanco]
  Cuerpo: SUBSCRIBE EEUROPE-BUSINESS

  2. O enviando un mensaje simple a esa dirección donde se activará el sistema de suscripción automática.

- Para abandonar la Lista, envíe un mensaje que diga lo siguiente:
  A (To): LISTMANAGER@HOOKUP.NET
  Tema o Asunto (Subject): [deje esta línea en blanco]
  Cuerpo: UNSUBSCRIBE EEUROPE-BUSINESS

- Los archivos antiguos pueden ser explorados en:
  http://magdanoz.bulgaria.com y en http://www.ijs.com/naafetee

Global-Marketplace-Digest de Trading House
http://www.tradinghouse.com/
Información: info@tradinghouse.com

Es una lista de intercambio gratuito de información comercial y empresarial de carácter global. Para participar en este Foro hay que suscribirse a la Lista.

- Para la suscripción envíe un mensaje respetando la siguiente estructura:
  A (To): majordomo@tradinghouse.com
  Tema o Asunto (Subject): [deje esta línea en blanco]
  Cuerpo: subscribe Global-Marketplace-Digest

- Para abandonar la Lista, envíe un mensaje que diga lo siguiente:
  A (To): majordomo@tradinghouse.com
  Tema o Asunto (Subject): [deje esta línea en blanco]
  Cuerpo: unsubscribe Global-Marketplace-Digest

Si desea recibir en diferentes direcciones de correo electrónico hay que enviar el comando: subscribe Global-Marketplace-Digest su_nombre_aquí a la dirección anterior. Inmediatamente recibirá las instrucciones para el envío de ofertas, demandas u otras oportunidades de negocio.

Trading House ofrece la suscripción a otras Listas de información comercial donde se puede acceder a contactos e información en regiones como Asia, Europa, África, Iberoamérica y Países Árabes. Se trata de: Asian Business, Euro-Business, Mercado-Mundial, Business Africa y Arabic-Business, respectivamente.

- Para la suscripción seguir las indicaciones establecidas en http://www.tradinghouse.com/

TBIRDS - International Business Discussion

Tbirds es un Mailing List dedicado a la discusión de temas relacionados con los negocios internacionales. También permite el intercambio de ofertas y demandas de oportunidades comerciales y ofertas de trabajo en el área internacional.

Entre los asuntos de interés que aborda este Foro destacan: NAFTA, GATT (barreras al comercio), Importación y Exportación, Finanzas Internacionales y Marketing Internacional, la problemática de las culturas cruzadas en las Joint Ventures Internacionales, Transferencia de tecnología, Derechos Aduaneros, etc.

- Para suscribirse a la Lista, envíe un mensaje respetando la siguiente estructura:
  A (To): listserv@listserv.arizona.edu
  Tema o Asunto (Subject): [dejar este espacio en blanco]
  Cuerpo: SUBSCRIBE TBIRDS su_nombre_aquí

- Para abandonar la Lista, envíe un mensaje que diga lo siguiente:
  A (To): listserv@listserv.arizona.edu
  Tema o Asunto (Subject): [dejar este espacio en blanco]
  Cuerpo: UNSUBSCRIBE TBIRDS su_nombre_aquí

Tradelink

Tradelink es un típico Mailing List de intercambio gratuito de oportunidades comerciales para la exportación, importación y cooperación empresarial. Presenta un gran movimiento de oportunidades de todos los países del mundo.

- Para la suscripción envíe un mensaje respetando la siguiente estructura:
  A (To): tradlnk@world-net.sct.fr
  Tema o Asunto (Subject): TRDLNK-SUBSCRIBE
  Cuerpo: [deje este espacio en blanco]

- Para abandonar la Lista, envíe un mensaje que diga lo siguiente:
  A (To): tradlnk@world-net.sct.fr
  Tema o Asunto (Subject): TRDLNK-UNSUBSCRIBE
  Cuerpo: [deje este espacio en blanco]

- Para solicitar información enviar un mensaje con el comando: TRADLNK-INFO en la línea del Tema o Asunto a: tradlnk@world-net.sct.fr

Import Export Bulletin Board (IEBB)
http://www.iebb.com/welcome.html
Información: webmaster@iebb.com y jay@iebb.com

IEBB contiene, por un lado, herramientas de comercio electrónico muy útiles para el envío y recepción de oportunidades de negocio y cooperación empresarial, y por otro un caudal de información muy valiosa para el desarrollo de estrategias de comercialización internacional.

La suscripción a IEBB tiene un coste que depende de los servicios que se contrate. Los no-miembros, sin embargo, pueden enviar (previo registro) oportunidades comerciales, así como ofertas y demandas gratuitas relacionadas con la formación de Joint Ventures y otro tipo de cooperación empresarial, a su Tablón de Anuncios. Los Tipos de oportunidades son: oferta de venta, oferta de compra, oportunidad de negocio. Éstas son mantenidas en las páginas Web durante 14 días. Cuenta con una excelente base de datos accesible mediante buscador.

Otros servicios-pagos que presta IEBB, son:

1. Oportunidades comerciales clasificadas, filtradas y remitidas por E-Mail: Se trata de un servicio muy práctico, mediante el cual IEBB remite todas las ofertas o demandas que se reciben a diario bajo la palabra clave que el suscriptor ha indicado.
2. Diario de Oportunidades de IEBB: Envío diario de todas las oportunidades recibidas en el día.
3. Envío de las oportunidades a UNTPDC-ETO, al Periódico Journal of Commerce y a nueve Newsgroups de Internet.

Asimismo, a través de IEBB se puede acceder a contactos *on line* mediante un sistema de Chat Rooms dedicado a promoción de productos y servicios.

Ofrece también información útil para los profesionales en comercio exterior relacionada a instituciones, empresas, información jurídica, información sobre Sitios Web interesantes, etc.

Partnerbase
http://www.partnerbase.com

Es un sitio dedicado a la búsqueda de socios comerciales para el desarrollo de Joint Ventures. En forma gratuita las empresas que lo deseen pueden incluir sus oportunidades comerciales en el

---

Partnerbase Partnership Opportunities
Classified by:
Region (Europe)
Below are profiles of potential business partners which match the criteria you selected.
If you would like to contact any of the partners listed below, simply click on the corresponding 'Contact Partner' button to fill in the Partner Contact Form. Your message will be automatically forwarded by Partnerbase to the company in question.

PARTNER PROFILE

Partnerbase ID: Px93601
Partner Location: UNITED KINGDOM
Industry Sector(s): Paper, printing and publishing Miscellaneous manufactured articles, Chemicals, rubber and plastics.
Turnover: $5.0 million +
Seeking partner in: Europe
Type of Partnership: Joint Venture

DESCRIPTION

We are extruders, printers, and converters of flexible polyethylene packaging. We are 1 of 10 UK companies in the group and there is a US operation. Our products are segmented into three types; those used by banks, courier companies, and retailers. The products we manufacture include: PATCH HANDLE CARRIERS - CUT-OUT HANDLE CARRIERS - RIGID HANDLE CARRIERS - FLEXILOOP HANDLE CARRIERS - DRAWSTRAP HANDLE CARRIERS - SIDE-GUSSETTED CARRIERS COIN BAGS - BULK COIN BAGS - NOTEWRAPPER BAGS COURIER ENVELOPES - MAILING ENVELOPES - TAMPER EVIDENT ENVELOPES - HOSPITAL SPECIMEN BAGS - PLAIN BAGS/WALLETS We are looking to set up a manufacturing resource in Eastern Europe (preferably Poland). We have extruding, printing and converting equipment available. We are looking for a business partner with experience in manufacturing.

Contact Partner (ENTER)

Cuadro 7. Formulario de Partnerbase

Tablón de Anuncios virtual o buscar, entre las ofertas que allí se han incluido el perfil de las compañías que más se asemeja al que la empresa necesita. Posee motores de búsqueda en base de datos, por palabra clave. El diseño de la herramienta de ingreso de las oportunidades de cooperación empresarial se expone en el Cuadro 7.

Trade Compass
http://www.tradecompass.com
Información: staff@tradecompass.com

Trade Compass edita un Megasitio de comercio electrónico donde los productos y servicios se organizan por *profesión* o por *categorías*. Asimismo, se puede acceder a todas las prestaciones mediante una forma simplificada que allí se denomina «Quick Navigate», desde donde se enlaza con los servicios más importantes, como búsquedas en el directorio de los miembros de Trade Compass, búsqueda de ofertas, demandas comerciales y oportunidades de cooperación empresarial (10.000 por semana), Foro de Negocios *on line*, enlace directo a STAT-USA, páginas de países del mundo, guías comerciales de los principales países del mundo, informes de marketing por países (más de 10.000 informes), análisis de los flujos comerciales por países (datos estadísticos de 190 regiones). Posee también un servicio de consultoría de comercio exterior por parte de expertos, información muy completa respecto a transportes marítimos, aéreos, terrestres y logística internacional, novedades en el mundo, bibliotecas electrónicas sobre negocios internacionales (con 14 categorías de información), agencia de viajes, servicios de seguros a la exportación, servicios financieros y muchos otros servicios útiles para los interesados en desarrollar negocios internacionales.

Como complemento, quienes quieran tener una actualización de las ofertas de productos y servicios de Trade Compass, pueden suscribirse en forma gratuita a Trade Compass Gateway simplemente enviando un mensaje a: gateway@tradecompass.com.

Asimismo, en el año 1997 ha lanzado una serie de servicios muy interesantes como:

1. Export Today Magazine, revista mensual de acceso libre que pre-

senta todo tipo de información profesional relacionada con actividades de comercio exterior. http://www.exporttoday.com
2. Trade Compas/Sterling Commerce Caravan es un servicio excelente de apoyo al comercio electrónico, basado en tecnología EDI, mediante el cual empresas de cualquier lugar del mundo pueden cerrar negocios u operaciones comerciales en forma *on line* utilizando los modelos de contratos y la documentación electrónica que hay allí (orden de compra, solicitud de embarque, facturas, declaraciones de envío, cartas de crédito, manifiestos, etc.). Mayor información en el URL: http://www.tradecompass.com/caravan.
3. Trade Compass Global Information Network (GIN). Trade Compass, conjuntamente con algunos de los principales Sitios Web especializados en información y servicios de apoyo al comercio exterior, se han puesto de acuerdo en dar reciprocidad e intercambio de publicidad de tipo «banners» rotativos entre los clientes de esta nueva red. Puede ser una opción interesante para empresas que quieran tener presencia permanente en varios Sitios visitados por profesionales del comercio exterior. Mayor información sobre este servicio en:

- Trade Compass. http://www.tradecompass.com/gin
- Asia Yellow Web. http://yellow-web.com
- BC TradeNet. http://www.bc-trade.net
- Export Today. http://www.exporttoday.com
- FreightWorld. http://www.freightworld.com
- Interage. http://www.age.co.il
- México Trade Monitor. http://www.mextrademonitor.com.mx
- Trade Compass UK. http://www.tradecompass.co.uk

The Trading Floor
http://trading.wmw.com/

Este Sitio Comercial ofrece la posibilidad de entablar negociaciones *on line* mediante Chat Rooms, contactos confidenciales, conferencias entre grupos privados, Tablón de Anuncios virtual de carácter gratuito de ofertas y demandas mediante técnicas multimedia, una muy extensa información sobre importadores y exportadores, y catálogos multimedia de productos y servicios. Posee motores de búsqueda en base de datos por palabra clave.

TradePort
http://tradeport.org/
Información: info@hq.baytrade.org

Este Sitio creado por Baytrade y por la Cámara de Comercio de los Angeles, California (USA), incluye numerosos enlaces con información relacionada a oportunidades de negocio en California y en el mundo, investigaciones de mercado, ferias y exposiciones comerciales, misiones comerciales, banca, transportes internacionales, empresas de importación y exportación, oportunidades de Joint Ventures, bibliografía sobre los diferentes temas del comercio exterior, disposiciones legales, consejos para el exportador o importador, Newsgroups, Mailing Lists y otras cuestiones.

Global Mercantile Exchange de Trading House
http://www.tradinghouse.com/
Información: info@tradinghouse.com

En Trading House se pueden enviar o explorar las oportunidades comerciales y ofertas de cooperación empresarial del servicio Global Mercantile Exchange en forma gratuita, o las novedades de Global News Bank, o información sobre oportunidades de empleo en Global Jobs & Careers Exchange. Se pueden intercambiar bienes o servicios a escala internacional a través de Global Barter, una novedosa herramienta de promoción comercial electrónica. También presenta otros servicios como Global Trade Services para el intercambio internacional de servicios, o Global Technology Exchange para el comercio de tecnologías o know-how, o Global Trade-Fairs & Events Exchange para la promoción de eventos comerciales, y Sub-Sitios relacionados con el intercambio de manufacturas, subcontratación internacional, etc.

Posee motores de búsqueda en base de datos general y específica para el sector industrial, ambas por palabra clave. Se puede acceder en los idiomas: inglés, español, francés y alemán.

Netsource Asia - The TradeCenter
http://www.netsource-asia.com/trade.htm

Netsource Asia edita un Tablón de Anuncios virtual de acceso gratuito muy visitado por empresarios de todo el mundo. En él se pueden encontrar oportunidades comerciales y de cooperación empresarial sobre todo tipo de productos y servicios. Las ofertas se deben incluir indicando si se trata de Exportación o Importación. Los mensajes no pueden exceder las 300 letras. En 1998 Netsource ha incorporado un servicio más completo que incluye una mayor seguridad en los mecanismos de promoción, a fin de evitar la presencia de anuncios no relacionados con los negocios, y las diferentes formas de marketing multinivel. Si bien el establecimiento de ofertas es gratuito, existe la posibilidad de suscribirse como Socio Pleno pagando 89 USD, y participar de privilegios especiales. Este Sitio Web está directamente relacionado con Netsource America, centrado en actividades comerciales de los Estados Unidos y se accede en http://www.netsource-america.com

DigiLead
http://www.digilead.com/
Información: info@digilead.com

DigiLead mantiene una base de datos *on line* de acceso gratuito y editada en idioma inglés, dedicada a la inclusión de ofertas y demandas de productos, servicios y cooperación empresarial.

Mercado-mundial
http://www.cgtd.com/global/index.html
Información: editor@cgt.com

Mercado-mundial es una revista en español, francés, italiano y portugués que cubre diferentes aspectos de la economía internacional y el comercio exterior. Es de suscripción gratuita y de distribución de oportunidades comerciales.

Los temas principales de este Foro de Discusión son: mercados emergentes; innovaciones en marketing internacional; información sobre los países y áreas geo-económicas en proceso de adaptación al sistema de mercado; liberalización de los mercados; privatización del sector público; papel de los gobiernos y administración en los negocios; tendencias globales en productos; mercados e industrias específicas; papel de nuevas tecnologías; telecomunicación, Internet en el futuro del comercio y desarrollo de la economía local y nacional, relación de la Península Ibérica (España-Portugal) con Europa, Latinoamérica, Europa del Este, Asia y África; relación de América Latina con los EE.UU., la Península Ibérica, Europa, Asia y África; cambios emergentes en las economías de la América Latina; bloques económicos como Unión Europea, Mercosur, Tratado de Libre Comercio de América del Norte (TLC-NAFTA), ASEAN, SAARC, ECO, etc. y el impacto sobre la economía global; compañías multinacionales y sus prácticas; mercados exteriores y su impacto sobre el mercado de trabajo; oportunidades en los diversos segmentos del comercio internacional; importación, exportación, inversión en los mercados emergentes; comercio exterior y su influencia sobre la economía nacional; búsqueda de nuevos productos, mercados, clientes; conectar con las firmas en todos los continentes; Joint Ventures, transferencia de tecnología y know-how, inversión, y cualquier tema propuesto por los miembros.

- Para suscribirse a la Lista, envíe un mensaje respetando la siguiente estructura:
  A (To): majordomo@primenet.com
  Tema o Asunto (Subject): [deje esta línea en blanco]
  Cuerpo: subscribe mercado-mundial su_e-mail_aquí

- Para abandonar la Lista, envíe un mensaje que diga lo siguiente:
  A (To): majordomo@primenet.com
  Tema o Asunto (Subject): [deje esta línea en blanco]
  Cuerpo: unsubscribe mercado-mundial su_e-mail_aquí

Para enviar mensajes a la Lista: mercado-mundial@primenet.com

Sistema de Promoción de Información Tecnológica y Comercial (Tips)
http://tips.org.uy
Información: tips@chasque.apc.org

Tips es una de las mayores redes de información comercial, tecnológica, financiera y de negocios que actualmente existe en América Latina. Posee varias herramientas de búsqueda en extensas bases de datos de esta región y de casi todo el mundo, y un servicio de difusión de oportunidades comerciales de tipo «empresa a empresa» a través de medios telemáticos e impresos muy eficientes.

Tiene su central de operaciones en Montevideo, y desde allí, un contacto directo y especializado con el resto de países del Mercosur. Por su extraordinaria capacidad tecnológica, Tips ha contado desde sus inicios con el apoyo de instituciones internacionales como PNUD y de la Comisión Europea, y actualmente es proveedor de productos y servicios telemáticos de la Comisión Europea, de la Agencia para el Desarrollo Internacional de Estados Unidos (USAID) para América Latina, de Agencias Gubernamentales de Promoción de Comercio Exterior de la región y de varias cámaras de comercio.

El coste del acceso a los servicios de difusión y búsqueda de oportunidades de Tips es de aproximadamente 15 USD por año. Vale la pena solicitar un *password* para prueba gratuita de los servicios por un período de un mes.

The Know-How Company
http://iypn.com/theknowhowco/index.html
Información: benelles@iypn.com

The Know-How Company es una empresa dedicada a la intermediación de derechos de propiedad intelectual, especialmente, licencias de conceptos y productos. En su Sitio Web se exponen conceptos y productos que están a la venta. Quien desee vender algún tipo de idea que tenga interés comercial a nivel global, puede ponerse en contacto con la firma en la dirección de correo electrónico de arriba.

Global Access to Trade and Technology Server
http://www.gatts.com/

Global Access es un sitio de Internet dedicado a difundir información sobre la comercialización de productos, servicios y tecnologías internacionales. Provee contactos con empresas y enlaces hacia otros Sitios Web de interés.

Negocios en Leningrado
http://www.mbs.umd.edu/Ciber/wp4.html

La legislación soviética permite la formación de Joint Ventures con diferentes grados de proporción en la propiedad. Si el socio comercial extranjero proporciona fondos que superan el 30% del total de los aportes, la Joint Venture gozará de una sustancial reducción de derechos impositivos.

La legislación rusa (RSFSR) otorga al Consejo de la Ciudad de Leningrado el derecho a registrar la Joint Venture con la participación del estado ruso o municipio como co-propietario, o en forma de cooperativa, holding compartido, o empresa privada. Durante los primeros dos años (en algunos casos tres), no se exige el pago de impuestos por la Joint Venture. Asimismo, se puede negociar el tipo de cambio del rublo a una divisa o moneda fuerte para la repatriación de los beneficios.

El socio «soviético» generalmente se hace cargo de todas las actividades de relación con los abastecedores, vendedores, agencias gubernamentales, inscripción y gestión de las licencias y las relaciones con los clientes.

Hamburguer Business Development Corporation (HWF)
http://www.hamburg.de/Firmen/HWF/Engl/hwf1.htm
Información: hwf.hamburg@t-online.de

HWF es una compañía de carácter mixto dedicada a apoyar proyectos empresariales de todo tipo en la región de Hamburgo, Alemania. Sus servicios son gratuitos. Trabaja en cooperación con otras instituciones públicas y privadas, como cámaras de comercio, asociaciones de importadores y exportadores, etc.

REFAC Technology Corporation
http://www.refac.com/
Información: refac@refac.com

Esta empresa radicada en Nueva York tiene como principal objetivo el desarrollo de negocios internacionales relacionados a transferencia de licencias y de tecnologías (negociación) y administración de licencias industriales y Joint Ventures en donde intervengan patentes, marcas y know-how.

Como servicio de gran interés, ofrece la explotación de tecnologías o propiedad industrial parcialmente desarrolladas o no-utilizadas y transformar ese capital «inerte» en un activo para los creadores o inventores.

Techno Industries Corporation (TIC)
http://www.teleport.com/~rouzpay/techno.htm

TIC es una empresa dedicada al desarrollo de negocios de tipo Joint Venture a nivel internacional. Ofrece su equipo de trabajo, ubicado en los Estados Unidos y en varios países del mundo, para la complementación de sus estrategias. Sus principales mercados son China y Europa del Este.

Corporación China de Crédito e Inversiones Internacionales / China International Trust & Investment Corporation (CITIC)
http://www.citic.com/
Información: citic@citic.com (Canadá)
Información: citifor@aol.com (USA)

CITIC es una corporación estatal china dependiente del Consejo de Estado, fundada en el año 1979 con el propósito de hacer efectiva la radicación de capitales internacionales y la formación de Joint Ventures en este país. Uno de los postulados principales de CITIC es brindar cooperación científica y tecnológica a los empresarios locales y relacionar a las empresas chinas con el sector bancario, financiero y comercial internacional a fin de que éstas puedan absorber capital extranjero. Pero uno de los aspectos más interesantes de esta corporación para los interesados en el desarrollo de Joint Ventures o transferencia de tecnologías, es que CITIC funciona también como un centro de relación entre la oferta y la demanda de cooperación empresarial. Por lo tanto, los empresarios que buscan socios comerciales en este país pueden solicitar el apoyo logístico de CITIC y luego realizar la presentación del proyecto ante el Ministerio de Cooperación Económica y Comercio Exterior (MOFTEC).

El servidor de WWW que utiliza CITIC está ubicado geográficamente en Canadá y desde allí no se ofrece información *on line* relevante. Es conveniente solicitar mediante correo electrónico la información empresarial que necesite, así como los datos necesarios para obtener colaboración oficial en los proyectos.

EleTech
http://www.arrakis.es/~ecr_pers/electech/espanol/cet.html
Información: etc@arrakis.es

En este Sitio Web se puede tomar contacto con una empresa española especializada en tecnologías que brinda asesoramiento y gestión en áreas relacionadas con tecnología electrónica, transferencia de tecnologías, nuevas fábricas y líneas de producción y ayudas de la Comisión Europea para el desarrollo de proyectos tecnológicos, implantación de las normas de calidad ISO 9000.

International Export Connections
http://www.teleport.com/~iexportc
Información: iexportc@teleport.com

International Export Connection Dewaniah edita un Tablón de Anuncios gratuito dedicado a actividades de comercio internacional. A través de este sistema se pueden enviar o conocer oportunidades comerciales relacionadas con: compra, venta, búsqueda de agentes, búsqueda de proveedores, Joint Ventures, oferta de empleo, embarques, publicidad, servicios legales, publicaciones, etc.

The International Franchise Research Centre (IFRC)
http://www.wmin.ac.uk/~purdyd/

Este Sitio Web, creado en 1993, tiene como principal misión promover e informar respecto a temas relacionados con el negocio de las franquicias internacionales. Para ser miembro del Centro es necesario asociarse por suscripción. A través de la página Web de IFRC se puede realizar, de todos modos, consultas específicas sobre el negocio y empresas, acceder a información documental, y acceder a enlaces con otros servidores y páginas que desarrollan esta problemática y ofrecen contactos con franquiciadores y franquiciantes.

Entre los miembros actuales figuran empresas de relieve como: Barclays Bank, British Franchise Association, Dyno-Rod, Franchise Development Services Ltd., Lloyds Bank, Midland Bank, Prontaprint, Rosemary Conley Diet & Fitness Clubs, Royal Bank of Scotland, The Swinton Group, and Wragge & Co, y otros.

Adviser Publisher (AP) - Brasil
http://manzolirico.com.br/
Información: manrico@portoweb.com.br

Esta empresa privada de Brasil ofrece en Internet sus servicios para la introducción de empresas extranjeras a partir de alianzas de cooperación empresarial. Según afirman, cooperar no significa hacer un contrato o negocio, sino trabajar juntos. Y lo que mantiene las empresas en un proceso de cooperación son las alianzas estratégicas, que las unen en este propósito, fortaleciendo la esencia de la competitividad.

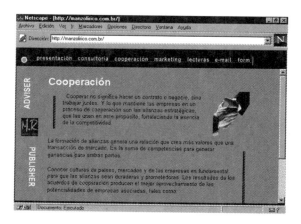

La formación de alianzas genera una relación que crea más valores que una transacción de mercado. Es la suma de competencias para generar ganancias para ambas partes.

Conocer las culturas de países, mercados y de las empresas es fundamental para que las alianzas sean duraderas y prometedoras. Los resultados de los acuerdos de cooperación producen el mejor aprovechamiento de las potencialidades de las empresas asociadas, principalmente en las formas de distribución, representación, intercambio tecnológico, abordajes conjuntos de terceros mercados, viabilidad de asociaciones y Joint Ventures.

Organización de Promoción de Negocios de Baden-Württemberg (GWZ) - Alemania
http://www.gwz.de/englisch/profil/2.html

GWZ es una organización de promoción de negocios de Baden-Württemberg, sudeste de Alemania, que desarrolla una intensa actividad en relación a la cooperación empresarial con todo el mundo.

Es una puerta de entrada para todo tipo de negocios que quieran establecerse en el estado de Banden-Württemberg, pero también para iniciar contactos para la formación de Joint Ventures con empresas de la región, ya que ofrecen unos servicios muy completos y prácticos para tales fines.

4.1.2. Recursos de Internet para la Promoción Global de Oportunidades Comerciales Generales de Productos y Servicios, incluso Joint Ventures, Transferencia de Tecnología y Know-how

misc.invest.marketplace
Newsgroup dedicado a la discusión de temas de carácter general relacionados con proyectos de inversión e inversiones de comercio exterior.

alt.business.import-export
Newsgroup especializado en intercambios de ofertas comerciales para la importación y exportación de productos y servicios en general.

misc.invest.marketplace
Newsgroup dedicado a la discusión de temas de carácter general relacionados con proyectos de inversión e inversiones de comercio exterior.

alt.business.import-export
Newsgroup especializado en intercambios de ofertas comerciales para la importación y exportación de productos y servicios en general.

alt.business.import-export.consumables
Newsgroup especializado en intercambios de ofertas comerciales para la importación y exportación de productos y servicios relacionados con el sector de bienes de consumo.

alt.business.import-export.food
Newsgroup especializado en intercambios de ofertas comerciales para la importación y exportación de productos y servicios relacionados con el sector de la alimentación.

alt.business.import-export.services
Newsgroup especializado en intercambios de oportunidades comerciales relacionadas con el sector servicios al comercio exterior.

alt.business.import-export.offshore
Newsgroup especializado en intercambios de ofertas comerciales

para la importación y exportación de productos y servicios en general.

cdb.foreign
Newsgroup especializado en intercambios de ofertas comerciales para la importación y exportación de productos y servicios en general.

clari.biz.world trade
Newsgroup especializado en intercambios de ofertas comerciales para la importación y exportación de productos y servicios en general.

biz.marketplace.international
Newsgroup especializado en intercambios de ofertas comerciales para la importación y exportación de productos y servicios en general.

relcom.wtc
Newsgroup especializado en intercambios de ofertas comerciales para la importación y exportación de productos y servicios en general.

misc.business.consulting
Newsgroup dedicado a la discusión de temas de carácter general relacionados con actividades de consultoría en negocios y relaciones comerciales.

rec.arts.books.marketplace
Newsgroup dedicado a la discusión de temas relacionados a publicaciones respecto a mercados virtuales y comercio exterior.

TradePort Mailing List
TradePort ofrece dos opciones para la utilización gratuita de sus servicios de Mailing List especializados en comercio exterior. Uno es *Tradeport-l,* en donde los miembros pueden enviar noticias y oportunidades comerciales de todo tipo; y el segundo es *Tradeport info,* donde los miembros sólo reciben información sobre comercio y cooperación empresarial internacional, boletines y novedades pero no es posible enviar mensajes.

1. Tradeport-l

- Para la suscripción envíe un mensaje respetando la siguiente estructura:
  A (To): Majordomo@merkury.saic.com
  Tema o Asunto (Subject): [deje esta línea en blanco]
  Cuerpo: subscribe tradeport-l su_nombre_aquí

- Para abandonar la Lista, envíe un mensaje que diga lo siguiente:
  A (To): Majordomo@merkury.saic.com
  Tema o Asunto (Subject): [deje esta línea en blanco]
  Cuerpo: unsubscribe tradeport-l su_nombre_aquí

2. Tradeport Info

- Para la suscripción envíe un mensaje respetando la siguiente estructura:
  A (To): Majordomo@merkury.saic.com
  Tema o Asunto (Subject): [deje esta línea en blanco]
  Cuerpo: subscribe tradeport info su_nombre_aquí

- Para abandonar la Lista, envíe un mensaje que diga lo siguiente:
  A (To): Majordomo@merkury.saic.com
  Tema o Asunto (Subject): [deje esta línea en blanco]
  Cuerpo: unsubscribe tradeport info su_nombre_aquí

Trade Bulletin Board - Cyber Commerce Corporation
http://www.cybercc.com/trade/bbs.htm
Información: chpark@cybercc.com

Es un Tablón de Anuncios virtual donde en forma gratuita las empresas que lo deseen pueden incluir ofertas comerciales de compra, venta u oportunidades de cooperación empresarial. Posee motores de búsqueda en base de datos, por palabra clave.

World Industrial Park
http://worldbusiness.net
Información: info@worldbusiness.net

Es un Sitio Web que edita información muy completa sobre empresas del sector industrial de Estados Unidos y de varios países del mundo. Sus páginas Web presentan un tráfico muy intenso de empresarios interesados en conocer las últimas noticias y tecnologías relacionadas con el sector industrial.

Posee un Tablón de Anuncios virtual llamado Global Marketplace en donde se puede enviar gratuitamente y analizar las oportunidades comerciales que allí se envían de todo el mundo. Aunque es gratis, para enviar ofertas es necesario registrar su empresa como miembro de World Business Network, cuya metodología está allí indicada. Pero pagando una inscripción de 150 USD por año, los miembros ejecutivos pueden incluir su página Web en World Industrial Park, ser incluidos en los 40 cuarenta motores de búsqueda más importantes de Internet y 5.000 anuncios tipo «banner» en el Tablón de Anuncios Global Marketplace.

World Trade Exchange
http://www.wte.net/
Información: wte_info@tradeline.net

Es una red de carácter internacional creada por la empresa norteamericana ITT y sus filiales europeas que provee gratuitamente información sobre pequeñas y medianas empresas, de sus productos y tecnologías. Actualmente más de 30.000 empresas ofrecen sus productos, tecnologías, oportunidades de formación de Joint Ventures y servicios a través de catálogos electrónicos, información corporativa, presentaciones multimedia, etc. Posee motores de búsqueda en base de datos, por palabra clave.

Marketnet
http://www.us-marketnet.com/

Es un Sitio Web editado en idioma español, inglés, francés y árabe. La simplicidad de su estructura permite el pronto acceso a información importante para la comercialización de productos y servicios a escala internacional. Posee Tablón de Anuncios virtual donde en forma gratuita las empresas que lo deseen pueden incluir ofertas comerciales de compra, venta u oportunidades comerciales. Presenta secciones de acceso directamente relacionadas con cada uno de los productos o servicios que generalmente interesan a los operadores de comercio exterior: Proyectos Industriales, Maquinaria y Equipos Usados, Tecnologías y Procesos, Stocks de Productos, Licitaciones, Ofertas de Empleo, Trueque de Productos, Oportunidades de Inversión, Franquicias, Negocios Inmobiliarios, Transporte de Mercancías, Agentes y Distribuidores. Asimismo, presenta secciones relacionadas con Mercados Internacionales, Seguros, Banca y actividades financieras, Noticias, Servicio de Traducción, Viajes y Turismo, Exposiciones Internacionales, Legislación y Catálogos Electrónicos.

Tradescope
http://www.owens.com/tradescp/submittl.htm
Información: email@owens.com

Tradescope ofrece la posibilidad de acceso ilimitado a las oportunidades comerciales distribuidas por el Departamento de Comercio y Agricultura de los Estados Unidos a través de sus bases de datos oficiales y a las licitaciones del gobierno japonés distribuidas por la Organización de Comercio Exterior de Japón (JETRO). El coste anual por este servicio es de 95 USD.

Asimismo, es posible enviar oportunidades comerciales y de cooperación empresarial, y también analizar las ofertas que allí existen sin coste alguno. Todas las ofertas enviadas se conservan durante 120 días. No pueden tener más de 40 palabras. Y deben estar relacionadas con la compra, venta, servicios internacionales u oportunidades comerciales internacionales.

Global Trade Opportunities Network (GTON)

GTON es un foro de intercambio de oportunidades comerciales entre importadores, exportadores y prestadores de todo tipo de servicios. El coste de suscripción anual para enviar y recibir oportunidades es de 10 USD, pero durante un período de evaluación de 30 días es gratis.

- Para suscribirse a la Lista, envíe un mensaje respetando la siguiente estructura:
  A (To): majordomo@esosoft.com
  Tema o Asunto (Subject): [deje esta línea en blanco]
  Cuerpo: SUBSCRIBE GTON

- Para abandonar la Lista, envíe un mensaje que diga lo siguiente:
  A (To): majordomo@esosoft.com
  Tema o Asunto (Subject): [deje esta línea en blanco]
  Cuerpo: UNSUBSCRIBE GTON

International Business Buy+Sell List

International Business Buy+Sell List es un Mailing List público y moderado que tiene por objetivo el intercambio de ideas y apoyo para llevar a cabo actividades comerciales entre empresarios de diferentes países. Es un foro interesante, ya que permite tomar contacto con exportadores o importadores o empresarios interesados en distinto tipo de cooperación.

- Para suscribirse a la Lista, envíe un mensaje respetando la siguiente estructura:
  A (To): intlbuy+sell-d-request@lofcom.com
  Tema o Asunto (Subject): SUBSCRIBE
  Cuerpo: [deje este sector en blanco]

- Para abandonar la Lista, envíe un mensaje que diga lo siguiente:
  A (To): intlbuy+sell-d-request@lofcom.com
  Tema o Asunto (Subject): UNSUBSCRIBE
  Cuerpo: [deje este sector en blanco]

TradeCom

Promueve contactos comerciales a nivel internacional y el intercambio de ofertas comerciales de productos, cooperación empresarial y servicios.

- Para suscribirse a la Lista, envíe un mensaje respetando la siguiente estructura:
  A (To): TradeCom-request@bigdipper.umd.edu
  Tema o Asunto (Subject): [deje esta línea en blanco]
  Cuerpo: SUBSCRIBE

- Para abandonar la Lista, envíe un mensaje que diga lo siguiente:
  A (To): TradeCom-request@bigdipper.umd.edu
  Tema o Asunto (Subject): [deje esta línea en blanco]
  Cuerpo: UNSUBSCRIBE

World Network of Chambers of Commerce and Industry
http://www.worldchambers.com/
Información: fischerg@ccip.fr

Bajo la coordinación del Consorcio para el Comercio Global de la Cámara de Comercio de París, se ha formado una alianza estratégica entre un enorme grupo de organizaciones empresariales, el Consejo Internacional de Cámaras de Comercio (IBCC) y la Corporación IBNet con el fin de coordinar y establecer las pautas de acción de la Red Mundial de Cámaras de Comercio en sus actividades de promoción internacional de oportunidades comerciales. Lo más relevante para actividades directas de comercio electrónico dentro de esta red puede verse en:

1. Global Business Opportunities eXchange (GBX)
http://www2.asianconnect.com/ibn/gw/ecbview.cgi
Es un Tablón de Anuncios donde de forma gratuita las empresas que lo deseen pueden incluir ofertas y demandas comerciales, y de cooperación empresarial. Posee motores de búsqueda en base de datos, por palabra clave.

2. IBCC-Net - Global Network of Chambers of Commerce
http://www.icc-ibcc.org/ibccnet.html
Es un sistema de intercambio de información entre Cámaras de Comercio e Industria con el objeto de profundizar la cooperación entre éstas y ampliar sus posibilidades de servicios en el entorno internacional. Actualmente más de 1.000 Cámaras de Comercio de todo el mundo ya están interconectadas mediante este medio.

Partnerseek
http://www.partnerseek.com/
Información: webmaster@ventureseek.com

Partnerseek es un Sitio Web, editado por The Synergizer, cuyo objetivo es reunir a empresas y a empresarios en un foro exclusivo para la búsqueda de socios para Joint Ventures, socios comerciales, o socios para inversiones de capital u oportunidades de inversión. El método seleccionado para el envío y exposición de las ofertas o demandas de cooperación empresarial es el típico Tablón de Anuncio, asimismo, consta de motores de búsqueda por palabra clave. Gratis hasta junio de 1998.

FREETRADER.COM
http://www.freetrader.com/free/fr07000.htm
Información: broker@freetrader.com

Freetrader.com edita un Tablón de Anuncios llamado Marketplace Exchange en donde empresarios de cualquier lugar del mundo pueden enviar oportunidades comerciales y de cooperación empresarial o analizar las que se enviaron con anterioridad. Este servicio es gratuito.

Promoción Internacional de Ofertas y Demandas para la Formación   155

Planet Business
http://www.planetbiz.com
Información: planetbiz@planetbiz.com

Es una fuente de información gratuita y muy completa sobre temas relacionados con el comercio internacional de productos, cooperación empresarial y servicios. Presenta un sistema de enlaces con las principales fuentes de información internacional sobre cada uno de los países de África, Asia, América, Europa y Oceanía.

Como complemento ofrece un Tablón de Anuncios clasificado por productos en donde se pueden enviar o analizar oportunidades de exportación, importación y servicios. Comprende sectores de: productos químicos, electrónicos, alimentos y bebidas, moda, maquinarias, materia prima, productos inmobiliarios, y otros.

Trade-Express
http://www.trade-express.com/
Información: tradex@squirrel.com.au

Trade-Express edita un Tablón de Anuncios muy extenso de acceso gratuito para el público general, mediante motores de búsqueda por palabra clave en base de datos se pueden analizar las oportunidades comerciales y de cooperación empresarial que allí se incluyen. Pero para poder enviar mensajes hay que pagar un derecho anual de aproximadamente 100 USD.

4.1.3. *Recursos de Internet en Europa para la Promoción de Oportunidades Comerciales Generales de Productos y Servicios, incluso Joint Ventures, Transferencia de Tecnología y Know-how*

Import-Export Bulletin Board de SWISS INFO.NET
http://www.swissinfo.net/iebbs/
Información: admin@swissinfo.net

Es un Tablón de Anuncios virtual donde las empresas que lo deseen pueden incluir ofertas comerciales de compra, venta u oportunidades de cooperación empresarial. Está situado geográficamente en Suiza. Posee motores de búsqueda en base de datos, por palabra clave.

Trade Zone France Companies
http://www.france-companies.com/trade/tradeuk2.htm
Información: nitex@france-companies.com

France Companies es un Sitio Web editado en Francia que permite, por un lado, la búsqueda detallada de productos y empresas en una extensa base de datos, y por otro, la inclusión en Tablón de Anuncios de oportunidades comerciales para la exportación, importación, búsqueda de socios comerciales u otro tipo de cooperación empresarial. Los servicios son completamente gratuitos.

X-Roads
http://www.businessroads.com
Información: xroads@businessroads.com

X-Roads edita en Francia una página Web dedicada a la difusión de oportunidades comerciales en el mundo. Asimismo, presta un servicio integral de asesoramiento, investigación de oportunidades y traducción. El envío de oportunidades es gratis. Sin embargo para acceder a los servicios completos, incluso búsqueda en sus bases de datos hay que pagar una suscripción de 250 FF por mes.

**Importaciones - Búsquedas y Licitaciones Internacionales /
Poptávky - Import a Tendry**
http://tradenet.chipnet.cz/Wanted.htm
Información: tradenet@chipnet.cz

TRADEnet y la Fundación para el Desarrollo de la Empresa de la República Checa editan un Tablón de Anuncios gratuito dedicado al intercambio de oportunidades comerciales de importación y exportación. Este Sitio destaca por la cantidad de oportunidades para la participación empresarial en proyectos y licitaciones de regiones y ciudades del Este de Europa y de la Ex Unión Soviética.

BCC TradeBridge - Russia

BCC TradeBridge es una lista especializada en oportunidades comerciales de productos, servicios e inversiones en Rusia. Se trata de una Lista moderada por sus editores donde las ofertas o requerimientos no pueden exceder un máximo de 20 palabras.

- Para suscribirse a la Lista, envíe un mensaje respetando la siguiente estructura:
  A (To): majordomo@bcc.ru
  Tema o Asunto (Subject): [deje esta línea en blanco]
  Cuerpo: SUBSCRIBE TRADE

- Para abandonar la Lista, envíe un mensaje que diga lo siguiente:
  A (To): majordomo@bcc.ru
  Tema o Asunto (Subject): [deje esta línea en blanco]
  Cuerpo: UNSUBSCRIBE TRADE

Spanbizpoint
http://www.spainbizpoint.com/biz2.htm
Información: spainbp@spainbizpoint.com

Spanbizpoint edita un Tablón de Anuncios en español y de acceso gratuito para el envío y análisis de ofertas y de demandas de importación y exportación. Es un buen recurso pero los conceptos de su formulario pueden llevar a la confusión. Sus editores indican que tienen preparado un nuevo formato de búsqueda de ofertas y demandas, estructurado en las 20 secciones y casi los 100 capítulos que establece el código arancelario internacional. Posiblemente con ello mejorarán sus prestaciones.

Spaindustry
http://www.spaindustry.com/
Información: infoqu01@sarenet.es

Es una base de datos *on line* de acceso gratuito mediante Internet en donde se pueden recoger los datos de 20.000 empresas importadoras/exportadoras españolas. Cualquier empresa que lo desee puede anunciar sus productos aquí. Posee motor de búsqueda en la base de datos.

TradeMatch
http://www.tradematch.co.uk
Información: sales@ipl.co.uk

TradeMatch es una base de datos *on line* diseñada para apoyar a empresas inglesas en la búsqueda de nuevos mercados, socios y consumidores a nivel internacional. Sus principales relaciones se refieren a países escandinavos, nuevos estados Bálticos y mercados emergentes como Polonia, Hungría, la República Checa. Lo interesante de esta base de datos es que está realizada con la participación de varias Cámaras de Comercio y Consejos de Exportación británicos.

Las empresas que deseen enviar la información sobre sus productos y servicios pueden hacerlo gratuitamente mediante una suscripción simple, pero para acceder a los servicios completos, como traducción de las ofertas, foro de discusión y publicidad complementaria de los productos TradeMatch cobra al empresario una cantidad anual no muy elevada.

Spain Traders Networks
http://www.spaintraders.com
Información: mlocsin@bigfoot.com

Es un Tablón de Anuncios simple en el que se puede acceder a oportunidades comerciales de productos y servicios de todo el mundo. El envío de ofertas es gratuito.

RETEL - Centro de Recursos Telemáticos
http://www.retel.com/negocios
Información: retel@retel.es

La empresa catalana Retel ha abierto un canal en Internet para las empresas, con el fin de apoyar sus estrategias comerciales. Ofrecen secciones donde el empresario puede registrar y consultar gratuitamente la información registrada: ofertas, demandas, stocks, acuerdos de colaboración, etc.

Promoción Internacional de Ofertas y Demandas para la Formación 159

Export Line
http: www.immagica.it/export-line/index.html
Información: export@immagica.it

Export Line es un Tablón de Anuncios de oportunidades comerciales establecido en Parma, Italia. Las ofertas y demandas se incluyen gratuitamente. La empresa editora de este Sitio ofrece un servicio personalizado de búsqueda y envío mediante correo electrónico.

4.1.4. Recursos de Internet en América Latina y América Central para la Promoción de Oportunidades Comerciales Generales de Productos y Servicios, incluso Joint Ventures, Transferencia de Tecnología y Know-how

Web de Negocios del Directorio de Argentina
http://www.grippo.com/wwwboard/wwwboard.htm
Información: admin@grippo.com

En este Sitio Web encontrará un clásico Tablón de Anuncios gratuito de ofertas y demandas que se corresponden a todo tipo de productos y servicios. Por estar ubicado geográficamente en la República Argentina, encontrará allí oportunidades comerciales muy relacionadas con ese mercado y Mercosur. Desde allí se puede acceder a más de 7.000 links de Argentina.

Asimismo, los editores de este Sitio Comercial mantienen la Lista de Negocios del Directorio de Argentina, que es un Mailing List gratuito de distribución exclusivamente en idioma español. Tiene por objetivo hacer circular anuncios, noticias, eventos y hechos reales por parte de empresarios de países de habla hispana respecto a los siguientes temas: oportunidades para importar y exportar, presentaciones de nuevos productos y servicios, representaciones de productos y servicios, datos claves de industrias y mercados verticales, historias de éxitos y fracasos comerciales, consejos para nuevos emprendimientos, promociones y ofertas interesantes y franquicias.

- Para suscribirse a la Lista, envíe un mensaje que respete la siguiente estructura:
  A (To): majordomo@rapidserver.com
  Tema o Asunto (Subject): [deje este línea en blanco]
  Cuerpo: subscribe negocios

- Para abandonar la Lista, envíe un mensaje que diga lo siguiente:
  A (To): majordomo@rapidserver.com
  Tema o Asunto (Subject): [deje este línea en blanco]
  Cuerpo: unsubscribe negocios

Una vez que se ha agregado a la Lista, recibirá todos los anuncios de los otros participantes directamente en su buzón de correo electrónico. Si usted quiere hacer un anuncio o consulta, envíe un mensaje como el siguiente, y éste será distribuido entre todos los participantes:

A (To): negocios@rapidserver.com
Tema o Asunto (Subject): Joint Venture (Seek Partner)
Cuerpo: Desarrollar el mensaje comercial.

Otra forma de suscripción es ingresando al Sitio Web arriba indicado, y si quiere analizar los antiguos archivos de oportunidades comerciales enviados a esta Lista hay que acceder a: http://grippo.com/negocios.

comercio.
http://www.tsyt.com/anuncios_frm.htm
Información: webmaster@tsyt.com

comercio. es un típico Tablón de Anuncios de ofertas y demandas comerciales de acceso gratuito y editado en español. Tiene un buen ritmo de accesos, especialmente, de empresarios de habla hispana de América Latina.

Contactos Comerciales (América Latina)
http://www.amarillas.com/concom/index.shtml
Información: jach@amarillas.com

Comint Ar, empresa radicada en la República Argentina, edita un Tablón de Anuncios de oportunidades comerciales para la exportación e importación denominado Contactos Comerciales. Sus principales usuarios son empresarios del Mercosur, de España y de México. Su acceso es gratuito y se edita en español. Es necesario llenar un formulario de registro con todos los datos de la empresa y los productos que ofrece. Ofrece acceso a la base de datos «Amarillas.com» mediante motores de búsqueda por palabra clave.

Zona Colón
http://208.17.151.138/oportu6.html

Zona Colón, que se edita en idioma español en Panamá, es un Tablón de Anuncios dedicado a oportunidades comerciales de exportación e importación. Es de acceso gratuito. No tiene gran flujo de oportunidades.

Asociación de Jóvenes Empresarios de la Provincia de Santa Fe - AJES (Argentina)
http://www.geocities.com/WallStreet/Floor/3669/index.html

AJES es una de las más activas asociaciones de jóvenes empresarios del Mercosur. A través de su Sitio Web es posible dar a conocer oportunidades de negocios, especialmente, relacionadas con Joint Ventures y transferencia de tecnología. Asimismo, esta asociación está en contacto directo con sus pares de América Latina y de la Unión Europea, entre quienes ya se están estableciendo los mecanismos electrónicos para la difusión e intercambio de oportunidades y proyectos.

Cámara de Comercio Argentino Catalana (CACOAC)
Información: Cacdac@mcye.gov.ar

Es una institución con sede en Buenos Aires, cuyos principales objetivos son la promoción de la cooperación empresarial bilateral entre la Comunidad Catalana y la República Argentina. Uno de los aspectos más interesantes de esta cámara son las extensas redes telemáticas que entrelazan a las empresas y empresarios involucrados en el proyecto, y el alto nivel de asesoría jurídico-empresarial. Por tal motivo, es una fuente a tener en cuenta para las acciones de difusión de propuestas para la formación de Joint Ventures y transferencia de tecnología, especialmente en el sector industrial.

Banco de Negocios SAVEAS
http://www.saveas.com.ar/negocios
Información: info@saveas.com.ar

El Banco de Negocios ofrece la posibilidad de publicar avisos particulares y/o empresariales, en diversos sectores, como si se tratara de clasificados, en forma gratuita. El sistema cuenta con un motor de búsquedas sobre bases de datos relacionales, que agiliza el proceso de obtención de la información. En español.

Anderson Sina - Trader / Broker
http://www.sinatrader.com/
Información: sina@sinatrader.com

Anderson Sina-Trader es un Sitio Web de información y contacto de una empresa privada de Sao Pablo, Brasil, dedicada a la creación de oportunidades de negocio a través de relaciones de cooperación empresarial.

Por lo que se deriva de su presentación en Internet, Sina-Trader se especializa en exportaciones e importaciones, operaciones logísticas, intermediación en transportes marítimos, solución de problemas

Promoción Internacional de Ofertas y Demandas para la Formación 163

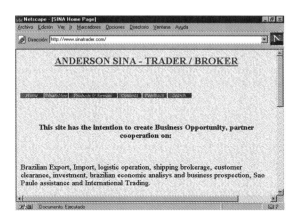

aduaneros, inversiones y análisis del mercado y la economía de Brasil para operadores de comercio exterior. También ofrece asistencia empresarial en Sao Pablo para misiones comerciales.

4.1.5. *Recursos de Internet para la Promoción en América del Norte de Oportunidades Comerciales Generales de Productos y Servicios, incluso Joint Ventures, Transferencia de Tecnología y Know-how*

STAT- USA
http://www.stat-usa.gov

Es un servicio del Departamento de Comercio de los Estados Unidos que proporciona acceso *on line* a diferentes bases de datos relacionadas con oportunidades comerciales públicas y privadas, estadísticas y con variables macroeconómicas de relevancia para investigadores de mercados internacionales.

Para acceder a la información es necesaria la previa suscripción que es de 150 USD por año o 50 USD cuatrimestrales. Las formalidades para la subscripción están indicadas en la página Web.

Las bases de datos más importantes que recoge STAT-USA son:

1. Banco Nacional de Información Comercial (NTDB): Es una de las más completas fuentes de información de los Estados Unidos respecto a comercio internacional. Aquí se incluye información sobre investigaciones de mercados internacionales, oportunidades de exportación, directorios de empresas americanas y extranjeras, informes completos sobre demografía, política y condiciones socioeconómicas de cientos de países del mundo.

2. Economic Bulletin Board (EBB): Es un boletín electrónico que distribuye información comercial, oportunidades de negocios, profundos análisis de mercado y de productos, y evaluación de las tendencias de los mercados.

3. Global Business Procurement Opportunities (Globus): Es un mercado virtual de carácter internacional en donde se presentan las principales demandas y licitaciones de entes públicos de los Estados Unidos y de empresas privadas de todo el mundo. En su conjunto mueve billones de dólares. Globus está compuesto por tres fuentes principales a las que STAT-USA da acceso:

- The Commerce Business Daily: Distribuye licitaciones, ventas de propiedades del Gobierno, remates oficiales, etc.
- The Defense Logistics Agency Procurements (DLA): Se anuncian Requerimientos oficiales y compras menores de 25.000 USD.
- The Trade Opportunity Leads: Es un mercado abierto donde importadores y exportadores de todo el mundo presentan sus ofertas y demandas comerciales a través de Tablón de Anuncios virtual.

4. Oficina de Análisis de Información Económica (BEA): Esta base de datos incluye análisis estadísticos sobre ingresos nacionales, regionales e internacionales, así como otros datos como rentas por habitantes o por productos en diferentes regiones, balanzas de pago, transacciones internacionales y otras informaciones macroeconómicas importantes.

Tradescope

http://www.owens.com/tradescp/submittl.htm
Información: email@owens.com

Tradescope ofrece la posibilidad de acceso ilimitado a las oportunidades comerciales distribuidas por el Departamento de Comercio y Agricultura de los Estados Unidos a través de sus bases de datos oficiales y a las licitaciones del gobierno japonés distribuidas por la Organización de Comercio Exterior de Japón (JETRO). El coste anual por este servicio es de 95 USD.

Asimismo, es posible enviar oportunidades comerciales y de cooperación empresarial y analizar las ofertas que allí existen sin coste alguno. Todas las ofertas enviadas se conservan durante 120 días. No pueden tener más de 40 palabras. Y deben estar relacionadas con la compra, venta, servicios internacionales u oportunidades comerciales internacionales.

Trade-Strategy

La principal finalidad de la Lista Trade-Strategy es establecer un diálogo abierto entre empresarios de todo el mundo involucrados con el sector del comercio exterior, especialmente con importadores y exportadores.

- Para suscribirse a la Lista, envíe un mensaje respetando la siguiente estructura:
  A (To): majordomo@igc.apc.org
  Tema o Asunto (Subject): [deje esta línea en blanco]
  Cuerpo: SUBSCRIBE TRADE-STRATEGY

- Para abandonar la Lista, envíe un mensaje que diga lo siguiente:
  A (To): majordomo@igc.apc.org
  Tema o Asunto (Subject): [deje esta línea en blanco]
  Cuerpo: UNSUBSCRIBE TRADE-STRATEGY

TradeLeads.com
http://www.tradeleads.com/maillist.htm
Información: membership@wmw.com.

Este es un servicio muy interesante para aquellas empresas que ven en los Mailing Lists una vía valiosa para desarrollar sus relaciones internacionales. Mediante una suscripción mensual de 29 USD, se les incluye automáticamente en 172 listas propias relacionadas directamente con el intercambio de oportunidades comerciales de exportación e importación, y oportunidades de cooperación empresarial. Permite también acceder a la completa suscripción en dos de los Sitios Web líderes del comercio electrónico global: Trading Floor y STAT-USA.

Trade Point USA
http://www2.tpusa.com/

Es uno de los centros de información comercial de los Estados Unidos editado y gestionado por I-Trade en donde se puede acceder a varios servicios de motores de búsqueda en base de datos y envío de oportunidades comerciales de productos y servicios, cooperación empresarial y transferencia de tecnología. Está directamente relacionada con la Red Global de Trade Points de UNTPDC-ETO, pero entrando en I-Trade podrá observar la existencia de muchos servicios (gratis o con costes muy reducidos) mediante los cuales los empresarios pueden hacer efectiva la promoción de sus inquietudes comerciales.

The IntlTrade Zone
http://www.std.com/intltrade/
Información: USA@worldnet.att.net

Este Sitio mantiene un Tablón de Anuncios y una base de datos exclusiva de ofertas y demandas de bienes o servicios. No cobra por el envío de ofertas comerciales, pero sí por la utilización del conjunto de servicios que presta, incluso, por ver las oportunidades archivadas en sus bases de datos.
Las oportunidades comerciales se envían a: ads@intltradezone.com

IntlTrade no permite más de 2 ofertas por semana, 50 líneas por oferta ni reenvío de oferta enviada dentro de los 60 días.

TradeUS
http://www.tradeus.com/tradeUS/index.htm
Información: itn@ultranet.com

TradeUs es un Sitio en que se puede encontrar todo tipo de información sobre empresas exportadoras e importadoras de Estados Unidos. Además, información sobre regulación jurídica de transacciones comerciales, ferias y exposiciones internacionales, revistas electrónicas y otros datos interesantes para el comercio con ese país.

Tiene un apartado especial donde se pueden enviar y analizar oportunidades comerciales de productos y servicios. Posee motores de búsqueda por palabras en base de datos.

Golden Bridge Trade Center
http://www.cyberus.ca/~golden_bridge/trade.html
Información: golden_bridge@cyberus.ca

Golden Bridge es un Tablón de Anuncios editado en Canadá en idioma inglés y francés. Tiene un excelente tráfico de empresarios de diferentes países del mundo interesados en la importación y exportación, y en cooperación internacional. El coste mensual de los servicios es de 10 USD. Presenta una sección interesante relacionada con la búsqueda de socios comerciales a nivel internacional.

Pronet International Business
http://www.pronett.com
Información: pronet@pronett.com

Es un Sitio Web establecido en Canadá que, entre otros servicios interesantes, presenta una poderosa base de datos *on line* de acceso gratuito dedicada al comercio internacional de productos y servicios, y cooperación empresarial a nivel global. Es posible acceder en idioma francés, inglés, alemán y español, asimismo, posee un traductor automático para las búsquedas.

BC Trade Network Bulletin Board (BCTN)
http://bc-trade.net/bctrade/postings/index.htm

Es un Tablón de Anuncios editado por exportadores de British Columbia, Canadá, con el apoyo de la empresa IBM. La inclusión de oportunidades comerciales es totalmente gratuita. Posee motores de búsqueda por palabra clave. Las ofertas y demandas, de todos los países, se establecen en inglés.

Centro Electrónico de Negocios NAFTA-Net
http://cenn.nafta.net/

NAFTA-Net edita un Tablón de Anuncios de oportunidades comerciales de acceso gratuito. En principio fue realizado para generar intercambios comerciales entre los países integrantes del Grupo NAFTA pero actualmente puede comprobarse que se envían ofertas y demandas de todas partes del mundo. Este Sitio ofrece también servicios de consultoría, creación de páginas Web, capacitación *on line*, información técnica sobre transportes, financiación internacional, asesoramiento jurídico, análisis de mercados, enlaces a bases de datos y varios servicios más.

International Trade Lead AutoSubmitter
http://www.gbot.net
Información: autosubmitter-request@gbot.net

La empresa Global Board of Trade ofrece la posibilidad de enviar automáticamente las ofertas y demandas comerciales a 68 Tablones de Anuncios o Sitios Web especializados en comercio exterior. El coste es de 20 USD.

4.1.6. Recursos de Internet en Asia y Oceanía para la Promoción de oportunidades Comerciales Generales de Productos y Servicios, incluso Joint Ventures, Transferencia de Tecnología y Know-how

KTNIC Marketplace On Line - Korea Trade Network
http://www.easycommerce.net/bbs/

Es un Tablón de Anuncios virtual creado por el Korea World Trade Center para el envío gratuito de oportunidades comerciales y oportunidades de cooperación empresarial de todo tipo (ofertas de compra, ofertas de venta, otras oportunidades de negocio). Posee motores de búsqueda en base de datos, por palabra clave.

Otro Sitio interesante respecto a este país es el de KOTRA, llamada Korea Traders Page http://www.kotra.or.kr/KOBO

Regent Commerce Network of China
http://www.china-inc.com/
Información: http://china-inc.com/company/newidea/newidea.htm

Este Sitio ofrece información sobre empresas, productos y servicios en China. A través del enlace «International Trade Leads» permite el envío gratuito al Tablón de Anuncios virtual de oportunidades comerciales de compra o de venta de productos, y de cooperación empresarial. Posee motores de búsqueda general por palabra clave para su base de datos de oportunidades comerciales y otro para el *newsletter* china-inc.com.

Otros Sitios interesantes en China son:
- China Business Bulletin Board
  http://odin.pat.dcu.ie%3A8080/cgi-bin/bbs.pl

- SinoNet
  http://www.sino.net/

China-Link Import/Export News

Aquellas empresas interesadas en relaciones con China y con la Cuenca del Pacífico pueden encontrar en Chinal-Link Import/Export News una importante fuente de información y contactos. Esta Lista es abierta y moderada y está dedicada a información comercial de la región.

- Para suscribirse a la Lista, envíe un mensaje respetando la siguiente estructura:

A (To): listserv@ifcss.org
Tema o Asunto (Subject): [deje esta línea en blanco]
Cuerpo: SUBSCRIBE CHINA-LINK su_nombre_aquí

- Para abandonar la Lista, envíe un mensaje que diga lo siguiente:
A (To): listserv@ifcss.org
Tema o Asunto (Subject): [deje esta línea en blanco]
Cuerpo: UNSUBSCRIBE CHINA-LINK su_nombre_aquí

China-NN - China News Digest

Es una Lista especializada en información comercial de interés sobre el mercado chino. Puede ser una fuente importante de contactos para el acceso a este enorme mercado.

- Para suscribirse a la Lista, envíe un mensaje respetando la siguiente estructura:
A (To): listserv@asuvm.inre.asu.edu
Tema o Asunto (Subject): [deje esta línea en blanco]
Cuerpo: SUBSCRIBE CHINA-NN su_nombre_aquí

- Para abandonar la Lista, envíe un mensaje que diga lo siguiente:
A (To): listserv@asuvm.inre.asu.edu
Tema o Asunto (Subject): [deje esta línea en blanco]
Cuerpo: UNSUBSCRIBE CHINA-NN su_nombre_aquí

AsiaOne Business Centre Bulletin Board
http://www.asia1.com.sg/cgi-bin/bulletin/board.pl

AsiaOne es un excelente Tablón de Anuncios virtual de acceso gratuito, en el cual participan diariamente varios cientos de empresarios con todo tipo de oportunidades comerciales. Los mensajes deben tener como máximo 50 palabras y pueden ser mantenidos en el Tablón de Anuncios de 1 a 4 semanas, según decida quien lo envía. Para el envío de ofertas y demandas AsiaOne pide que se seleccione un password de 10 letras o números fácilmente recordables.

Taiwan Trade Opportunity
http://manufacture.com.tw/post.htm
Información: service@manufacture.com.tw

Taiwan Trade Opportunity presenta por un lado la posibilidad de acceso a una extensa base de datos de productores-exportadores de Taiwan, y también un Tablón de Anuncios virtual donde en forma gratuita se pueden enviar oportunidades comerciales de compra, venta o servicios.

Para enviar una oferta hay que llenar un formulario electrónico y después de 24 horas se publica. Los editores revisan cada una de las ofertas vertidas en la base de datos con el objeto de que no incumplan las regulaciones de envío. Esto da mayor seriedad al sistema. Las oportunidades comerciales permanecen en la base de datos durante 30 días.

Traders Bulletin Board International and Australian Business
http://www.cnctek.com/tradersboard/index.html
Información: info@cnctek.com

Este es un clásico Tablón de Anuncios donde de forma gratuita pueden ser enviadas ofertas comerciales de productos o servicios, a la vez que analizar las ofertas y demandas que se han enviado. Posee motores de búsqueda por palabras clave en base de datos.

Globalstrategies
http://www.globalstrategies.com/
Información: mail@globalstrategies.com

Ofrece un servicio integral de apoyo a la promoción de productos, servicios y oportunidades de cooperación empresarial en el mercado de Japón. Mediante una suscripción-paga se accede a los servicios de inclusión de página Web traducida al idioma japonés e inclusión de la misma en los principales centros comerciales telemáticos de Japón.

Foro de Promoción del Comercio con Asia y Oceanía
http://www.jetro.go.jp/atpf/info/index.html
Información: tda@jetro.go.jp

La Organización de Comercio Exterior de Japón (JETRO) ha desarrollado un Sitio Web específico para promocionar actividades comerciales en todos los países de Asia y Oceanía. Ingresando en la dirección URL de arriba se accederá a un mapa con enlaces e instituciones de promoción de comercio exterior de 19 países de la región.

PPPindia's Online Trade Bulletin Board
http://www.pppindia.com/trade/trade.html

Plans Proposals & Projects (PPP), empresa de la India, edita un Tablón de Anuncios de acceso gratuito dedicado al intercambio de oportunidades comerciales de importación y exportación. Su estructura es muy simple y está generalmente bastante actualizado.

4.1.7. Recursos de Internet en África para la Promoción de Oportunidades Comerciales Generales de Productos y Servicios, incluso Joint Ventures, Transferencia de Tecnología y Know-how

Asociación de Comercio Global (Sudáfrica)
http://andromeda.marques.co.za/clients/gta/index.htm
Información: ernst@niobe.marques.co.za

En este Sitio se encuentra una base de datos sudafricana a través de la cual se puede acceder a directorios de empresas y oportunidades comerciales de todo tipo, especialmente relacionadas con la exportación, importación, formación de Joint Ventures y transferencia de tecnología. Asimismo se pueden enviar gratuitamente oportunidades de negocio. Posee motores de búsqueda por palabra clave.

África - Sudáfrica
http://www.exinet.co.za/trade/trade.html
Información: exinet@aztec.co.za

África - Sudáfrica edita información relacionada con comercio exterior, formación de Joint Venture y transferencia de tecnología con Sudáfrica. Posee un Tablón de Anuncios simple en donde se publican ofertas y demandas por países. Envíe su oferta a la dirección de correo electrónico: exinet@aztec.co.za

4.2. Páginas Amarillas Electrónicas y Directorios de Empresas Exportadoras de todo el Mundo

En los siguientes Sitios WWW encontrará información respecto a empresas y productos de diferentes países del mundo. Generalmente los datos que allí se recogen incluyen nombre, dirección, teléfono, fax, correo electrónico y en muchos casos las páginas Web de las empresas. Se trata de bases de datos con motores de búsqueda por producto o servicio, sector de la empresa, o nombre.

Páginas Amarillas de Asia
http://www.yellow-web.com/index.html

Páginas Amarillas de Australia
http://www.yellowpages.com.au/

Páginas Amarillas de Chile
http://www.chilnet.cl/

Páginas Amarillas de India
http://www.webpage.com/tradeindia/tradeindia/eyp/index.html

Páginas Amarillas de Israel
http://www.yellowpages.co.il/cgi-bin/main.pl

Páginas Amarillas de Holanda
http://www.markt.nl/dyp/index-en.html

Páginas Amarillas de Filipinas
http://is.eunet.ch/astarte-bin/pbo/apps/show?HTML=yellowsearch.html&APPNAME=yellow

Páginas Amarillas de Rusia
http://www.cbi.co.ru/database/default.asp?label=organization

Páginas Amarillas de Rumania
http://www.romanianyellowpages.com/~mozaic/

Páginas Amarillas de España
http://www.paginas-amarillas.es

Páginas Amarillas de Europa
http://www.euroyellowpages.com/

Páginas Amarillas de Singapur
http://165.21.1.10: 80/~yellow/Welcome.htm

Páginas Amarillas de Japón
http://www.nyp.com/

Páginas Amarillas de Nueva Zelanda
http://nz.com/NZ/Commerce/YellowPages/

Páginas Amarillas (Big Yellow)
http://152.163.202.23/select/yellow.05.html

Directorio de Exportadores Coreanos Cyber Commerce
http://www.cybercc.com

Páginas Amarillas de Honduras
http://www.pag-amarillas.com

Páginas Amarillas de Paquistán
http://www.one7.com

Páginas Amarillas de América (EE.UU.)
http://www.abii.com/lookupusa/ayp/aypsrch.htm

Páginas Amarillas de Internet (EE.UU.)
http://iyp.imall.com/

Páginas Amarillas de Italia
http://www.paginegialle.it/fe-docs/ricerca/index.htm

Páginas Amarillas del Oeste (EE.UU.)
http://yp.uswest.com/

Páginas Amarillas On Line (EE.UU.)
http://www.ypo.com/

On`Yellow Pages (EE.UU.)
http://www.onvillage.com/onvillage/onyp

Original Yellow Pages (EE.UU.)
http://206.141.250.39/

Usa Net (EE.UU.)
http://netaddress.usa.net/NA/Subscribe/Step1
Directorio Europeo de Negocios (Europages)
http://www.europages.com/

EuroLink (Unión Europea)
http://www.syselog.com: 80/eurolink/

Directorio de Negocios del Reino Unido
http://www.milfac.co.uk/milfac/

Directorio de Negocios de Países Árabes
http://www.us-saudi-business.org/

Directorio de Exportadores de Taiwan
http://manufacture.com.tw/

Directorio de Internet de Hong Kong
http://www.internet-directory.com/

Directorio de Negocios de Turquía
http://www.businessturkey.com/

Directorio de Exportadores de Suiza
http://www.swissinfo.ch/swissinfo/firmen.htm

Directorio de Exportadores del Mercosur
http://www.merco-sur.com/

Directorio de Negocios PRONET (200 países)
http://www.pronett.com/region/region.htm

Directorio de Exportadores de México
http://www.mexico-trade.com/directory.html#trade

Directorio de Exportadores de Irlanda
http://homepages.iol.ie/~aidanh/business/index.html

Directorio de Negocios de Argentina
http://www.externa.com.ar/

Directorio de Exportadores de España
http://www.accessnet.intercom.es/exportnet/central.html

Directorio de Empresas de Cataluña
http://www.cambrescat.es/html/p-31.htm

Promoción Internacional de Ofertas y Demandas para la Formación   177

Directorio de Comercio e Industria de Vietnam
http://www.cgtd.com/global/vietnam.html

4.3. Sitios Web utiles para Actividades Comerciales y Negocios de Carácter Internacional

Traducciones Español - Inglés - Francés
http://www.geocities.com/athens/delphi/8974

Horas del Mundo. Consulta Interactiva
Horas del mundo: http://www.stud.unit.no/USERBIN/steffent/verdensur.pl
o gopher: //gopher.aystin.unimelb.edu.au/1/general/time

Tipos de Cambio, Divisas Convertidor de Monedas. Consulta Interactiva
http://www.houstonet.com/calculator/converter.html
http://www.xe.net/currency

Acceso a los Mercados - Niveles de Barreras Arancelarias por País
http://mkaccdb.eu.int/

Cartas de Crédito: Un sitio para consultar cualquier duda relacionada con cartas de crédito:
http://picasso.wellsfargo.com/inatl/wrldalmn/intro/types/

Guía Internacional de Marcas y Patentes de Invención
http://www.thomson-thomson.com/netscape/docs/main/InternationalGuide.html

Directorios Telefónicos de todos los Países del Mundo:
http://www.replink.com/telecom.html
http://www.pangaea.net/data/phone1.htm

Códigos Telefónicos de todas las Ciudades del Mundo
http://www.ATT.COM/traveler/iacf/ccodes.html

Directorios de Fax de todo el Mundo
http://www.info-lab.com/

Informes sobre la Seguridad de cada uno de los Países del Mundo
http://travel.state.gov/travel_warnings.html

Mapas Interactivos de Todas las Ciudades del Mundo
http://www.mapquest.com/

Días de Vacaciones en el Mundo
http://www.rubicon.com/passport/holidays/holidays.htm

Ferias Internacionales
http://192.246.56.247/tshowform.html
http://www.tscentral.com/
http://www.expo.co.uk/dtiotp.html
http://www.expobase.com

Anexo 1

Formulario Oficial de Solicitud de Ingreso al Sistema de Promoción de Negocios del Programa BRE de la Unión Europea

Para ingresar al sistema BRE, se debe contactar con un corresponsal local o remitir una copia completa de este formulario al siguiente número de fax de Bruselas: **+32-2-296.25.72**

AUTHORIZATION:
I authorize the BRE first to publicize the summary of the business cooperation sought without disclosing the name of my company or firm, and then to communicate to any interested company all information given in this form, except the details I have underlined.
DATE: NAME:

SIGNATURE:

APPLICATION FORM - (COOPERATION PROFILE)
_ *PLEASE TYPE - DO NOT USE HANDWRITING* _

1. COOPERATION PROFILE

	Your reference[1] :
Company:	....
Legal status:	.... Date of establishment: ....
Address:	....
Postcode:	.... Country:
Telephone:	.... Fax:
Telex:	....
Contact person:	....
Languages spoken:	....
Workforce:	....
Turnover:	.... ECU/USD: ....
Subsidiaries: Yes/No	....
Bank details: Name of bank:	....
Contact person:	....

1. Please give your reference (max. 12 characters), which will be used to acknowledge receipt.

Formulario oficial de solicitud de ingreso al Sistema de Promoción de Negocios 181

International activity?	Yes/No	....
Since when?		....
In which markets?		....
Previous agreements?	Yes/No	....

2. TYPE OF COOPERATION SOUGHT

Please indicate the type of cooperation sought:

Financial:
    Business creation
    Take-over
    Merger
    Joint venture
    Other: (please specify)

Technical:
    Research and development
    Transfer of knowledge
    Product design
    Manufacturing agreements
    Patents
    Licences
    Civil engineering

Commercial:
    Distribution agreements
    Marketing agreements
    Commercial assistance
    Supply of equipmentl
    Other: (please specify)

3. DESCRIPTION OF THE COOPERATION SOUGHT

4. TARGET COUNTRIES[1]

*Please indicate the countries in which you are interested
(see attached codes)*

1. Countries in which your Cooperation Profile will be disseminated.

Model cooperation profile (guidelines to be followed when entering a CP)

AUTHORIZATION:
I authorize the BRE first to publicize the summary of the business cooperation sought without disclosing the name of my company or firm, and then to communicate to any interested company all information given in this form, except the details I have underlined.

DATE: NAME:

SIGNATURE: **THE CP MUST BE SIGNED!**

APPLICATION FORM - (COOPERATION PROFILE)

1. COOPERATION PROFILE

Your reference[1]: (number specific to the company)

Company: *(1) Name of the company or correspondent* ....

Legal status: *of the company* .... Date of establishment: *of the company* .....

Address: *(1)* ....

Postcode: *(1)* .... Country: *(1)* ....

Telephone: *(1)* .... Fax *(1)* ....

Telex: optional ....

Contact person: *(1)* ....

Languages spoken: *(1)* ....

➡ **From here on, data on the company only!**

Workforce:..

Turnover:....................................... ECU/USD: ....

Subsidiaries: Yes/No ....

Bank details: Name of bank: ....

Contact person: ....

---

1. Please give your reference (max. 12 characters), which will be used to acknowledge receipt.

Formulario oficial de solicitud de ingreso al Sistema de Promoción de Negocios 183

International activity?	Yes/No	....
Since when?		....
In which markets?		....
Previous agreements?	Yes/No	....

2. TYPE OF COOPERATION SOUGHT

Please indicate the type of cooperation sought:

Financial:
    Business creation
    Take-over
    Merger
    Joint venture
    Other: (please specify)

Technical:
    Research and development
    Transfer of knowledge
    Product design
    Manufacturing agreements
    Patents
    Licences
    Civil engineering

Commercial:
    Distribution agreements
    Marketing agreements
    Commercial assistance
    Supply of equipmentl
    Other: (please specify)

3. DESCRIPTION OF COOPERATION SOUGHT

Example: ...... (*give the nationality of the company and not of the correspondent*) company, specialising in ... (*give the sector of activity*) seeks cooperation agreements as regards ....(*specify the type of cooperation sought*) in the field of ... (specify the exact sector concerned).
[Where possible, indicate the precise area in which the cooperation is to take place].
NB: 1.   The text must not exceed 150 words, i.e. approx. 10 lines
       2.   The text must be typed!

4. TARGET COUNTRIES[1]

Please indicate the codes of the countries in which you are interested
(see attached codes)

1. Countries in which your Cooperation Profile will be disseminated.

Anexo 2

Formulario Oficial para Solicitud de Información sobre el Programa ECIP de la Unión Europea

EUROPEAN COMMUNITY INVESTMENT PARTNERS
ECIP
Technical Assistance Unit
Montagne du Parc 4
B-1000 Brussels (Belgium)
FAX 32-2-545 34 11

Request to receive the list of ECIP financial institutions and eligible countries

Name of the company:--
Attn. Mr./Ms.---
Street:---
Town:---zip code:---
Country:---

For Facility 1 only Chambers of commerce or professional associations can obtain application forms from the Technical Assistance Unit.

For facilities 2, 3 and 4 additional information and application forms can only be obtained from an ECIP financial institution.

Facility 1B is available to governments and public agencies of the eligible countries and requests for information and funding can only be submitted by them.

Anexo 3

Modelo de Formulario a Enviar al Mailing List de TradeWinds

Es importante conservar la forma y espacios del formulario original. Es posible escribir el texto del anuncio en español ya que TradeWinds llega a todos los países de habla hispana, pero es aconsejable presentar parte también en inglés para lograr una mayor difusión de la oportunidad comercial.

START FORM
Note that the line below a field indicates the maximum length of that field.
Place values ONLY at the right of «: » (with sole exception of «product description»).
Product Category: Offer
(Valid categories: «Demand», «Offer» «Miscellaneous»)
Contact: Mr. Oscar Gutierrez
Company: Industrias Gutierrez SL
Address1:   C/ Alfonso I, 527 Piso 4
Address2:
City: Madrid
State: —
(Use 2 character abbreviation for state.)
Zip: ——
Province: Madrid
Postal Code: 28020
Country: SPAIN

Bus Type:	Manufacturer
	(Type of business.)
Target Cntry:	World
	(Target country for offer.)
Opp Type:	T117
	(Opportunity type - see chart below.)
Phone:	+34 976 584758
Fax:	+34 976 584759
Email:	Gutierrez@nextime.es
URL:	http://www.nextime/gutierrez
Product Name:	Energy Saving Products (Licence)

PRODUCT DESCRIPTION - (Start next line, 35 characters per line, 5 lines):
Industrias Gutierrez SL primary manufactures cutting pointer screws. The main feature of the product includes highly energy saving screws by applying acceleration principle to reduce the strength needed for the work. We are interested in transfer the thechnology worldwide.
END FORM

Glosario

Bookmark: Es el sistema que utilizan las aplicaciones WWW para archivo de los URLs de páginas Web que interesan a los usuarios. En español se denomina marcador.

Broker: Comisionista o intermediario comercial.

Canales de Voz: Es la versión sonora de IRC. A través de este sistema es posible mantener conferencias de voz en tiempo real (como relaciones telefónicas) con la ventaja de que se utiliza el protocolo TCP/IP de Internet, lo que permite un ahorro enorme en comunicaciones a larga distancia. Uno de los sistemas más comunes es Iphone (Internet Phone).

Capital-riesgo: Capital que se invierte en un determinado proyecto de I+D o en un nuevo negocio basado en una innovación.

Carta de Intenciones (LOI): Es una comunicación detallada que emite el interesado en el desarrollo de un acuerdo empresarial a fin de dejar constancia de las voluntades y compromisos que les une.

Cc: Es la contracción de Carbon Copy o Copia de Carbónico. Sistema utilizado en las aplicaciones de correo electrónico para distribuir un único mensaje a múltiples usuarios.

Chat Rooms: Sistema que utiliza IRC para las comunicaciones entre usuarios. Son las «salas de conversación» públicas o privadas donde se debate sobre temas de todo tipo.

Comando «help»: Es la palabra clave que se incorpora en el Tema o Asunto o Cuerpo del mensaje para solicitar ayuda en los Mailing List o Listas de Correo.

Comando «subscribe o SUBSCRIBE»: Es la palabra clave que se incorpora en el Tema o Asunto o Cuerpo del mensaje para solicitar la suscripción en los Mailing List o Listas de Correo.

Comando «unsubscribe o UNSUBSCRIBE»: Es la palabra clave que se incorpora en el Tema o Asunto o Cuerpo del mensaje para abandonar un Mailing List o Listas de Correo.

Comercio Electrónico: Es toda forma de transacción comercial o intercambio de información utilizando nuevas tecnologías de comunicaciones entre empresas, entre empresas y sus consumidores o entre empresas y la administración pública, así como los mecanismos de pago telemáticos, dinero digital, métodos de seguridad en el comercio *on line* y operaciones bancarias cibernéticas. Comprende la aplicación de todas las tecnologías de intercambio de datos (EDI, Correo Electrónico), de acceso a información (bases de datos, Tablones de Anuncio), y captura automatizada de datos (códigos de barra, reconocimiento de caracteres ópticos o magnéticos).

Commodities: Mercancías. Productos sin transformación o con la mínima transformación.

Copyright: Derechos de autor. Protección del contenido de obras originales contra el plagio, distribución o comunicación pública total o parcial de una obra literaria, artística o científica, sin autorización del autor.

Cuenta POP: Acrónimo de Post Office Protocol o Point of Presence. Es el sistema de reconocimiento de una dirección de correo electrónico.

Glosario

Cuerpo del Mensaje: Zona de la estructura del correo electrónico en donde se escribe el texto principal del mensaje.

EDI: Acrónimo de Electronic Data Interchange o Intercambio Electrónico de Información. Es un sistema normalizado de traducción de documentos electrónicos en relaciones comerciales de tipo «empresa-empresa» y «empresa-administración». Enfatiza la utilización de información electrónica como reemplazo de la documentación impresa en papel y la seguridad de las transacciones.

EDIFACT: Acrónimo de Electronic Data Interchange for Administration, Commerce and Transport o Intercambio Electrónico de Información para la Administración, Comercio y Transporte. Es un sistema normalizado de traducción de documentos electrónicos que Naciones Unidas ha establecido para el intercambio de documentación administrativa y comercial. Comprende el conjunto de normas acordadas, directorios y guías para el intercambio electrónico de datos estructurados, en particular de los relacionados con el comercio exterior de productos y servicios entre sistemas de información independientes y computarizados.

E-Mail: Contracción de Electronic Mail (Correo Electrónico). Sistema de telecomunicaciones que permite a los usuarios intercambiar mensajes con otros usuarios de ordenadores (o grupos de usuarios) mediante redes de comunicación.

Enlaces o links: Es el sistema de hipertexto que permite pasar de una página Web a un URL determinado.

ETO: Acrónimo de Electronic Trading Opportunity (Oportunidades Comerciales Electrónicas), que es un sistema desarrollado por UNTPDC para unir los diferentes Trade Points.

FAQ: Es el acrónimo de Frecuently Asked Questions, es decir, las respuestas a las preguntas más frecuentes que realizan los usuarios y se exponen en diferentes utilidades de Internet a fin de facilitar la resolución de problemas y dudas de nuevos usuarios.

Foros de Discusión: ver Usenet.

Gopher: Servicio de distribución de información que permite el acceso a colecciones de información jerárquica dentro de Internet. Gopher utiliza protocolos muy simples y se caracteriza especialmente por los enlaces mediante hipertexto.

I+D: Acrónimo de Investigación y Desarrollo.

Incoterms 1990. Conjunto de 13 Reglas neutrales y codificadas recogidas por la Cámara de Comercio Internacional (CCI) para la interpretación de las formalidades comerciales. Recogen las distintas modalidades de entrega de las mercancías, situando con precisión en el contrato de compra-venta internacional las obligaciones respectivas del vendedor y comprador. A efectos prácticos facilita las aplicaciones EDI.

IRC: Acrónimo de Internet Rely Chat. Es un protocolo internacional que provee conferencias sincronizadas entre usuarios mediante aplicaciones especiales (mIRC, iChat, etc.).

ISO-9000: Conjunto de normas de calidad de International Organisation for Standardization (ISO) u Organización Internacional para la Normalización.

Know-how: Conocimientos que pueden estar concretados en elementos tangibles o intangibles, siendo las personas su soporte principal.

Licencia: Es el derecho que el titular de una patente de invención o de un know-how concede a un tercero, para que pueda utilizar dichos conocimientos para su efectiva explotación comercial en una zona geográfica y por un período de tiempo determinados.

Lista: Es la contracción de Mailing List o Lista de Correos

Mailing Lists: Es un servicio que utiliza el correo electrónico como medio de comunicación entre grupos de usuarios con intereses comunes. El Mailing List puede ser moderado, es decir que los men-

Glosario 193

sajes son enviados a un individuo que selecciona si el mensaje va a ser o no enviado al resto de los integrantes de la Lista.

MLM: es el acrónimo de Multi Level Marketing o Marketing Multi-Nivel. Mecanismo de promoción masiva, con alto grado de agresividad, utilizando todas las utilidades de Internet.

Motores de búsqueda: Sistema de acceso telemático a información de bases de datos.

Newsgroups: ver Usenet.

On line: Conexión a un medio telemático.

ONGs: Acrónimo de Organizaciones No Gubernamentales.

Páginas Amarillas: Bases de datos de Internet que contienen información básica sobre empresas de todo el mundo, como dirección de correo electrónico, número telefónico, dirección postal y datos de productos.

Precio CIF: Acrónimo de Cost, Insurance and Freight. Regla Incoterm 1990 que significa Coste, Seguro y Flete. Las obligaciones esenciales del vendedor son pagar el transporte hasta destino, entregar la mercancía a bordo, pagar los derechos de exportación, los gastos de carga y descarga en destino. Las obligaciones esenciales del comprador son aceptar la entrega de la mercancía ante entrega de factura y conocimiento de embarque y pagar los gastos de descarga si no están incluidos en el flete.

Precio FOB: Acrónimo de Free of Board. Regla Incoterm 1990 que significa Libre A Bordo. Las obligaciones esenciales del vendedor son entregar la mercancía a bordo, aportar la licencia de exportación, pagar los derechos de exportación y pagar los gastos de carga del puerto de embarque. Las obligaciones esenciales del comprador son designar el transportista, pagar el flete y pagar los gastos de descarga en destino.

Prototipo: Modelo original en el que se ha introducido algo nuevo y que posee las características esenciales de lo que se intenta producir.

PYME: Acrónimo de Pequeña y Mediana Empresa.

Rappels: Descuentos a distribuidores.

Red: Abreviación de Internet

Regalía o Royalty: Obligación de pago del adoptante o receptor de una determinada tecnología al cedente de la misma, por el uso de una patente, marca o know-how y que, en general, se establece en forma de canon sobre ventas.

Relación empresa-empresa: Relación de comercio electrónico entre empresas.

Reply: Sistema de contestación directa utilizado en las aplicaciones de corro electrónico para responder mensajes.

Saltos publicitarios o banners: Sistema de publicidad utilizado en WWW que consiste en el establecimiento de pequeños espacios en páginas de mucho tráfico y que enlazan con el Sitio Web del anunciante.

SEAL: Acrónimo de la Infraestructura de Seguridad Electrónica a través de Enlaces Autenticados de UNTPDC (*Secure Electronic Authenticated Link*).

Tablón de Anuncio: Es el nombre en español de Bulletin Board Sistem (BBS), que consiste en un servicio *on line* de transferencia de correo electrónico, ficheros y otras utilidades. Los Tablones de Anuncios de oportunidades comerciales se caracterizan por la posibilidad de envío y recepción de ofertas y demandas, que por su exposición gráfica y enlaces directos con los que participan en el mismo, permiten una ágil relación entre las partes interesadas.

Tecnología: Conjunto de información y conocimientos que pueden ser utilizados sistemáticamente para el diseño y fabricación de un producto, para la aplicación de un proceso o la prestación de un servicio, y que comprende todas las técnicas íntegramente asociadas a la gestión y comercialización.

Telnet: Protocolo normalizado de Internet para servicios de conexión con terminales de ordenadores remotos.

Tema o Asunto: Parte de la estructura del mensaje del Correo Electrónico donde se establece el objeto del mismo.

Tiempo real: Las prestaciones se realizan en el mismo momento en que se está operando con una aplicación telemática.

Trade Points Network: Red mundial de centros de comercio exterior, que está bajo la dirección y coordinación de UNTPDC, y creado en la Asamblea Internacional de Naciones Unidas sobre Eficiencia en el Comercio Exterior de Ohio (EE.UU.) en octubre de 1994.

Transferencia de tecnología: medidas que, por una mejor rentabilidad y eficacia del potencial científico y técnico, dan lugar a una modificación de la utilización actual y potencial de los resultados de la I+D; la transferencia de tecnología tiene pues por objeto materializar más rápidamente las invenciones en productos comercializables (innovaciones). La forma usual de comercializar la tecnología es por medio de la licencia de patentes.

UNTPDC: Acrónimo de United Nations Trade Point Development Centre o Centro de Desarrollo de Puntos Comerciales de las Naciones Unidas, institución creada por UNCTAD para el enlace de los Trade Points e implantación de la Infraestructura SEAL.

URL: Es el acrónimo de Universal Resource Locator (Localizador Universal de Recursos). Es un sistema unificado que permite identificar objeto WWW, Gopher, FTP, Newsgroups, etc.

Usenet: Contracción de User's Network o Red de Usuarios. Conjunto de miles de foros electrónicos de debate y discusión llamados Grupos de noticias o Newsgroups; los ordenadores que procesan sus protocolos y las personas que leen y envían noticias de Usenet.

WWW: Acrónimo de World Wide Web o Telaraña Mundial. Sistema de acceso e intercambio de información creado por investigadores del Consejo Europeo para la Investigación Nuclear (CERN) en Suiza. Trabaja con protocolos de comunicaciones de tipo HyperText Transfer Protocol (HTTP) e HyperText Markup Language (HTML) que permiten la inclusión de texto, imágenes multimedia, audio, gráficos, audio, vídeo, etc.

Bibliografía

Alonso, M. *Una franquicia para mi nuevo negocio.* Gestión 2000. Barcelona, 1997.

Andrieu, O. *Cómo buscar y encontrar en Internet.* Gestión 2000. Barcelona, 1997.

Archibugi, D. y Michie, J. *La Internacionalización de la Tecnología: Mito y Realidad.* ICE (26). Madrid, 1994.

Asoc.de Gerentes de Tecnología Universitaria de EE.UU. Resultados de encuestas e investigación. Documento de trabajo, 1997. http://www.tmo.umich.edu/techtransfer/index.html

Cañadas, M. *Cómo crear empresas rentables.* Gestión 2000. Barcelona, 1997.

Collado, A. *Negociar con Éxito una «Joint Venture» Internacional.* Staff Empresarial (54). Ed. Betne SA. Barcelona, 1997.

Comisión Europea. *Crecimiento, Competitividad, Empleo. Retos y Pistas para Entrar en el Siglo XXI. Libro Blanco.* Oficina de Publicaciones Oficiales de las Comunidades Europeas. Luxemburgo, 1994.

Cosumano, M., y Elenkov D. *Linking International Technology Transfer with Strategy and Management.* ICRMOT Working Papers. http://web.mit.edu/icrmot/www/wp_list.htm. 1992.

Fenyo, A. *Conecte su red local a Internet.* Gestión 2000. Barcelona, 1998.

Geringer, M. «Selection of Partners for International Joint Venture». *Business Quarterly*, otoño, 1988.

Lefebvre, A. *Intranet cliente-servidor universal.* Gestión 2000. Barcelona, 1998.

Lewicki, R., y Litterer, J. *Negotiation.* Homewood, Illinois. Ed. Richard D. Irwin, Inc., 1985.

Molero, J. *La Exportación de Tecnología como Factor Estratégico del Desarrollo Industrial: Un Análisis Sectorial.* Instituto de Comercio Exterior de España (752). Madrid, 1996.

Medina, N. Transfer of Technology to Latin American Countries: Can Joint Ventures Be a Substitute for Intellectual Property Rights. *Journal of Global Marketing* (1) Vol. 10, 1996.

Pallot, M. *The European Society for Concurrent Engineering* (ESoCE). http://www.ispo.cec.be/ecommerce/concur.html., 1997.

Schumpeter, J. A. *The Theory of Economic Development*, (paperback edition) Oxford, O.U.P., 1961.

Sidro Cazador, V. *Gestión Tecnológica de la Empresa.* Manuales del Instituto de la Pequeña y Mediana Empresa (IMPI) de España (21). Madrid, 1988.

Susbielle, J.-F. *Telefonía en Internet.* Gestión 2000. Barcelona, 1997.

Tyre, M. *Managing the Introduction of New Process Technology: International Differences in a Multi-Plant Network.* ICRMOT Working Papers. http://web.mit.edu/icrmot/www/wp_list.htm. 1991.

Valdés, A. *Empresas Conjuntas: Una Revisión de la Literatura.* Instituto de Comercio Exterior de España (755). Madrid, 1996.

Walmsley, J. *Handbook of International Joint Ventures*, Graham and Trotman Ltd., Londres, 1982.

So I Will Recognize His Voice

A Collection of Short Stories

By Dan Phillips

Dedication

This book is dedicated to the men that we look up to; that we want to emulate.

Lisa Godwin, unbeknownst to her, gave me the title to this book. In a conversation with her once, she said, "I pray to God a lot. That way, when he calls me, I will recognize his voice."

Lisa's husband, Bo, was a man to look up to. While he lived, he mentored hundreds. When he passed, thousands more grieved.

My grandfather, William F. O'Brien, was a man I looked up to, and so did the whole town he lived in. Sometimes when I consider my actions or words, I think to myself, "What would Poppa do?" While he lived he coached thousands. When he passed, generations mourned.

My father, who when I was six, adopted my little sister and me when he married our mother. His heart is in the right place. It's in his soul, not on his sleeve.

For my children, my prayer, "Lord help me to be a good man, a man they might look up to."

Works of Fiction

The short stories in this collection are all works of fiction. Any resemblances to any person or situation are strictly coincidental.

Introduction

One of my hobbies is writing. I write magazine articles and white papers and RFP's and sometimes books. I don't know why, perhaps it is one of my fruits and at a time like this I hope that is true. This is the fourth "religious" book I've written, though the first one that is fictional, and, a collection of short stories. My previous books were more about introspection; two of which are study guides for other books by another author. This book started out to be a novel, I had hoped, but I am either too lazy or too deficient of attention to write a full novel, so instead, settled on short stories.

I started writing books for two reasons, really. The first is in hopes of enabling others to view their relationship with God in a different light, from a different perspective perhaps. The second is all personal; I hope to chronicle my growth as a Christian. As I keep writing books, the thoughts in those books reflect the time spent in scripture, in devotionals, in small group study, in church, and, listening to sermons. I have enjoyed, what I believe to be, a fair amount of growth since I first put religious thoughts to paper some eight or so years ago. I am happy with my pursuit of spiritual maturity, and I hope that God is too.

My Friday morning Men's Group is a big contributor towards my spiritual growth. One of our initiatives is to select Christian books, read them and then discuss them. An incomplete list of authors would include Dietrich Bonhoffer, Joe Kissack, David Platt, Richard Rohr, Andy Stanley, Richard Stearns, Philip Yancey, and, William Paul Young. I mention that discussing books is one of our initiatives. We are very happy to also be an active group, donating time, treasure and talent to a variety of organizations and people in need. We are not arm-chair Christians and being active with these men has led to much of my maturity; and for that I thank God for introducing them to me.

In addition to outstanding authors I have been blessed to be exposed to several wonderful Pastors. I read Charles Stanley's devotional most every day and have watched him occasionally on TV some Sundays. And, his son, Andy Stanley is another great man to listen to. At my own church, for many years before his retirement, William Self was a big influence on me. And today, at our church, we have a young, dynamic Pastor in Shaun King.

This book is a collection of short stories. When I hear, or read, a phrase or a verse that strikes me, the impact on me many times unravels in the form of a story, or a parable. For example, I was impacted by a book we were reading in which we talked about the Holy Spirit and how this part of the trinity is given to us as a guide, a voice of sound reason, and an interpreter of the world around us. That led me to the story "Ruah" in this book. Ruah is a Hebrew word meaning wind or breeze and was used as the word for "spirit."

Please understand and accept that I am no theologian. I make no assumptions that these stories neither reflect Biblical passages nor explain any concepts of any religion. The stories in this book are simply that, stories. They are pure fiction and any relation to any real person or historical event is purely coincidence. My hope is to take spiritual concepts and bring a pictorial narrative to them to offer a perspective that might differ in some way from the reader's understanding of that same concept.

Thank you for selecting this book out of the thousands you could have chosen. My hope is that one or two of these stories bring you a message that you need to hear at the time you need to. I hope that you enjoy this and share some of it with friends.

May God bless you by seeing you safely in your home with the acceptance of your loved ones;
May you keep God in your heart, mind and actions today and tomorrow.

Dan Phillips

Other Books by the Same Author

Your Walk:
And the Struggle It Takes

Studying the Shack

Studying Cross Roads

Table of Contents

On the Edge of Normalcy	1
Surplus	15
Vision	25
Too Cold Outside for Angles to Fly	43
Ruah	57
The Three of Him	85
The Child is the Father of the Man	105
Final Exam	121
Serial Killer	129
Tapestry	139
The Last Person	181
Love and Fame	191
Clay	203
Believe	215
Satan's Test	231
The Farmer's Sons	257
The Hitchhiker	271

On the Edge of Normalcy

I just started reading a book and I had to put it down. There was a thought that was presented, it was that God is the author of the story and we are just characters in the book. As the author, he chooses when and where to insert us in the storyline. And, as a character, we don't have access to the entire story; we are really just lucky to know if we will show up on the next page or not. I had to put my book down because it made me think that there was a much better book to read. That book was authored by God. And, being human, all I really wanted to read was the part my character had in the story.

So, it got me to thinking. I started replaying memories of my life. You know, when as a kid you get in a fight with your sister. Or, when you wrecked your first car. Or, the time your mother walked in as you were kissing that girl too late at night on the living room sofa. I remembered some Halloweens, especially going to a Haunted House in the neighborhood where I grew up. I remembered my college graduation day. They were all great flashbacks but they didn't really stick out in the plot. They didn't really have those cliffhanger moments like mystery novels have. They didn't have those surprise nuggets of self-awareness that sometimes sneak into who-dunnit books.

If God had penned my life on the pages of time I hoped that there was something interesting to write there; that I wasn't just a waste of ink. So, just like when you query a database, I tried to filter the memories I had. My thoughts started gravitating to what could be called, "Ah Ha!" moments. What I found was that these "Ah Ha!" moments didn't really pertain to the moment I remembered them. What I'm trying to say is that the moment in which a deeper meaning hit me intellectually was from something that I had experienced in the past. The "Ah Ha!" was something that had been revealed to me before but was just at that moment surfacing in relevance and awareness.

For example, as a teenager I volunteered in a hospital for a summer. I'm a guy, so I wasn't a Candy-Striper, but it was my job to transport, via wheelchair, patients from their room to wherever their next test was to take place. Why they trusted a 16 year-old to get someone bad enough to be in a hospital up out of their bed and into a wheelchair, I don't know! But, with experience I got used to assisting octogenarians up, out, and down and rolling them along to where we would do it all in reverse.

A couple of weeks into the summer I got a call to go to 7-West. 7-West was the wing in which people with mental illnesses were housed. Once off the elevator, they even had a locked door. I was supposed to pick up a man and bring him down to

X-Ray. This guy, Warren, was in his late 50's, maybe early 60's. You know, to a kid, all adults look too old. This first time I rolled Warren, he didn't say much, but you could tell he was looking for something; like he had misplaced whatever it was. On the way back, he was even a bit more agitated.

"Have you seen it boy?" he asked with a husky voice just above a whisper, like it we were co-conspirators.

"Seen what, sir?"

"Baaah! What do you know?" And that was it for that trip.

During the summer I transported Warren several times a week. Once when I came to get him, his wife was in the room visiting. She looked rich, and the rock on her finger did nothing to dissuade that assumption. So, I did some asking around and found out that Warren was a very important man. He owned some big company, with some big house and some big cars that drove him from meeting to meeting. I gathered that he worked very hard and had done very well. But the man in my wheelchair was just a shadow of that guy.

Sometimes, he was more lucid than others. "Boy," he'd spurt out when he thought no one else could hear us, "Boy, I can't seem to find it. Where did it go?"

"Find what, sir?"

"I have all of these people that work for me. All of these people that do whatever I tell them to do. But I can't remember. I can't remember who I am. I can't find me. I've left me someplace and none of those people will tell me where I am." With that, he slumped in his chair and said no more that trip.

It turned out that Warren had a brain tumor. You could tell it was serious by the way the hospital staff acted around him. I got to roll him to his new, private room off of 7-West when things started coming close to the end. They must have been giving him some strong drugs because Warren really wasn't himself much anymore. He rarely went looking for his lost possession now. I remember one of the last times I saw him, before he passed.

"Boy, come here. Listen. I worked and worked. I really can't remember what I did but I know I spent most of my life at work. I have a wife and two kids and I don't really know them at all. My wife tells me that we had a couple of houses and a private airplane. She tells me that I loved to fly at night to Paris; that I loved to watch the sunrise after I left in the dark. I don't know. I have all of this stuff but I don't know who I am. Am I a good guy? Am I a prick?"

He lay there staring up, not at me, but vacuously at the ceiling tiles. I thought he was done with me, but as I turned to go, I could catch, just under his breath, "Who am I? Who am I? Who am I?"

Years later the memory of Warren hit me when my tech company skyrocketed and an IPO put more money into my bank account than I ever thought possible. I didn't know what to do with all of that money, but it was burning holes in my pockets. I was getting ready to buy an estate, a villa, heck; it could have been called a resort. It was definitely a piece of real estate that I didn't need. The paperwork was in front of me and there were a whole lot of zeros after a 9 on the price line. With pen in hand, and that commission-due realtor breathing down my neck, standing over my shoulder, Warren popped in my head. And what I heard him say, now so many years later, was, "I gained the whole world, but lost my soul."

Much to the chagrin of that realtor, I didn't buy that property. I stood up and walked out and then walked and walked. I had earned, or maybe been given, financial freedom but I didn't know what to do next. I really didn't know who I was. I didn't have the title of CEO anymore; I didn't have a role to play every day. Like Warren, I went looking for me. I needed to do some soul searching.

I tried a few churches here and there. I found that the churches that appealed to me more were the ones that spoke towards mission work. I didn't know if I could find my soul at any church, and I wasn't really sure that doing some kind of mission work would help either. I opted to keep my options open about church. But, I did find a shelter that gave out two meals a day downtown.

After some phone calls and return calls a woman named Mandy told me to show up at this shelter before lunch one day. I put on what I thought would be appropriate clothing; you know, nothing too nice, not too flashy, not too expensive; something that might fit in with that crowd. I got in my shiny BMW and headed to the address. And, I got to thinking. What did I know about appropriate clothing? I didn't even know the kind of people that would show up there. How was I going to relate to them? How was I going to get past the smell? What if there were really crazy, or dangerous, people down there? Where was I going to park my car?

Somehow I made it down there that first day. Mandy was nothing like what I had expected. She was more like Kathy Bates than Doris Day, which is whom I pictured when speaking with her on the phone. I guess I was a bit late because she was at full, fast speed motion. Where, in my previous life an introductory meeting, at worst, would be conducted in a private office with refreshments, this was in a seedy, cafeteria-like room and on the fly. Shortly, and I mean nanoseconds, after I said hello, I was in an apron and carrying chaffing dishes out of a steamer to a food line. Then, like the bell to recess, the doors opened and hungry people moved in quickly.

Either the food smelled bad, or the homeless people, or both. I didn't know if I should look them in the eye, or avoid eye contact. How much food was I supposed to spoon on a plate? Do I speak with them? What do I do if they talk to me, or even worse, ask me a question, or even worse than that, ask me for money?

When I caught a moment, I scanned the room for Mandy. She was out from behind the counter where I stood. She was walking between the tables and talking with one man here, another over there, a woman seated in the corner. From where I was I couldn't hear her, but you could tell that she spoke with them as if they were friends, or family.

At the end of that first day, exhausted, I asked her, "Is this what you do every day?"

"Yep, twice a day, five days a week for me," she replied with what looked like smiling eyes.

I started showing up once or twice a week and working with Mandy and her crew. I have to say that I never really felt comfortable there. My clothes were so much better. I got to come and go, in my own car, as I pleased. Many times I couldn't understand what they were saying; it was like a different language to me. I kept my distance. I just couldn't learn how to interact with the people I fed.

"Mandy, how do you do this?" I asked after working with her for months. "I just don't seem to fit in. And you seem to be at once one of them while still being the person in charge of all of this. I don't know how you do it."

She actually stopped moving, which was very rare. She looked down for a couple of seconds before facing me with her reply. There was thought behind this, as she said, "We are all children in God's eyes. You happen to have gone to better schools and have more toys than these people here. I happen to be blessed to be a ring leader, to gather all us kids together to share God's grace. You have to leave who you are at the door; let me rephrase that, you have to leave who you think you are at the door. You have to strip yourself of what you think is right, or what you think you deserve, or how you think you should be treated. You have to leave the outside, outside and in here just be one of God's children, just like all of them."

I worked side by side with Mandy for a couple of years. Several years after that I had joined a church and we were on a mission trip to the Dominican Republic. Our mission trip was to show the love of God by bringing a sustainable fresh water solution to Haitian workers living in poverty in the DR. On the flight down, unbeknownst to me, I was sitting next to my future wife, Toni. She was fairly new to our church and this was her first mission trip, her first leap of faith so to speak. She was nervous and we spoke non-stop during the flight.

At one point, after a long breath, talking to me but looking out the window she said, "I don't know why I came. I don't know how to do this. What if they are really bad off? What if they are like dying in front of me? How can I relate to them, I mean here I am this white woman who can barely make it past her own "first-world-problems" and I'm going into a third world? How do I act? What do I say?"

At that moment, memories of Mandy came back to me and I replied, "Spirituality is much more about unlearning than learning." And then, I started to tell her about how we are all God's children.

Toni and I were about as happily married as any couple could be. We had married late in life, so we had no children, but we did have a Golden Retriever that we spoiled like we were grandparents. Toni was a teacher and loved her students and her job. I was still comfortably wealthy with the money I had made many years prior, and the conservatively, sound investments I had made since. We lived and we loved and we genuinely cared for each other with no bounds.

It was summer vacation for Toni when we found the lump in her breast. The doctors said we were fortunate to have found the cancer fairly early, but they had recommended an immediate and strong course of action. That plan had us going to the hospital frequently for treatments, and a long stay for the removal of both of her breasts. I had a lot of time to myself when I brought her to the hospital. She'd be tied to tubes and many times she was so tired she slept. So, I would walk the halls of the hospital and sometimes go to the Sanctuary and pray.

On one of my walks, in the Oncology wing of the hospital, I literally ran into this skinny, little, bald headed child. At first, I couldn't tell if it was a boy or a girl, being bald headed and scooting away as quickly as if caught red-handed in the cookie jar. I walked that hall several more times that day and finally caught up with her. Or, I should say, I spotted her with her parents, holding her gently by her arm and escorting her back to her room.

Jenny was eight years old and we became fast friends. She had leukemia but she wasn't going to let it beat her. I didn't have much experience with kids, but Jenny was the most determined kid, really one of the most determined people I had ever met. She was simply vivacious, infectious with her happiness. She felt sorry, not for her, but for the other kids that were in the same hospital ward as she was. It was as if she were a mother hen and these other children her chicks and she was there to protect them.

She started a website where she posted pictures of her bald head, and the bald heads of many of the other children. She challenged other people to a dare. She wanted us healthy people to dare our friends to pay us to shave our heads, and then to donate that money to the kids on her website. She was a true marketing genius at only eight. In less than a month, she had most all of the students in her last year's second grade class bald; and many of their parents too. Her fund was being used to help with the medical costs of her chicks.

Toni was shocked one of the days I had brought her to the hospital with a full head of hair and then picked her up a few hours later bald. Toni was going bald too, which made us look quite the odd couple.

As Jenny got sicker and sicker, her determination only grew stronger. She didn't know the word legacy, but she was establishing exactly that. So many people were touched by her that after she passed her parents were able to establish an organization in her name that provided funds to families of children with leukemia to help offset medical bills.

Like anybody that is fighting their way through cancer, Toni had her ups and downs. She was on her way to recovery, and for that we were both grateful, and prayerful. In one of her down moments, with trepidation and the beginnings of tears welling in her eyes, she asked me, "Will you still love me without breasts? I have breast cancer, am I just damaged goods now?"

I ran my hand along my scalp, where the fuzz of hair was just growing back and I thought about Jenny. With my love for Toni bursting through and crackling my voice, I thought I felt Jenny reply for me, "No, dear, I love you all the more. We are at a point now where we have a decision to make. You can choose to be wound identified, or you can choose to use your wound to redeem the world." And I went on to tell her more about Jenny and how her legacy is impacting the world she knew.

The morning sun is beginning to warm the air, the mist flowing away, as I sit on the front porch. The book I was reading is closed on the table in front of me. But, the story, God's story, is still with me, living again with these memories, and many more. I noticed a pattern with my "Ah Ha!" moments. It seems that the "Ah Ha!" moments were all born when I was with people on the edge or normalcy. I couldn't really remember many truly meaningful moments when I was with "normal" people, only the people on the edge. Just maybe God shows up more out there on the edge.

Toni, ready to start her day, and the dog, Sade, come bounding out the front door. Toni has the dog leash with her. We've been walking a lot lately, since Toni has been formally announced by the doctors as being in remission. We've been walking to get us ready to walk in our first, Race for the Cure, with the Susan Komen foundation. I stand and stretch and tell her, "OK, my story for our walk today is this: the ultimate meaning of our lives is found when we can discern where our story lines intersect with God's big story."

Toni, with that gleam in her eye, smiling replies, "Oh boy! Is the walk going to take us that long?"

So I Will Recognize His Voice   On the Edge of Normalcy

Surplus

She was exhausted. Work was just killing her. That and the kids and the husband and the house; it was just all too much. The weekends weren't much better, with the laundry and the cleaning. She might get a break sitting at her daughter's soccer game, or her son's baseball game. But, she was just so tired all of the time.

Finally, she had had enough and trudged upstairs to bed. Her husband was still in his "man-cave" watching some team play some other team in a sport she had never had interest in. She performed her nightly rituals and wasn't even interested in the TV. She said a quick prayer of thanks to the man upstairs and closed her eyes.

Dreams are funny things. One place seems to morph into another and characters come and go. Claire had vivid dreams, at least she thought so of the ones she could remember. Sometimes she felt as if she was outside of herself, actually watching her participate in her own dreams. That's kind of where she was now, in a dream but aware that she was dreaming. That's when God began speaking with her. He was speaking to her, not in her dream, though she was dreaming. Her dream just happened to be a favorite Bible story, Jesus feeding the five thousand with two fish and five loaves of bread. The funny part in the dream was watching the disciples bring back baskets and baskets of left overs and thinking where could she store them and would her family eat left overs.

As far as what God had told her, just like with many dreams her memory of the words faded upon awakening. His presence, his aura, his light in her soul was still with her, but his words seemed just out of grasp. "Soul," that was one of the things he spoke about to her. Something about how everyone has a soul, that he had breathed his spirit into each one of us. But, for the life of her, she couldn't utter a sentence that came close to summarizing what he had said. But, she started her day empowered, feeling special, that God had come visiting and sat down with her for a spell. Even her bleary eyed husband noticed a lightness in her step that morning and asked her, "What's up?" to which she just didn't have an answer.

The kids were packed and off to school. Her coffee toting husband had driven off to a business meeting somewhere. Claire was in her car and off to work. She liked her job well enough, but today, winding her way through traffic, her mind was back on her dream. Was it a dream? The office she worked in was downtown and after getting off the freeway she had a mile or two of city blocks before her parking garage. No different than most any other fair weathered day, there were panhandlers at several stop lights. They must be territorial because it was usually the same guy, in the same clothes at the same light close to her office. Today she caught the light red, and was the first in line, which put her right next to the guy with his cardboard sign. In pencil, traced over and over again to stand out against the brown cardboard, the sign read, "I'm a Christian too. God Bless."

She rolled down her window first, before looking in her purse. Her first thought was that might have been a mistake. As the man approached with his street grimed hand stretched palm up she found that all she had was a twenty dollar bill. It was too late to back out now, but for some reason it just didn't seem to bother her. With a smile on her face and her elbow resting on the car door frame looking out, the man said, "Thank you sister, our father has shined on both of us today."

When she told her cubby-mate at the office the story of giving the twenty dollars to that man she was just flabbergasted. "Claire, what got into you? You know all he is going to do with that money is go buy some booze and get drunk. He's just gonna keep on begging and bothering everyone."

Claire didn't think so. Her encounter with God in her sleep flashed in her mind as she replied, "He called me sister. He is a believer just like I am. How could I not help him?"

"Claire, he's probably a druggie, or at best a drunk. What do you think he's gonna do with that money?"

"I don't know. All I know is that God has blessed me and my family and at that moment I felt that I needed to share some of the gifts that God has given me with that man." Where did all that God talk come from Claire wondered. It was not like her to speak so openly about her faith life at work, or really with anybody. Something has definitely gotten into her today!

The work week wore on and more often than not Claire was stopped near the front of the line at the red light every day. And, every day, the same man stood there with his cardboard sign. And, every time she gave him some money from her purse. It got to the point that she organized her purse to more easily withdraw his donation each day. It got to the point that she began thinking about him, and wondered about his plight, every morning as she left her driveway to begin the trek to work. It got to the point that on Friday morning she asked him, "Where do you live?"

The next Friday morning, at their weekly conference at work, the owner of the small company Claire worked at began a conversation about coming up with a morale booster. He was looking for an event in which most all of the employees could participate in, something fun; something to bond them together. Several ideas were bantered about and the one gaining the most votes was a dessert party one afternoon at work. Claire raised her hand, and meekly at first, but then with more determination stated that she thought that everyone should bring gently used clothes and something cooked to a homeless shelter that was close to the office. As she finished the first part of her pitch she was met with some blank stares and with uncomfortable silence.

Not daunted, she stood up. She began to tell them about the man she had met, Bobby. Robert Dupree was born and raised on city streets not so far away. He put five years into the Army before he couldn't take the desert anymore. Upon his return he had started a little company of his own and used everything he saved from Uncle Sam to get it started. When the financial crisis hit, he lost everything. He hasn't seen his wife or his daughter in more than four years now. Most nights, when he can get in, he stays at the Methodist Men's Shelter. On nights that he can't, he camps out under an overpass a few blocks away.

She told them that she had been giving him money every day, which was met by gasps from most of the women in the room. She told them that he was the nicest man and always had a smile on his face. She told them that though he sometimes drank, he hated doing so. He was trying to save some money to buy some new clothes. He had his eye on a low rent, pay by the week hotel near city center. He thought that he might be able to get a job now that things seemed to be picking up. Then, she ran out of steam and she kind of floundered, surrendering, she sat back down. The silence was still echoing around the room.

The meeting adjourned and no real decision was made towards the morale booster. Claire did get a few stares as people went back to their offices and cubicles. As Claire was about to go through the door of the conference room, her boss asked her to stop and wait as he wanted to speak to her.

"Oh no!" she thought to herself. Her family couldn't really afford for her to lose her job, they needed both incomes to get by. She struggled to maintain her composure while that last few coworkers exited. The boss closed the door and motioned for her to sit down again. "Tell me more about your idea," he said.

A month had gone by and Saturday morning was just awakening with the sun coming up. Claire had been given the authority to make the company's morale booster a community service project. Her husband thought she was crazy, but he was on board. Her kids thought that the idea was neat, and with some apprehension, were ready to visit their first homeless shelter and see their first homeless people. Claire had met with Bobby and Bobby had introduced her to the man responsible for running the shelter. She learned that there were 60 beds, on a first come first served basis, but that the shelter really had about 100 men that frequented it, at least for meals. Some of the men were pretty much what some expected of homeless people, mentally or emotionally challenged and addicted to one bad habit or another. But, some of the men were really just down on their luck, perhaps just one paycheck away from making it back in the day.

Claire had divided up her fellow employees into four smaller groups. One group was responsible for getting gently used men's clothing. A second group was to find, or make, enough food to feed over 100 men both lunch and dinner for one day. Another group was to find some professional services people, doctors, nurses, barbers, dental hygiene techs, and so on that would give of their time for that day. The last group was to canvass the local retailers, businesses and office buildings looking for any paying odd jobs that could be offered to these men. All of her employees donated money during the month, and the boss used company funds to match their efforts.

Claire and her family had arrived in their car and parked outside of the shelter. As her husband and kids got out grabbing the clothes and food that stuffed the car to the point of a useless rearview mirror, Claire found herself unable to open the car door. What if the men didn't show up? Worse, what if her fellow employees didn't show up? What if there wasn't enough food? What if she failed? She sat frozen until her husband opened her door, saw the look on her face and asked if she was OK.

A deep breath and a quick prayer and she got out.

They had fed almost 200 men at lunch. She didn't know where all the food came from, but it kept coming. Her team responsible for the food had their cellphones plastered to their ears the moment they saw the line of men out the door. After lunch she watched as Bobby got his hair cut. It was a while later when he came by in what looked like a new suit and shiny white teeth. It was almost like back stage at a fashion show as men walked back and forth in new-to-them shoes and pants and jackets. Off to the side, at several tables, interviews were taking place. Bobby was excited when he told her he had landed a job at a local fast food restaurant, with a promise of management training if he kept a spotless record. Dinner time was approaching and the line outside looked twice as long as it did for lunch. For some reason, it didn't bother her.

After dinner was served, clean up began. It was just amazing how much food was leftover. She thought, "What are we going to do with all of these leftovers? Would the men want to eat them again tomorrow?" And, that brought her back to her dream, the one in which God spoke with her. Bobby had taught her that a piece of God, a soul, resides in every one of us. And God had taught her that with what little she can give Him, how much more he can do with it. She smiled to herself thinking about just how much that twenty dollar bill had bought her.

So I Will Recognize His Voice   Surplus

Vision

She had been pregnant once before, but she preferred not to think about that anymore.

xxxxxxx

I was new to this place, though I was very comfortable, and knew I fit right in. I'm not really sure where it is to tell you. I have never known anyone to come back from this place to tell me. I knew everyone and they knew me, which took some getting used to.

I'm not sure how to describe just where I am at this moment, but you might think of it as a cathedral. People are sort of organized by pews, but different. Different like one of those 3D chess boards; how it is so much different, and played differently than the conventional flat chess board. People are where they are supposed to be, where you'd expect them to be, but really just all over the place.

He is always here, and no matter where I seem to go in this immense place, in or out of the cathedral, I seem to find him. Or, maybe, he finds me. Most likely he never seems to leave me…now. I can remember times when it seemed as if he left me, or more accurately I left him and really wasn't looking for him either. But here, in this place, he is always with me.

Why, just the other...I want to say moment, or it could have been day...you see, I can't seem to keep track of time in this place. Really, time is just irrelevant, so I just don't bother anymore. Anyway, he came to me to make sure that I was seeing clearly. He was checking on my vision. Oh, the sights you can see if your eyes are working like he plans for you. My vision is much better than it was before, but I still expect improvement.

For example, my wife, Beth. I knew she had been pregnant once before we met, but my eyes just couldn't see the whole story. I'm not really sure that they see the whole story now, but I do see so much more than I did before.

xxxxxxx

Beth was a junior in college. It was a small school, but was well known for their basketball team. The coach was great and many high school superstars would wait anxiously every spring to see if they would get a scholarship to play for him. That being said, many a parent prayed that their son would get the chance to learn under this man. But all of that is another part of the story.

Beth had been dating a starting player on the team. He was a senior, and though he got very good grades, he had his eyes on the pros. She had met him at a fraternity/sorority mixer the second semester of her freshman year. They had been pretty much exclusive since that time on.

As his senior season was coming near an end, and pro scouts were taking more and more seats during the games, the boyfriend's head began to swell. The coach saw this and called him in for a talk. When he told Beth about the meeting, she could hardly believe it was him telling the story. Once, where he was warm and genuine, he was now cold and harsh. He was incredulous that this "old, long forgotten coach had the audacity to call me to his office; in front of everybody!"

Things got worse quickly. One of the season's final games was coming up and the coach had threatened him that if he didn't change his attitude he'd be sitting on the bench. Game day came, and pro scouts lined the first row near center court. Beth had her customary seat but couldn't find her boyfriend on the court at all. Instead, he was in his warm ups sitting at the end of the bench and she could tell he was fuming. At the end of the game, in which he didn't play, he was the first out of the locker room. He asked Beth for her car keys, snatched them, and walked so fast he left her behind.

Beth had to walk back to her dorm room alone. The next morning, she found her car in the parking lot, smashed on one side, with the car keys sitting in the driver's seat. No note, no phone call, no boyfriend anymore. In a hung-over fog, when she had asked him what had happened, he didn't apologize, didn't tell her how or why, but just dumped her on the spot.

A week or so later, she was at a party that had many people, and most of the basketball team, including her ex was there. He wouldn't look at her; wouldn't even acknowledge her presence. Against her better judgment, she had a few drinks and began to flirt with one of the other basketball players. Flirting lead to dancing, dancing lead to kissing and kissing lead to them leaving together to go back to his room. She had only ever been with her ex before. This boy was rougher and definitely wanting her in a sudden way. She'd had enough drinks to foster some courage, or fool's pride, and put up with his rough demeanor. He said he had protection, but didn't, and forced himself upon her. Fortunately, for her, it was over quickly. He uttered some apologies and tried to make light of the situation. In his mind he was trying to set the stage for an encore. She sobered up, cleaned up, and left him near to passing out in his bed. She was unsuccessful in holding back the tears as she managed her way back to her dorm.

Finals were coming up at the end of the school year. Beth began to feel nauseous in the mornings and thought she was getting the flu. She checked with the school nurse, and in a pace faster than she could cope with, was informed that she was pregnant.

xxxxxxx

This clear vision, this better sight, it takes some getting used to. I can see Beth's episode in that bedroom as if I was there, like a fly on the wall. If I close my eyes, I can even feel her sense of revenge against her boyfriend and how it then turned into trepidation followed by false courage. And, I am shocked when the school nurse tells her the news. This vision is a strange thing. When I picture Beth like this, now at this time, I can make out a little girl in this place with me. She looks so much like Beth that she reminds me of our daughter. I don't know her name, or even if she has one, but I love to watch her play with him. He plays with all the children. They clamor for him and seek him out to sit and listen to him, or to chase him through what looks like a clover covered field.

I've never seen or felt her ex-boyfriend in this place with me. I'd like to ask him where the ex is but I think that I already know the answer. And what's really strange, is that I swear that there is a place in this cathedral of a gathering for that boy, that rough boy that took advantage of Beth that night. I don't know how I know that, but I can see where he will be, like a seat that has been reserved just for him.

This improving vision, like I said, it takes some getting used to.

xxxxxxx

Beth couldn't concentrate through finals week. It was a blur. If she wasn't vomiting, she was crying, leaving very little time for study. She was due to go home, to be with her parents for the summer. What was she going to tell them? What would she tell her sister, and her brother?

Once the exams were over, she began to think of her alternatives. The thought of abortion came and went quickly. She was Pro-Choice, for other women, but she was all Pro-Life for her. Not for the first time, but it had been awhile, she prayed. She didn't know what to ask for. She started off praying that this was a mistake that she really had the flu, but she knew better. She prayed for the strength to tell her family, but really struggled with that. She dared to envision a future in which she was a mother and had this little child. But that vision just didn't feel right either. She prayed that she would be a good mother. She prayed about adoption. Her prayers didn't garner any answers but she felt better, much better praying so she kept it up.

Her parents couldn't have responded any better to her story. She thought she caught a glimmer of disappointment in her father's eyes, but if there was, he hid it quickly and loved her more. Her mother just held her and let her talk. Her mother sat with her every now and then when Beth prayed.

The summer went on. Beth had a job; she was working in a retail store, selling clothes. She loved the perks, getting huge discounts on designer clothing. However, this summer, she didn't buy much of anything. This summer she thought that she might need to save her money. Abortion was out, which left only two alternatives; adoption or keep the baby for herself. She ate well and slept well. She took walks with her mother. She even attended some pre-natal classes. Time cemented her resolve about this baby. She was going to love this baby no matter what. And that love had already started. And that love blossomed the day she felt the kick.

xxxxxxx

I love my Beth. That Beth; that summer; that maturation from a girl to a woman. That's the Beth I fell in love with. She faced troubles head on. She kept her strength up regardless the burden. She found him and loved him so much sooner than I ever did. In fact, she introduced me to him.

He is with me right now and shares his vision of his and Beth's love for each other that summer. Oh, does he love her. Oh, how she so much wants to love him, to trust him, to rely on him, but something always holds her back. But, he loves her all the more.

I can see the birth of motherhood in Beth. I can feel the stirrings in her. She is so very beautiful, gleaming with child, glistening with determination. How I wish I could have been there with her. I've never loved her more.

xxxxxxx

It was late in the summer and the clothing store was setting up for the last sale of the season. Beth was working a long day, moving racks of dresses, lifting boxes of jeans. It was past closing time and Beth and a few of the girls and the store manager were trying to finish up to go home. Tomorrow would be a very busy day, another long one. Beth was chatting along with one of the girls when the conversation became just one way. She hung up the dress in her hand and turned to the other girl. The girl looked at Beth and then looked down to her pants that were bloodstained and the red was spreading quickly.

Her parents made it to the hospital just a little too late. Beth had lost her baby. It was a girl it turned out, but she had lost it. She tried to be brave. She tried to be withdrawn from the moment. This pregnancy was a mistake anyway, she never really wanted it; she hadn't planned for it. She was holding it together until she saw the tears in her father's eyes. Then it hit her; then it all came crashing down. Then, death carved love right from her heart.

xxxxxxx

I sob for Beth. And, he holds me just like he held her then. I can feel his love for her right now as he held her then. Through teary eyes I can see Beth in her bloody gown on that gurney in total loss. I can see the pain and anguish of her parents. Her Dad is here with us now. His vision is better than mine but still he has tears freely flowing down his face. He has a place in this cathedral, a fairly prominent place at that.

As the three of us comfort each other I can see the change in Beth starting. She could have sat paralyzed in misery. She could have been defeated. She could have given up on school, given up on life, given up on love. Instead, she prays. and as she prays with him an inner strength grows. It is a light, with an amber hue, it shines. It doesn't flicker, it doesn't waver; it penetrates. She is bolstered with that light and welcomes it to be a part of her. I can see that light in her soul. I can see grit in her and strength and faith that life will be better than this. I'm not sure, but as my eyes focus more I see just a hint of me in her brightness.

Beth finished college, with a degree and without a boyfriend. A few years out of college, she joined a coed softball team sponsored by her employer. That's when we first met. The team I was on played her team a couple of times that season. I played first base, and so did she for her team. It got to be a joke, kind of like, "We have to stop meeting like this," whenever one of us got on base. I know I was falling for her by the end of the season. And now, as I see her then, I feel that she was interested in me as well. But, she had sworn off men, she hadn't even dated since losing her baby. I could see that she thought of that child as "her baby" and not "that baby." I love her mothering instincts in that moment, just as I loved them with our child.

xxxxxxx

Beth called her parents one night. As usual, her mother asked her if there were any boys in her life. Beth, more out of impatience, but definitely with a bit of anxiety, mentioned this man that plays softball. He would stay after some of his games, if her team played later, and watch. Once, she reciprocated and stayed late to watch him play. At the end of the season, they had even shared a soda and popcorn from the concession stand. As she cautiously tested her emotions as she put these thoughts into words for her mother she could just see her mother's smile with the phone glued to her ear.

The Pastor at Beth's church was a warm, friendly, and easy to talk to man much into his 70's. He wanted to retire, but his congregation was not in a hurry to find his replacement they loved him so. Beth visited him one afternoon. It was the first time she had ever told anyone, outside of her family, of the events of that lost baby. She didn't bring enough tissues and the old Pastor was kind enough to hand her his handkerchief. It's kind of funny, she still has the handkerchief; she holds it in her keepsake box. That conversation was a turning point for Beth. She began to love herself again. She started to accept that God loves her. At the end of the meeting the Pastor told her that he wanted to meet this young softball player.

Beth called that man that night from her home. She was rewarded immediately by his pleasure in her calling him. She said that she wanted to ask him out on a date, and they went on and on about who was supposed to ask who first and so on. Then, he just said, "Yes." Then she told him that the date was for this Sunday, she wanted to take him to her church. That was when she had thought she had lost him. But, it only took a second or two, and he said, "OK."

xxxxxxx

That Pastor sits here with me now as we look back on that phone call. He never did get to retire, that congregation just loved him to death, and he is more than fine with that. He shares with me his impressions of Beth, during that first meeting and during our marriage counseling with him. I can tell he is so proud of her. I can even tell he's proud of me for having turned my life to Jesus. Beth and he were big factors, the biggest factors, in my finding my way to God. There are sometimes when the Pastor plays with that little girl that looks so much like Beth, and so much like my daughter. I get the feeling that I should know her; that I should know her better through him, but my eyes can't quite focus in on her yet.

But the Pastor lets me see through him how much Beth loves me. Seeing through him that way just fills me up with such joy I can't hold it. Some of the people around me notice that my emotions run high and they smile with me, nodding in appreciation as if they know exactly what I'm feeling.

xxxxxxx

Beth wore a beautiful white wedding gown and he was so handsome in his tuxedo. As her father walked her down the center aisle at her church, she took a moment to glance at all of the people, all of the special people in her life that chose to be with her on this day. The wedding and reception were a blur but it was a fantastic time. She couldn't believe that she was married, and so lucky to have such a man. It was a scary time for her, when he proposed. She had told herself that if ever that time came she would reveal her story; the loss of her first child.

He listened to her as she cried her way through the story. He even shed tears for her. He held her for such a long time, and they rocked back and forth in their embrace as often long time partners do on a dance floor. It was then that she knew he was right for her. It was then that she had said yes.

It wasn't long before they were pregnant; that she was carrying his baby. Happiness would sometimes give way to anxiety and fear but he just continued to hold her in the wee hours of the night. A baby girl it was and they were both so very happy. She thought that their daughter had his eyes. He thought that she looked just like Beth, and most people agreed with that. Still, she saw her husband in her baby's eyes and it comforted her.

xxxxxxx

Her Dad and I are just beaming watching Beth giving birth to our new, little girl. It was his first grandchild and a peacock couldn't have spread his wings any wider than Poppa did. I was there, in that room for the birth, and Poppa was just down the hall in the waiting room, regardless, we love just watching that moment again and again. It's not often that you get to see creation.

xxxxxxx

Meagan grew up so fast, it seemed to Beth. No sooner out of diapers than trudging off to school. She could not have hoped for a better home. Her husband, in between softball tournaments, worked honest and hard. Beth, once school had started for Meagan, went back to work as well. The money could have been better, but not at the expense of the love and relationships they had at home.

It was a Saturday morning and they were to take Meagan to gymnastics. Her husband sounded so tired and she talked him into staying in bed. She would take Meagan to the class, buy some donuts on the way back, and bring him breakfast in bed upon their return. A quick kiss and a faster, "Love you!" and Beth and Meagan were off. Her husband passed in his sleep.

The doctors struggled to find a reason and came up with some medical terms. None of it really mattered to Beth. She was crushed. Meagan was destroyed.

xxxxxxx

I swear it hurts more now than it ever did. Poppa and he and I sit here numb, with rivulets on our cheeks. I don't think I was afraid of dying as much as I was afraid of leaving, but, so young, to be honest, I never really thought about it. Others in this cathedral slowly crowd in around us. Spiritual warmth turns to light, embers at first, but gently, slowly growing into brightness that envelopes us all.

xxxxxxx

It was hard, so very hard. The first year after her father died, Meagan just didn't know what to do. Her mother cried often, probably more than that because she always tried to hide the tears. Many, many nights, her mother slept with her in her bed.

It was a spring morning some years later. Beth had asked Meagan what she was doing that Saturday morning, if she could join her on an outing. On the way to a ballpark, Beth told Meagan stories of her softball playing father. She told her that was how they had met. Meagan couldn't believe that her mother had ever played softball. And, she was even more surprised that, that was what the plan for the day was. Beth was going to play softball on the team her workplace had put together. Before Beth headed to the field, she told Meagan, "I'm going to play for your Dad. I hope he's watching up there. I'll play for him and you watch for him to keep him in our hearts."

xxxxxxx

This cathedral I find myself drawn to is in honor of Beth. The souls that frequent here grow in number as Beth gets older. The seats here fill up with the souls of all of the people that have made an impact on Beth, or she on them. Some souls are here often, like her father and me. Jesus is always here, and I'm not really sure how he does it because he is everywhere. And that little girl, the one that looks so much like Meagan, she is always here. My vision improved and I can see that she, still unnamed, is the baby that Beth lost. She just makes everyone so very happy as she is always smiling and ready to play with anyone.

This vision thing; it really works well for Jesus and he helps all of us to see better, to see as he does. Poppa is much better at it than I am, and he is very patient with me when I can't quite see what he sees. Perhaps, if I had worked on seeing like Jesus does while I was still living I would be better at it now. It's a very simple concept really. Open your eyes to see a person's past, their present, and the promise of their future. It means that you need to appreciate everything, every lesson a person has learned to get to where they are as you are seeing them. And, it means that as you look at them; see them for who they are in the moment, not your projection of who they should be. And finally, see the promise of their impact on the future; how they will provide so many more opportunities for love.

As I said, time is irrelevant here which probably makes it easier here than there, but still…

"Too Cold Outside for Angels to Fly"
(quote from an Ed Sheeran song)

Krissy, born Kristin, was 23 and on her own, not for the first time, but perhaps for the last time. She was born to white suburbia and attended mostly white, high performing public schools. She was a pretty girl and was both a Middle School and High School Cheerleader. Family life was normal, school life was normal, church life was normal. That is, until a party in her senior year at high school.

Krissy was a very responsible teen, doing her homework, driving carefully, attending cheer practice and those multitudes of games, all without a hitch. Her parents trusted her, and when the opportunity arose she was permitted to attend whatever parties she wanted. Of course, her mother had to know who was hosting the party, the phone number of the parents, and she had to be home by midnight. Krissy had been to several jock/cheerleader parties before, but the party on that night was a bit different.

xxxxxxx

Claire was in her mid-thirties. Though she wasn't pretty, really kind of plain looking, nothing makeup could really fix, she was a smart girl. She was mostly introverted, homely, some called her, including her single mother. Her luck with boys was not good at all. In middle school she thought that a boy she liked also liked her, but after she ventured a tentative "Hello," the public ridicule that boy launched marked her for life. On top of that, the girls in Gym class continuously made fun of her, only like the top clique girls can. The final straw was that she was sexually molested by a boy in high school. It wasn't rape, but the difference to her was negligible.

Clarie started college, living at home, attending the closest Community College not knowing what she wanted to do with her life. She had two classes that first year that set a path for her. One was a mix of Sociology and vocational Social Work. The other was a World's Religion class. Claire and her mother never really attended church, well, Christmas Eve and Easter were the only times they went. Clarie never even got a new Easter dress; they just went and sat through the sermon. But, from her studies Claire found comfort in the strict, conforming ways of the Catholic religion and actually attended a few services that first year in college.

xxxxxxx

The party was at another Cheerleader's house, out around the pool. Girls in bathing suits, boys too, hormones wild. One of the jocks had brought a friend, a guy from another school. Krissy found him "dreamy" as the girls all described him from afar.

She caught him looking at her several times. Eventually, she separated from the pack to see if he might come over, and he did. After some not at all awkward talk, and some swimming in the pool, she found herself with him, sharing a chaise lounge, pretty much separated from everyone else.

Some talk and some kissing kept her interest, and her spirits, piqued. The exploratory conversation went into challenges of who did the craziest things, who could outdo the other with stories of bravado or epic failures. Eventually the boy told a story of having sex while high on cocaine. That turned into a challenge, him chiding her that she was too afraid to try it.

Krissy wasn't like many of the other girls in that she wasn't promiscuous. She had one boyfriend back in her junior year and they'd had sex a couple of times. Then, she had one night of break-up sex with some other boy, and that had been the extent of her experience there. And, she had never tried cocaine. She had drank some, and tried a joint once, but didn't like how her arms felt numb after taking a few hits and that pretty much ended that experiment. She really didn't want to try cocaine, and she wasn't planning on having sex with this boy, but she did both.

xxxxxxx

At the conclusion of her two years in Junior College, Claire joined a Convent to become a Nun. Her two years had shown her that her calling in life was to help others and that Jesus was to be the only man in her life, the only one worthy of her love, and the only man she would allow to love her.

Her desire to help others drove her further and further into the city. Her efforts brought her from mostly lower middle class to run down neighborhoods of color. She, through her church, helped children and their single mothers, most of whom were addicted to one drug or another. She had heard a prayer once that included the line, "Lord, let our hearts be broken by the same things that break yours." From that time on, she thought of herself in that light, trying to see as God sees, to feel his grief and work towards helping that poor individual causing it. She wasn't truly a leader, but her Sisters all knew her for having her heart and her soul in the right place.

xxxxxxx

It was a good thing that Krissy was near the end of her senior year in high school when she met that boy. After that party, she started to hang out with him more and more. Sure, the morning after she was truly upset with herself for what she had done. But, by the next weekend, she found the desire to be with him, and to have that experience again, too strong to buck. For the last few weeks of school, her work, and grades suffered. She had already been accepted to the State University, so her parents weren't too worried as she sloughed off the last few weeks. Though, they were quite upset that she had come home very, very late after the graduation party, and really didn't seem to be herself when she woke up the next afternoon.

The State University was huge, with more than 30,000 students, of which over 8,000 were freshmen. Even so, it was really just like a high school on steroids and she blended right in. She did the Greek thing and got into a Sorority. But, she tried out for Cheerleading and didn't make it, which really upset her. Without that commitment, without that outlet, Krissy found that she had a lot of free time. College was like three hours of class a day, and after that she could do whatever she wanted to do. And, that meant party.

She was one of the prettiest girls and attended every Frat party she could. And at every party, she had suitors lined up trying to impress her, she thought. Alcohol flowed freely, and cocaine was readily available. Soon, she had a reputation as a party girl, one that loved the high and would most likely reward the person bringing the high with a romp in the bedroom. One night Ecstasy was introduced and she ended up servicing a line of Frat boys.

She was missing classes and her classwork was below passing. Rumors of her reputation had also made it to her assigned school counselor. That meeting with the counselor shook Krissy pretty hard. She still thought of herself as a good person, responsible and capable. She promised to do better, a promise that lasted two weeks at best.

xxxxxxx

As humbly as she could, Clair took joy in her successes. On the few instances where she could bring food and love to a family and see God work with them, to see the mother try to better her life and that of her children's, she rejoiced. But, the odds were heavily stacked on the side of failure. And, for each one of those failures, she grieved. She had known a few people that had either died at the hands of overdoses or violence. But more often than not, the children that were found in a shelter or under a bridge one day were never seen again.

She did not blame God for those failures, and she didn't blame herself. She felt that blaming anybody would mean that she would have had to judge them and she knew that judgment was not hers to levy.

Her work began to lead her towards women and children, not only suffering from poverty and drugs, but also suffering from sexual abuse. Many times the mothers of the children she tried to help had to sell their bodies for the money needed for the drugs they were addicted to. And, to her horror, she also knew of stories of children being sold into prostitution. All of it saddened her so. All of it burdened her heart so. All of it motivated her.

xxxxxxx

Until the letter arrived at her parent's house over the summer, Krissy had thought she had made it through her freshman year, barely. But, the letter did arrive, and it was none too pretty. She was being dismissed from college, not only for poor academics, but for behavior detrimental to the standing and reputation of the university.

It was not an easy summer. Krissy was able to get accepted into a vocational junior college that had a Graphic Arts curriculum. After a very trying summer, one in which she was only able to get high a couple of times, she started school again in the fall. Also, she had picked up a part time job at a local print shop where she hoped to gain experience that would help her with her pursuit of a Graphic Arts job when she graduated.

The junior college more interested in collecting tuition that turning out contributing adults kept Krissy for her two years and gave her a degree in Graphic Arts. During her tenure, Krissy had found a boy in school, and a different one that came to the print shop, that supplied her with cocaine for sex. With her degree, and her experience, Krissy found a job with a marketing firm that could use her skill set. This company was a couple hours' drive from home and she relished the idea of living on her own.

Her parents, not exactly happy to see her go, were happy to see her go. Krissy found an apartment with a roommate before her move and took her bedroom furniture with her. Krissy and her roommate hit if off well, at first. They both liked to party, and finding the occasional strange man in the shared bathroom the morning after was more of a chuckle than a concern. Her roommate was good, until Krissy started being late on her share of the rent.

xxxxxxx

Clair took more and more of an interest in the souls she was charged with. Many times this meant intervening in family squabbles and other incidents. Several times she took children from their mothers and brought them to shelters and into the foster system. Sometimes she had to step in between a mother and a "boyfriend" to stop him from beating her in front of her children. Her Sisters warned her that she was getting too involved, that it was too dangerous what she was doing. Unspoken, she felt that God would protect her, that she needn't worry for her own safety.

One day, she saw one of the mothers she knew, a mother of two skinny, little girls, standing on the edge of the street. Next to her was a man and they seemed to be in a heated argument. He started to get rough with her and Clair was able to approach them as he had a grip of her arm and was dragging her into an apartment building. The woman was hurting, craving for her addiction, but she was also terrified. Clair could see the turmoil on her face and in the tears streaming down her pot marked cheeks. Clair was able to diffuse the situation and walked the woman back to where she had stored her daughters while she worked.

The next day, Clair was approached by both the man from the day before, and another man, a very scary looking man. They were able to manipulate her into an alley. That was where she learned that the really bad guy was the pimp of the woman she helped the day before. That was when she learned that a Nun's clothing was no protection from the Devil. Bruised and disheveled, it was a couple of hours before Clair made it back to her Convent. The Sisters immediately took her in and cared for her external wounds. But, Clair was wounded on the inside too.

xxxxxxx

Krissy began to skimp on groceries to save money for rent. Her addiction to cocaine had turned into an addiction of Crack. And sex, previously all the currency required, didn't always pay for that habit. The more she smoked, the less attractive she became and the more her favors had to be replaced with cash. Her roommate carried her for two months, after Krissy had sold all of her furniture to try to pay some back rent. But, in the end, Krissy lost her job the same week she lost her apartment.

She had befriended a guy at work. He was sort of a loser, nobody really paid attention to him. He came and went each day without really raising an eyebrow. He liked that Krissy liked him. Krissy talked him into letting her stay with him.

He didn't care that she couldn't pay any rent. And, he even cared less when he found that she was going to share his bed. For him, he had hit a streak of good fortune. That lasted for several months, just until the fourth or fifth time he caught her lighting up in his own apartment. He never partook of the drugs, never wanted to. He thought he could love Krissy, and that his love might cure her. But, Krissy never loved him, and the drugs stole her heart away anyway.

As the leaves began to drop, signaling the onset of fall, Krissy found herself literally on the street. She had a pillow case of clothes and about $15 in her pocket, stolen from his wallet the night before, and nowhere to go.

xxxxxxx

It took Clair only a week or so to heal her physical wounds. But, her faith had taken a hit as well, and that was going to take a while longer. She had believed that God would protect her. She had thought that God wouldn't give her more than she could handle. That episode in the alley had brought back old memories, of being ridiculed and molested as a teen. She thought that she had released all of those fears to God, but found that they had easily come to the surface again.

As autumn approached, she tentatively went back out into the neighborhoods. She was pleased to see that some of her children were still there, and appeared to be none the worse for wear. And, as usual, she said prayers for those children, and their mothers, that she could no longer find.

The Convent was gifted with an old, used car. It was decided that Clair, on occasion, could use that car to go downtown on her outings. The Sisters had thought that the car might give her both some protection and a base from which to work from. Clair accepted that offer and found that truth lay in both hopes. In fact, the car gave such a feeling of security that she tended to stay downtown later into the evenings, and with darkness coming sooner each night, she stayed past dark several times.

xxxxxxx

A white girl in a dark part of town; a pretty white hooker in a very bad part of town, could rake in some good money. Krissy spent her first homeless night in the Bus Station. There, she was first picked up by a guy that said he could take care of her. She could get her fix and spend a night in bed. She thought she knew better, she even thought about calling her parents, but that Crack called hard upon her and soon she was walking down the street with this new guy.

A couple of nights later, the guy withheld the Crack from her. He gave her some clothes to wear and told her where to stand outside to get some tricks to get the money to pay for her need. At this point it didn't really matter to her. In her mind she tried to keep a party mindset; she tried not to think about what she was actually doing.

As the weeks went by, the nights got colder and colder. She worked very hard to first get money for her pimp to get her fix, but also to spend as much time with whatever man so she could stay out of the cold. Winter, and winter in her heart, was fast approaching.

One day, with the sun cracking through a shade in the window, splintering her eyes strung out red from the night before, the door to the apartment crashed in. The man, the man that had beat Clair, the pimp, forced his way in and waving a pistol beat the man that had been pimping Krissy and took her away. She was hardly coherent enough to understand that she had left one pimp to be sold by another, worse one.

Once the new pimp had got her back to his place, he stuck a needle in her arm and the rest of her cares went away.

xxxxxxx

It was well into the New Year and winter's clutches wouldn't release the city. Streets were frozen and only the brave or desperate ventured out late in the day. Clair had had a good day, for her. She was able to get several broken families into a new shelter and made sure that they got some new clothes, blankets and a warm meal. She walked back to the car and began to drive back for the night. She caught a glimpse of blonde hair, real blonde, not a platinum wig, across the street. It was a girl. She could have been pretty once, Clair thought, but it was obvious that an addiction, or addictions, had stolen whatever beauty she might have been blessed with.

The girl wasn't wearing much; a lot of skin was showing. She shivered as she nervously paced back and forth. As Clair watched, Krissy crumpled to the ground. Clair instinctively reached for the car door handle and pulled on it to get out of the car just as she saw a man come to Krissy. He bent over her and spoke to her, but Krissy didn't move. He yelled at her, and she still didn't move. He kicked her, and Krissy vomited on the sidewalk.

Clair had had enough and got out of the car. That was when the pimp, the man that had beaten Clair, looked up to see if anyone was watching him. That was when he pulled out a short baseball bat. That was when his eyes met Clair's eyes. That was when Clair stopped dead in her tracks.

Ruah

Year 2023

The auctioneer had rarely ever seen such frenzy. It was crazy. And all of it over an artist that he had never heard of until just days ago. And the best part, this was just the first of three of this artist's pieces that were being sold. Today was going to be even better than he had imagined!

Year 1898

Tommy had just turned 16. He was a man now, his father had told him. Tommy and his family lived in northern Massachusetts. He had attended some years in school, and could read some. He was also very good at drawing things. His last teacher even thought he could become an artist. But, he was needed on the farm more than he was in school and that's where God found him one day.

He had just read a little book about a fella they called Johnny Appleseed, who was born not too far from where he lived. On this particular day, he was out tending to the herd of cows the family owned, and he was responsible for. It was a farm day just like every other day. Birthdays, holidays, sunny days, rainy days, there were all the same on the farm; the animals knew no different.

Out in a field, where Tommy was fixing a hole in the fence, at a place where the cows kept knocking down to get to greener grass around a little spring fed pond, Tommy heard a voice. His father was a "God fearin' man," so Tommy knew the Bible pretty well. His mother had even read stories out of it at night when he was younger. Many years later, Tommy would describe this voice as telling him, "Stop what you are doing and follow me. Follow me to show the gospel to my children. Follow me to bring love to your brothers and sisters. Follow me and you shall have no wants."

Year 2013

Katelyn was a vibrant young woman, on her own and the proud renter of her first apartment on the outskirts of San Francisco, where she worked as a lab specialist for a research facility. This was her first real job and her first time, other than school, living on her own outside of her parent's house. She loved going to antique stores and flea markets and garage sales in search of neat items to decorate her apartment. There was even a TV show she loved to watch, one in which people would bring old or unique items to experts to have them appraised. Sometimes these pieces would be appraised at some outrageous amount. Katelyn often wondered if she would be so lucky to find gold like that.

On this sunny, but San Francisco cold summer morning, that's where Katelyn was, out shopping. She was going to hit the garage sales first and then hit the antique shops later in the day. She had planned her pursuit the day before, reading the Classified Ads for the Garage and Yard and Neighborhood and Estate Sales. She had the route laid out in her GPS in the car and was off.

She had pretty much exhausted her list of stops with not much to show for it. She had always figured, especially on big ticket items, meaning over $20 to her, that she would leave the sale where she found it, and if she thought that she really wanted it, she would go back to get it. If it was still there, it was meant to be. If not, tough luck! And that's where she was, deciding whether or not to go back after this antique looking Singer sewing machine or not. The thing was, she had seen several of those machines and really didn't think that it was so unique to purchase one for her own. She was about to turn around and head into town for the Antique shops when she spotted a poorly placed Estate Sale sign. The sign said it was for today and tomorrow and had an address scrawled in crayon across the top of an arrow.

So, she followed the arrows until she got to quite an old house. You could tell it had been around for a long time by the size of the lot the house sat on and the size and age of the trees that shaded it. The sale didn't appear to have been too busy, because other than a very old woman, there was only one shopper there. Katelyn decided she had nothing to lose, so she parked and walked up the long driveway. The other shopper bought a couple of crocheted doilies and walked out of the house leaving Katelyn alone with what she assumed was the owner of the house.

Katelyn introduced herself, and Emma Gray did so likewise. They spoke a few pleasantries and Katelyn asked if she could walk around the house to see what she might like. Emma asked if she would like the "two-penny" guided tour and Katelyn accepted. Knickknacks and furniture, mementos and memories, one man's treasure and another's trash, all was found in the home. Along the way, Katelyn learned that this was indeed Emma's home, that her husband of fifty-two years had just passed and Emma said she needed some downsizing! This house had been in her late husband's family since it was built back in 1912. Emma had moved in some thirty or so years ago after her in-laws had passed and left the house to her husband, and now it was hers. They weren't blessed with any children, so it really was left to her.

Through the kitchen and into the dining room, and then to the living room; Katelyn entered first, and when she turned back to ask Emma a question, something caught her eye. On the wall that separated the dining and living rooms, under a wooden cross, hung an old frame with age tinted glass covering what looked like a colored pencil drawing. She couldn't make out what the drawing was but she immediately recognized the style and the colors. She immediately flashed back to another drawing in another house that being her late Grand Pa's house about forty miles south of here.

Year 2023

The auctioneer had the gavel in his hand, but hadn't even lifted it yet. There were still six bidders actively bidding against each other with no end in sight.

"$500,000," yelled a grey suited man raising his paddle high.

"510," yelled a well-dressed woman near the back.

"$525,000," countered another woman, sitting on the aisle, flush on her cheeks.

The young woman that had brought these pieces to the auction house sat in the front row looking like she was at mid court at a tennis match. As the numbers screamed past $600,000, if anyone had taken the time to look closely, they could see a tear starting in the corner of one eye.

Year 1898

It was close to the noon day meal when Tommy had heard the voice, so he left the herd in the field and went back home to eat with his mother and father. Sweet homemade bread with molasses, green beans and yellow squash, a block of cheese his mother had churned, and, a slab of beef were spread on the table where his mother and father sat waiting for him to clean up and sit down. After a prayer of thanksgiving they all dug into the serving plate closest to each and then passed them around in a way that had been practiced many a year. About half way through what Tommy had on his plate, he just had to tell his folks what had happened.

He told them he had heard God speak to him. Immediately his mother felt his forehead and then opened his eyes wide with her fingers to peer into them. He shook her off and kept with his story. He was leaving after the meal. He was going to get some of his clothes and a few other things and start walking. He didn't know where to, but he knew that God knew. He didn't know what he was going to do other than to find people that needed his help. He didn't know where to find them, but he knew that God knew. His father said nothing and only looked straight at him. His mother, tears in her eyes, asked him if he was sure this is what God wanted him to do.

After the meal, his father stood, put out his hand to shake Tommy's, pulled him in for a quick hug, patted him on the shoulder, and walked out to his chores. Tommy helped his mother clean up from the meal, and then went to his room to pack. It didn't take long and his mother came to his room to check on him. She sat on the bed near his stuff and told him the motherly things she needed to say. Tommy finished up, bent over to tighten the knots on his shoes, grabbed his pack, kissed and hugged his mother and walked out the door.

The last time he saw his parents was when he was about a quarter mile away. His mother was on the front step, one hand on her hip, the other shading her eyes from the sun. His father was bent over a plough, pulled by two horses, trying to get one more crop in the garden before the cold winter.

Year 1999

Katelyn was nine and it was summer time because she wasn't in school. Her parents left her at Grand Pa's and Nana's house, which they would do for a couple of weeks each summer back then. They had an attic and Katelyn played up there many times. There were clothes for her to try on and old books for her to peruse. And she found, curled up in a corner, an old paper roll, that when opened revealed a gorgeous portrait, drawn with colored pencils.

During this visit she had moved boxes and old furniture around up in that attic to form her own little living space. She took that drawing, rolled it back on itself several times to straighten it out, and with some tacks hung it on the beams that housed the chimney from below. She put on one of Nana's old dresses, and a feathery hat and called Nana up to see her place. When Nana arrived, and appreciated Katelyn's style and decorating she noticed the drawing and gasped.

Carefully she removed the drawing, not with anger towards Katelyn, but with love and caring towards the parchment. With just a nod in Katelyn's direction, Nana tenderly held the drawing and descended the stairs back down to the house. Katelyn, unsure of what she had done, quickly shook off her make-believe and followed Nana down. She found Nana, hugging Grand Pa, in the kitchen, with the drawing on the table before them. Neither said anything, but just looked at the picture in-between glances at each other. When Katelyn entered, they went to sit and invited her to join them. It seemed that there was a story to be told.

Year 1898

Tommy walked quite a piece that first day. To the only town he had known; clear through to the other side. A couple of miles out, as dusk approached, he found a spot to camp for the night. He lay his pack down and unrolled his bed mat, where he found that his mother had stuffed in some bread and cheese and the few dollars he knew she had kept in a mason jar on the mantle above the fireplace. At least he had some dinner and some money if he came across hard times.

He wasn't afraid, and he really wasn't concerned. He was in peace with his decision and felt that God would provide for him. He really didn't know how God would do it, and if he thought much about it, it might make him change his mind. Instead, he tried praying.

After some time in prayer, which really wasn't anything formal like the traveling preacher would spout once every month or two in a tent set up just outside the market in town, but more like a conversation, albeit one-way, he felt as if he should draw. He felt that God had placed a person's face in his mind and he wanted to draw it. He felt that God wanted that face drawn with His love all around it. Tommy didn't know how to draw love, but he did know how to draw a face. So, by a fire he had coaxed to life, he took out his stubby colored pencils, the ones his teacher had given him after she had complimented him on his skill, and one of the few pieces of thick drawing paper his mother had bought him a couple of winters back and he fixed on drawing the face he could see in his mind. When he finished the face, and was happy with it, he still couldn't figure out how to draw love. So, he lay back and tried to picture what love looked like and dreamily fell asleep.

The fire had almost died and the breeze was cool when his dreams included the cries of a woman. And those dreams, those cries, woke him in the middle of the night. The wind carried these sad, sad lamenting sobs to him from somewhere that must have been close. He stashed his belongings under a fallen log, and like a hound to a scent, put his head up and followed the cries upwind.

There was a one room cabin several hundred yards away from where he had camped. The door was open and a slant of lantern light spilled across the ground, on which was a man's body and a woman slumped on top of him. It was the woman that he had heard. And, when he announced himself, and came to her side, the woman's face was the one he had drawn just hours before.

Tommy camped near that cabin for several weeks. He helped her to bury her husband who had just dropped dead where Tommy first saw him. He helped her to mend the fences to keep her livestock. He fixed the leaks in the roof of the cabin. He showed her how to make a small vegetable garden, and how to keep the rabbits and deer from eating her yield. He hunted for her and dried and salted enough meat to last her the winter, he hoped. More than anything, he became a shoulder she could cry on, at any moment, at any time of the day.

One night, during prayer, he saw her face with the glow of God's love all around her. He could see the colors of love, the whorls, the flashes, the brilliance, the cadence of the flow of color. He took out the paper he had drawn her face on and finished the piece. For some reason, he didn't know why, he signed it, "*Ruah 1.*" Before the morning light, he placed his drawing safely by the cabin door and left, walking where God lead him, down the path.

Year 1999

The portrait on the kitchen table was of Nana's grandfather. Katelyn could see him clearly, and could see the resemblance between him and Nana. They both had the same eyes and nose, and both tilted their head the same, just slightly to the right, just past vertical, attentive and inquisitive so to speak. Nana told her the story.

Her grandfather had fought in World War II, and had been badly injured. He had been gone for a couple of years before being flown back, now sitting in a wheelchair. Nana's grandmother was not the strongest woman, suffering from colds and allergies her whole life. While he was at war, their home deteriorated quite a bit without a man to keep it in repair. Her grandfather had gotten a lift into town from a neighbor and had wheeled himself into the General Store. He was buying some lumber and nails and other fixin's to work on his house and started talking to the shopkeeper to find out if he knew of any handyman that could help him.

An older gentleman, perhaps close to sixty, had been standing in the corner of the store and overheard the conversation. He walked up to Nana's grandfather and introduced himself and said that he would be more than happy to work for him. The man's name was Tommy.

Tommy moved into the attic above the garage and lived there and worked there for a couple of months. Nana pointed out to the back deck where a wheelchair ramp still stood and told Katelyn that Tommy had built that. When he wasn't working, and if her grandfather was out and about, Tommy would read from an old worn Bible stories to her grandmother as she lay on the couch in the parlor.

Tommy had never asked for any money, he was just as happy as could be working the day long and sharing a few meals. Her grandparents were quite sad when Tommy said he had to leave. All he would take, when they pressed him; all he asked for was a new set of colored pencils he had seen in the General Store. When they gave him that box, they had hid some money inside even though Tommy never asked for it. The morning after he left, they found this portrait of Nana's grandfather. In the colors surrounding his face you could almost make out what heaven must look like. And, when you glanced away, you could swear you could see Jesus standing in the background.

That portrait was signed, "*Ruah 416.*"

Year 2023

The six bidders were now down to four, but the frenzy was no less. The last bid was $720,000 when the grey suited man in the back, stood, cleared his throat, and boldly said, "$900,000."

The hush, dense and thick, lasted only for a moment before the other three bidders starting raising paddles and calling out numbers.

Year 1899

Tommy had just turned seventeen. And, he had just made his way into Pennsylvania. The terrain was much the same as Massachusetts, if not a bit rockier. He had found a comfortable pace for walking this last year and found that he could spend time talking with God without worrying too much about one footfall after the other. He still didn't have a plan on where he was going, and still, really, didn't care much. The road had been good to him so far.

People were very nice and meals, and sometimes a bed, weren't too hard to come by.

As what was becoming usual, at the fire one night God showed him a face to draw. So, he drew it. When he finished, he knew he simply had to wait and God would show him where to find the person he drew.

She was just a waif. Her parents both had died and the little town she lived in had gotten tired of her stealing and running off anytime someone wanted to just talk to her. Tommy was passing through when a matronly woman, running a Boarding House, had her by her ear dragging her out of the kitchen door. The girl's mouth was still busy chewing, and her hands looked like they'd been stuck in a cherry pie.

She wasn't crying, but she sat upset on the ground, back against a tree trunk in the center of town. Tommy sat next to her. He shared a couple of apples he had in his pack and she ate ravenously. Spunk is what she had, manners were what she lacked. It turned out that she thought she had some family in a town near Philadelphia called Passyunk. Tommy told her that he would take her there. She frowned at that, and at best was undecided; that is until Tommy opened his pack and showed her all of the apples he had hidden within.

It took several days to get to Passyunk only to find out after arriving that the family she thought she had there had moved on years past. He was told of an orphanage closer to Philadelphia that would take her in. So, they walked on.

The orphanage was next to a Catholic church and was run by the nuns of that church. The priest was quite elderly and rarely left his room. The orphanage had ten or so children in it, but it was in bad repair. Tommy brought the girl and she was accepted. Space was very tight in the sleeping quarters for the orphans and adding one more girl made it tighter. Tommy had seen something called a "bunk bed" during his travels and went on to build several of them over the next couple of weeks.

When it came time for Tommy to move on, he accepted a Bible, only slightly worn, from the Mother of the nuns. And, the next morning when the little girl awoke, on the wall near her face was her portrait. All of the nuns were astonished by the gift. It was more stunning than the stained glass they had seen in some of the bigger churches in the city. Many of them saw the hand of God in the making and prayed deeply in gratitude for Tommy. The little girl asked, but no one could answer, what the meaning of what was signed in the bottom corner, "*Ruah 8.*"

Year 2013

Katelyn, in the middle of her question to Ms. Gray, immediately walked to the portrait on the wall. The glass covering was old, and the light wasn't too good in the corner here, but she could tell she had seen this artist's work before. She could see that this one too was a portrait, and that the background was vibrant in color. Emma came up next to her and admired the portrait as well. When Katelyn turned to her, Emma quickly told her that this was the one thing that was not for sale. Katelyn told her that she didn't want to buy it, but she hoped that she could get a closer look.

They took the frame off the wall and set it on a table. Emma asked Katelyn if she would do the honors of releasing the drawing from the frame because her hands were too shaky these days to be of any good. Free from its bondage, from the back, Katelyn could tell it was quite old, but that the feel of the paper reminded her instantly of the drawing she found in the attic at Nana's house. When she turned it over, the drawn face was almost like a picture, and the colors in the background were just stunning. She checked in the corner and found, "*Ruah 418.*" Emma began to tell the story.

It was World War II and Emma's father, not knowing he was a father, left her mother when the Army called. Yes, they had had a hasty wedding, and obviously an amorous, if not too short, honeymoon.

But her father had gone off to war, and her mother had got a job working in the Richmond Shipyard. About the time she figured out she was pregnant with Emma, about the time she was too sick to continue working, about the time she was going to write her husband about the good news, was when she learned that her husband had been killed overseas.

Days later, she walked out of the doctor's office after her visit and it was raining pretty hard. She needed to get to the bus stop to get back home. An older man, scruffy at best, raised his coat in the air to shield her from the rain as they both headed to the bus stop. He too got on the bus. She thanked him and sat down, and he across the aisle from her. She didn't know why, but she started talking to him. Conversation was easy and before she knew it, she had told the whole story; married, pregnant, widowed, not working. His name was Tommy and he got off at the same stop she did.

Every day until Emma was born, and then some, Tommy would stop by her house. And every day he brought her some food. Sometimes it was just bread and cheese. But, sometimes it was fruit and vegetables too. She remembered once her mother telling her about the morning he brought by bacon and eggs and bread and jam and he stayed the morning while she cooked and they ate together. The whole time the landlord never stopped by for the rent. It had skipped her mind for a few weeks, but then she remembered and wondered why.

After Emma was born, on a very clear morning, with sun and birds in the air, her mother opened the door, expecting Tommy to stop by as was customary. Instead, rolled up leaning against the door jamb was this portrait of her. When Emma got old enough, her mother told her the story. He mother believed that if you looked at the drawing just right, and just above her head, you could make out the gates to heaven in the mix of colors there.

Year 2023

The auctioneer, somewhat reluctantly, slammed the gavel down for the third time. The first piece, "*Ruah 427*," sold for $1,125,001 to the woman on the aisle, with her flush now down her neck and peeking above her collar. The grey suited man was the last to bid against her, but now he steeled himself for the next piece, "*Ruah 379.*"

Year 1902

Tommy had walked from Massachusetts all the way down to Florida. He was now in a place called Tarpon Springs, Florida. He didn't know much about the sea, or boats, but the town was full of Greek immigrants working at sponge harvesting. He had become pretty good at wood working though.

The night before making it in to town, the face he drew was that of a young boy, maybe ten or eleven years of age. The boy loved his mother but feared his father. His father would come in from the sea most every evening and stop by a saloon before coming home. Most nights he wouldn't get home until after dark with the stench of saltwater, gasoline, rum and body order permeating the house as soon as he arrived. He was loud, and abusive to the boy's mother. The worse his father got, the more the boy gravitated towards his mother and the angrier the father got accusing him of being more girl than man. His father wanted a man out of this boy.

Tommy found him on the edge of the water. The boy, upon seeing Tommy, shrunk back, afraid of what this man might do to him. But, Tommy sat, took out his pencils and paper from his pack and began to draw. There was a dock, and some boats, and some pelicans; there was sand and shells and gently rolling waves. Tommy seemed to capture them all on paper, and captured the boy's attention as well.

Tommy showed that boy what a man could look like. He introduced him to Jesus and read to him his favorite Bible stories. Tommy told the boy that Jesus was a carpenter, and that he liked to work with wood as well. He told the boy that Jesus found some of his disciples on the shore, tending their fishing nets, just as he had found the boy near the water. With the boy in tow, Tommy picked up the odd job or two around town and taught him some skills, when really what was being learned was self-confidence and self-esteem. Tommy had that boy lift more wood than he thought he could. He had that boy work longer into the day than he thought he could. He had that boy work for others more than he had imagined he could.

On the day that the boy was going to take his mother to a new town, a place that her family came from, a place away from his father, a portrait was found just outside his door. The boy could tell it was drawn by Tommy. It was his face, and the colors around him in the drawing just gleamed and glistened, like the sunset on the ripples in the bay. The boy didn't know what "*Ruah 53*" meant, but he sure liked his drawing.

Year 2013

Katelyn was now more intrigued by the signatures than anything. The one Emma had was numbered 418. The one her Nana had was numbered 416. What did that mean, she wondered?

A few weeks went by and she decided to start an investigation on this Ruah artist. She started by going to some of the longer established art galleries in San Francisco, and the surrounding area. She brought #416 with her and began showing it around. Most galleries didn't know anything about the artist. Quite a few of them offered her some money for it, with the promise of more money if she could get more drawings. But at one gallery, the dealer there knew exactly what she had because he had one too. His was number 413. It wasn't from his family; he had found it in a yard sale a couple of weeks back. He was so struck by it that he hadn't put it out on display yet.

Katelyn got the name, phone number and the address of the man that had sold #413. She called that night and the story he told her was about an older man named Tommy, right around the time of 1940. It was a wonderful story, but Katelyn's mind was working on figuring out how to learn more about the artist. She took out a map, and located the three spots where the three drawings had been found. A pattern developed; it revealed a path from #413 to #416 and then to #418 that moved generally northward, and was chronological. That got her motivated. And, a quick internet search for Tommy Ruah that delivered no results did nothing to stop her.

Year 1906

Tommy was near Cleveland, Ohio, in a small town called Glenville. "*Ruah 112*" was a portrait of a young man. A man that grew up to be a Lutheran

Minister. A man that when Tommy first met him was walking out of jail after a night of drunk and disorderly. A man who hung his portrait in his study and looked upon it before writing every sermon he spoke.

Year 2020

Katelyn had spent seven years now chasing Ruah. At first, it was just a hobby. Then, it became almost an obsession, and now it was a calling. She had saved and saved her money, only spending on bare necessities, and the occasional road trip. After discovering the pattern, she had a decision to make; to search north, or to search south. She felt that north was easier because if she was right, the stories and the drawings would be more recent, and, she wouldn't have as far to travel.

A month or so after she started her search, she got very lucky and found #420 almost in her back yard, at another Estate Sale. It took some time to find her next drawing, #437, which was up near Seattle. But that spurred her to conduct some road trips. After doing some research to find out what roads were built in the late 1940's, and what small towns and stops there were along the way, she spent her weekends driving and stopping at small towns and all the shops and galleries and sales she could find. This garnered her a couple of more drawings. But the real excitement hit a couple of years into her campaign.

She had posted some of her Ruah pieces on some social websites. She even recorded a short video in which she narrated the story she had pieced together on Ruah. The video, after a few months, had several hundred thousand views and that was when she got an email from a woman in St. Louis. She had "*Ruah 286*" and had a Tommy story too, from 1919. Then, she got another email, this time from a man near Washington, DC, who had "*Ruah 22*" and his Tommy story took place right about 1900.

Now, when Katelyn looked on her map, and inserted all the numbers, and dates, she had, she could trace Tommy back through the years all of the way to the east coast.

Year 2022

Katelyn's search had made the local news channel. She had a collection of almost thirty of the drawings, though she didn't know what to do with them. She had located many more than her thirty, but those weren't going to be sold; they were to be handed down to family with their own Tommy story. During her search, she found people of all kinds, rich, poor, healthy, sick, young, and old. What struck her most was how Tommy had helped each and every person and she wondered if there was a way that he could still help. Three of the drawings she had located belonged to people that were in dire need. One had major medical bills to pay. Another had lost everything he had in the recent economic troubles. And the third was handed down to a sole heir of twelve years old after her parents were killed in a car accident.

Someone had mentioned to her during her TV interview that she could get rich if she sold them all off. She didn't think about that at first, mainly because she loved the drawings, and the stories that went with each one. As the drawings progressed, you could see more and more of what had to be called God's love for the person in the portrait shine through. There was really no other explanation. And, where Katelyn's faith life was dormant before she started the search, now it was alive and strong. But, the thought of selling the drawings stuck with her, and she thought about the three people she had met that were in so much trouble.

It took a while to contact them, to explain what she thought she could do, and to persuade them. She set up an arrangement with an auction house and set up escrow accounts for each person for any sales to be deposited in. The auction was set for early next year.

Year 2023

The day before the auction, Katelyn received a phone call from a number she didn't recognize. The call was from a woman in Ferndale, Washington. She had "*Ruah 444.*" As she and Katelyn got to talking, Katelyn perceived that this story was a bit different from all of the rest.

She remembered as a kid, back in the early 1950's she had an Uncle Tommy that lived in her house. She was just five or six at the time, but she remembers him clearly. Uncle Tommy wasn't really her uncle; it's just what her mother told her to call him. Uncle Tommy was pretty old and pretty run down, but he'd get up every morning and go outside to tend to this and that. Mostly, she remembered him napping every afternoon in a chair by a window with afternoon sun.

Uncle Tommy had a drawing he was working on. It was a picture of a young man, maybe a boy. You could tell that this boy was alive, you could see it in his eyes; they just lit up. Uncle Tommy worked and worked on the background though. She remembered that it seemed to take him weeks to finish with all of those colors. On the day before he passed, her mother asked him who the picture was and he told her it was him, a long, long time ago. He said he was sixteen when he started his walk with God and this is the picture of himself on the day he started.

Her mother asked Tommy what he meant by his walk with God and Tommy told her a few of the stories of his travels; that is in-between falling asleep here and there. Uncle Tommy wanted to go to bed, but her mother had one last question; why? She remember Uncle Tommy, struggling out of his chair, and turning towards her mother, and simply said, "Love. Love is why."

Uncle Tommy died that night. When her mother tells the story today, she starts by telling how selfish and conceited she was before this older man found her coming out of a beauty parlor one day. She tells of how, somehow, he found a way into her heart and her home. Uncle Tommy needed someone to care for him and God had chosen her. Her mother had "*Ruah 443.*" The woman also said that if you looked at #444 long enough you could see the hands of God reaching down to the boy in the picture. She thought it odd that an old Tommy would draw a young Tommy with God's hands reaching for him.

Year 2023

The auctioneer banged his gavel for the last time. The three Ruah drawings all captured more than one million dollars each. Deposits would be made in the bank accounts the pretty young woman in the front row had set up.

Katelyn stood on legs not sturdy. A sunbeam had started faintly through a window at the beginning of the auction and was now so pronounced it was almost like a rainbow indoors. On the auctioneer's podium a crystal glass of water sat. As the sunlight hit the crystal, the refractions spread colors on the wall behind. Colors, like the love of God.

So I Will Recognize His Voice   Ruah

The Three of Him

Johnny only cried once. That is all he would allow himself to cry. He was 7 years old and his father, whom he thought he adored, moved out. His parents divorced and his father barely said goodbye to him. He watched the final argument and meltdown between his parents from the top of the stairs, near to his bedroom door. He didn't catch every word but he definitely felt the hostility in their exchange.

After the front door slammed and the tires squealed out of the driveway, after he heard his mother's sobs from her now single bedroom, he lay down on the floor with his pillow, looking out the window to the stars. Then, he cried. Not long, not hard, but gentle tears spilling out and catching in his ears.

They, as a family, had attended church now and then. He knew that God lived up there in the stars in some place called heaven. He had heard that God made everything better if you just asked him to. So he did, ask.

He didn't know how to pray, so he just talked to who he thought God was. He prayed that his Dad would walk back in through the door. He prayed for his Mom to stop crying. He prayed that God would take his heartache away, right now. He waited. The front door never opened and if anything the moans from his mother grew louder, and there was even the smashing, crashing noise of glass breaking.

He decided then that God wasn't going to help him. So, he figured he'd cried enough and it was time to stop, so he did. Instead, he came up with a little rhyme to help sooth him,

All I have is me, myself and I,
And that's all I got 'til the day I die

He felt more grown up. And, as if in acquiescence, his mother had stopped crying, at least he couldn't hear her anymore. He figuratively pat himself on the back, praising himself for these two accomplishments.

xxxxxxx

God watched Johnny that night and saw him as only he can. He saw both the little boy and the promise of the man he was going to be. Suffering enters everyone's life, and some have more than others, by the grace of God. Johnny was going to grow up without a father. To do that Johnny needed to be self-reliant; he had to be strong. God heard all of Johnny's prayers that night, and as only he can, he let Johnny feel as though he had grown up that night, the he was responsible for himself and that somehow his efforts had calmed his mother that night too. With a knowing smile, in Johnny's tiny voice, God replayed, "*…me, myself and I…'til the day I die*" over in his head a few times.

xxxxxxx

Johnny didn't have a Dad around to teach him to throw, or catch, or hit, or shoot hoops. His mother opted to remain single and dedicated her efforts on raising her son alone. Johnny was a good reader, loved books, and a good student. So, when Gym class came around in Middle School, he was a bit out of his league.

It turned out that Johnny wasn't very good at any team sport. The school year started off with volleyball, and went into basketball and ended up with scoop ball, a game like lacrosse. Halfway through just the volleyball season the rest of the boys figured out that Johnny wasn't all that good and he found himself being picked last for teams, and being placed in a spot that had little action, or impact on the game. It wasn't so much that he was uncoordinated; it was more that he had had no experience with team sports and the strategies they employ. He was more bystander than participant and even lacked the knowledge to be a cheerleader for his own team.

As with any group of children, there always has to be a pecking order. In sports, that list went from the most athletic down to the most awkward. Johnny got his fair share of ridicule and abuse. Near the end of the school year, during scoop ball, the team captain decided that the position where Johnny could make the least negative impact was at goalie. The game was close, and heated. The Gym class period was to end any minute. Johnny let in the goal that lost his team the game; that really lost his team captain's stature and for that he made Johnny pay dearly.

His mother knew that something was bothering Johnny when he came home from school that day, but he wouldn't say what it was. Johnny said very little to his mother, put his books in his room and sat on his bed. Surely, if there was a God he would strike down that boy that hurt him so. God would at least teach that boy a lesson. How? Johnny didn't care, but he sure wanted something done. But God wouldn't answer him; he wouldn't tell Johnny that he'd do anything.

"Enough of this nonsense," Johnny thought to himself. Why was he thinking about God anyway? Instead, he retreated back to what had saved him before:

> *All I have is me, myself and I,*
> *And that's all I got 'til the day I die*

Johnny and his Mom lived in a "Swim and Tennis" community. For some reason, Johnny left his room and went into the garage. There, he found an old tennis racquet, one that belonged to his father. There was a can of tennis balls too. With the intent of at least breaking the racquet, or smashing some tennis balls, he marched off to the tennis courts and found a practice wall there. He hit the balls hard and then harder. The problem was that the harder he hit the balls, the further he would have to go to retrieve them to hit them again. So, instead, he tried controlling his swing so that he could hit the ball several times against the wall before having to retrieve an errant shot. The exercise actually turned from one of frustration to one of personal accomplishment and gratification. He controlled the racquet and the ball. He moved to where the ball was going and hit it. He could make it as easy or as challenging as he wanted to.

xxxxxxx

God heard Johnny's prayers that afternoon. He saw what the ridicule did to Johnny, on the inside, and in the future. He grieved for Johnny at that moment, but only for a time. God saw the heart of that team captain too. God smiled knowingly as Johnny hit those tennis balls against the wall over and over again. He smiled more as Johnny's coordination improved and his gratification grew. He delighted once again in Johnny's little verse and looked forward until the day it would actually come to fruition.

xxxxxxx

Johnny was a very good student in High School and took the hardest level classes he could. He was going to graduate very close, if not at the top of his class, with a much better grade point average than a 4.0. He really enjoyed, and excelled at all projects and assignments in which he worked alone. He didn't necessarily feel good about study groups; he sort of felt that he was there to help the strugglers when there was no one there to really help him. And, he didn't like projects that required collaboration with other students at all. The only grade he ever received less than an A happened in an Economics class in which one of the group members on a project neglected to complete his portion of the work. From that point on he made sure that even in collaborative assignments he got every little detail completed, even if it wasn't his assignment.

Another place he excelled at was tennis. By his Senior year he held the top spot on the Tennis team. From his junior year on he was undefeated in singles and had won State Champion. Johnny's senior year in tennis was following the same success. He made it to the semi-final match of the State Championship without even losing a set. His mother sat in the crowd watching him, but also eyeing the college scouts that were appraising her son, planning on offering scholarships. Johnny would have his pick of either or both academic and tennis scholarships; she was so proud.

Johnny easily won the first set of the semi-final match, and was up in the second set as well. After a very strong serve his opponent was only able to return a weak, head high lob. Johnny raced from the service line towards the net to smash the ball in for the game point when his Achilles tendon snapped instead.

What followed next was a very fast pace: pain, a stretcher ride to an ambulance, a longer ride to the hospital, a cast on most of his leg, and tears from his mother. Once home, his mother was going to set up the couch for him to rest, but, Johnny, crutches and all, hobbled up the stairs to his bedroom. He would have like to fling himself on his bed, at the same time throwing the crutches across the room. But, instead, he gently sat and lifted his heavy, immobile leg as gently as he could and lay down, laying the crutches as close to himself as the bed allowed.

He had had a plan. With his grades, and his ability in tennis, he was going to go to a California college. He thought he could get a full ride to almost any college he could be interested in. But, the doctors told him that competitive tennis was pretty much out of the picture for quite a while, if not for the rest of his life.

He started to say something, something directed towards God, but stopped himself. "Why bother?" was what he whispered to himself. If he was upset, he wasn't even going to show it to himself. He swallowed the pain and chased it with his mantra:

All I have is me, myself and I,
And that's all I got 'til the day I die

xxxxxxx

God was saddened by Johnny's injury. He really liked to watch Johnny play. When Johnny played tennis, God could see the freedom in his spirit. He could see the joy and pleasure in Johnny, not so much in that he defeated his opponents, but that he had played so well. Single minded athleticism, drive, determination and self-motivation were gifts God had provided Johnny and he loved watching Johnny use those gifts in action. When Johnny lay on that bed, coming home from the hospital the first time, and he almost uttered God's name, God's ears perked up, only to be hurt when Johnny quickly turned from him in that time of need. Since He wasn't invited to be with Johnny that night, he left him, but did so humming that little verse in his head as he went, smiling, knowing when it would truly come true.

xxxxxxx

College was everything he thought it was going to be. John, now, graduated Summa Cum Laude with a double major in Business and Marketing. He was single minded focused throughout his college years, without even dating or going Greek. Invisible to him a girl, Eden, who was in several of his classes, had kept a close eye on him. During the graduation ceremony she spotted him several rows away and made up her mind to speak to him before the day, and the opportunity, passed.

After the speeches and the caps were tossed, when mayhem settled down to the search for family and loved ones, as John spotted his mother across the square and started that way, Eden suddenly stepped in front of him. He recognized her of course but hadn't really paid her or anyone else really, much mind. She congratulated him, and he her, and she asked him about his plans. He had his pick of job offers but had narrowed it down to a large, local firm. She mentioned that she had also received a job offer from them but hadn't decided yet. The conversation came to an awkward pause. Abruptly, Eden approached him, hugged him, kissed him on the cheek and whispered in his ear, "I hope to see you soon." And, as fast as she had appeared, she left.

Fazed, John started to walk, slowly, again, towards his mother. When they met, she asked him, "Who was that very attractive young lady?" Stammering, John replied, "Just a friend."

While they were walking back to the car, his mother said, "Thank God! John, you are so blessed, I thank God every day."

Missing a step, he looked at his mother befuddled. She had never really talked about God before. He never knew her to be religious. But more than all of that, he was a bit insulted. God didn't have anything to do with his successes. It was all him. He was the one that worked hard and sacrificed. He didn't remember God pulling all-nighters with him. He didn't reply to his mother, but if she looked she would see that his expression had soured from pride to a hint of hurt or affront.

John's mother surprised him by taking him out to a nice restaurant after the graduation ceremony. It was the first time he had ever had a glass of wine with his meal. His mother asked once more about that pretty girl, but they mostly talked about his future plans. He was going to accept the job offer from the big firm in the city. That firm dealt with technology primarily in the health care industry. He would not necessarily start at the bottom, but he did face a big learning curve. He would need to find an apartment downtown, and he had pretty much settled on that decision as well.

After dinner, they arrived back at their home. John feigned tiredness and went to his room, but he was really trying to avoid more questions about his future, and, truthfully, he was still a bit miffed about the "Thank God" comment from his mother. So, in his bedroom once more, again looking out the same window and perhaps at the same stars, he thought about God. Why would his mother make a comment like that? Why shouldn't he get the credit for his hard work and relinquish any credit to a god he never believed in? Why did God have to steal this moment from him when he was never there before?

xxxxxxx

God celebrated Johnny's success. He relished that John used his gifts so well. He even had a little smirk when his mother dropped that comment about him. He had been working on Johnny's mother for quite some time now and the Holy Spirit was beginning to connect with her now. He was weaving a very fine tapestry for Johnny, but just because He could see the future didn't make living in the present any less emotional or genuine. He knew that Johnny would be upset, but He hoped still that John would begin to soften. Instead, Johnny's behavior reinforced what God already knew. For Johnny, it was all about:

All I have is me, myself and I,

And that's all I got 'til the day I die

And, God knew how that was going to turn out.

xxxxxxx

Three years had passed since that graduation day and John had moved quickly up the ranks at his job downtown. He had started on the operations side of the business, making sure that the equipment his company both sourced and manufactured met delivery schedules and customers' expectations. From that, he moved into some of the client needs assessment and device design work, still more operations than design, but he was given an opportunity to learn a lot, which he did. At the moment, he had moved over into the marketing side of the business, compiling features and benefits analysis on both his company's and their competitors' product lines. He was hoping to gain experience in some of the market analysis and campaign strategies soon. On more than one occasion he'd had lunch with the President of the company, just the two of them.

And, in just a few weeks, Eden and he were to be married. As he looked back on that relationship, he really didn't know how he had reached this point. He wasn't complaining, if anything he thought that they were a really good fit, but he couldn't remember what he'd done to get this far.

Eden, on the other hand, had staked her claim on that graduation day and did very little to sway off course. She had been sizing John up the last two years or so in college and just knew that he was going to be something special, that he would be making a name for himself. She had the potential to be very successful in her own right, and the fact that they both enjoyed the same business verticals made keeping in touch that much easier. From that kiss on the cheek at graduation to the proposal she quickly accepted, and had subtly engineered, she had victoriously carried out her own marketing and sales campaign.

It was about this time that John's boss told him about a rather large, new project that was in the works and that the President of the company had suggested to him that John be on that team. John was proud that he had created a reputation to date that would entice the President to put his name forward. John didn't even think that the start date of this project was the first Monday of his honeymoon. When he excitedly told Eden the news that night he was shocked that she wasn't as excited as he was, that is until she told him about the conflict with their honeymoon. He made the argument that this was an opportunity too good to pass up. She made the argument that a honeymoon is the start of a lifelong relationship and a once in a lifetime event. She left that dinner alone disbelieving that her fiancé would even consider skipping out on their honeymoon. He went back to his apartment fuming that his fiancé would think that a week on the beach was more important than his job and surely his next promotion. From his bed, not in a whisper but aloud, he found comfort in:

> *All I have is me, myself and I,*
> *And that's all I got 'til the day I die*

Fortunately for both John and Eden, the project was pushed back two weeks for other reasons. They didn't need to come to an agreement, but, a memory was etched in Eden's mind nonetheless.

xxxxxxx

That project John started on just after his honeymoon turned into his full time job with the company. The kids now, a boy and a girl, were 5 and 3 years old. Eden had become a stay-at-home mom after J Jr. was born. John, or JK as some of his superiors took to calling him, quickly had become Project Lead and eventually turned that into a very profitable branch of the business. For his Christmas bonus he received a figure in the mid-six figures. And that got him thinking.

At the beginning of the project, JK would look for ways to improve product design, or enhance operations related to the delivery, or whatever, and he found that the higher ups, and specifically the President, saw things only their way. After several failed attempts, JK began keeping a ledger of the many improvements he thought up. At this point in time he figured he could make a much better product, one that would garner higher demand, at a profit margin north of what the current project was enjoying. The bonus he got, and the ledger and plans he had, set him on a path to entrepreneurism.

A month after he received that big bonus, just at the end of January, he put in his two-week's notice. It was a shock to his employers and even after a couple of lunch meetings with the President, JK was still set on leaving. He had spent the month speaking with a few key people he thought could help him and calling on both company clients and new prospects for sales leads.

Eden was taken aback when he told her he had quit his job and was going out on his own. The shock quickly wore off to anger that he had not even told her of his plans; that she didn't even get to weigh in on the decision. She had hoped to send their children to private schools but now feared that they wouldn't be able to do that. She was not happy, and in her book, when the mother is not happy, nobody should be happy.

JK on the other hand was upset with her that she didn't see how great an opportunity this was for him.

He had explained everything to her and all she had heard, or replied to, was that he quit his job. It was his job anyway, so what did she have to say about it? He'd never done it before, but he left the house and headed to a bar. He didn't know what to order, but whatever he ended up with he had too many and the next morning, the first of his new enterprise, was spent hung-over with no sympathy from Eden at all. Even his little old verse did very little to quell the headache and nausea that morning.

xxxxxxx

God was sorely disappointed in Johnny. He could see the pain, the doubt, the separation that his reluctance to share had caused Eden. Johnny had lived his mantra to the fullest. He was developing an all engulfing ego, one that was destined for failure. God didn't like to see his children cause themselves so much pain, but, part of being human was the way in which they learned and many times that was by the hard way.

xxxxxxx

JK's new enterprise, starting with a hangover, didn't fare much better. At first he thought he could do it all by himself. He got himself an office, out of the house, and furnished it with expensive trappings. He found that the suppliers he contracted with at his old company wouldn't contract with him for fear of losing that sure account for his potential orders. He found that the companies he was selling to in the past, which had expressed interest in his venture, didn't stomach the risk of moving from a sure platform to an unproven one. And, as hard as he tried, implementing some of his ideas for better features and greater efficiencies into his new solution wasn't as easy, or as successful, as he first thought. Lack of sales led to boredom in the office. And, that boredom led to frustration that was better handled with a stop at the bar on the way home, a destination that got later and later each day.

A couple of months had gone by and JK had spent quite a bit of his startup capital and had nothing much to show for it. Eden was less and less happy with him as each night he missed dinner with the family and smelled of alcohol when he finally did walk in the door. She told John that she was going to take the kids to her parents' house for a week or two and that she hoped he would use the time to figure things out. He passed off the news as nothing much to concern himself with and went to bed. Eden slept that night in the guestroom, and had the kids and her packed and gone before he woke the next morning.

At first, JK was more upset that he had to make his own coffee than being in an empty house. But, as he began to realize that Eden and the kids were gone, his anger grew. She never understood him, he thought. Why did he need her anyway? Before he knew it he was repeating to himself:

All I have is me, myself and I,
And that's all I got 'til the day I die

But, as he took a shower to prepare for the day, he decided to use this event to kick himself in the pants and make a change. At the office he summed up his finances and decided that he could hire a Product Development guru he had heard of, hoping it would turn his fortunes around. The new guy convinced JK that their product needed a complete overhaul and laid out a development plan, with a budget. JK looked over the plan, and analyzed from several angles. The plan was expensive, and without any sales coming in, to complete it would take him to the end of his savings. He told himself that he should check with Eden before deciding what to do, but, he rationalized, since she wasn't home, he'd just pull the trigger on his own.

Eden came home in a couple of weeks, and John seemed more up, more enthused, happier than she had seen him for quite a while. And, the bar wasn't a stop on his way home anymore. That lasted for a couple of months.

That was when JK found out that his new Product Developer had been skimming off the top with a couple of the new vendors he brought in. That was when JK was told by the only supplier he trusted that his product was pretty much worthless, and that to fix it, it would take a couple of hundred thousand dollars more. That was when JK took a second mortgage on the house, cashed in his retirement fund, fired the new guy, and hit the bar hard on the way home. That was when JK found a pile of invoices, real ones, which the former employee didn't submit for payment and the collections calls started, at work, and at home. When Eden found out how much he owed, and then got out of him some of the things he had done, she left him again, without a word this time.

xxxxxxx

God watched with sorrow in his heart. Johnny, John, JK, his son, lay on the floor in his living room dumbfounded. After the anger of Eden leaving, after the shock of a collections agency coordinating the depletion of all of his savings, after he became lonely perhaps for the first time in his life, John just lay down. His mantra didn't help him, in fact, it made him all the more aware of just how alone he was. Without really knowing it, Johnny lashed out and shouted at the top of his voice, "God, God, why?" In an angrier voice, full of venom, he yelled, "God, if there is really a God, how could you?" In a whimper, barely a whisper, he moaned, "God, God,…, God, what am I supposed to do?"

Finally, after everything he could think to do by himself; finally, after he thought about Eden and his children; finally, after he remembered his mother and how she had sacrificed for him; finally, in a whimpering voice so close to Johnny's he asked, "God, …, God, please, please help me."

That was when Johnny, for the first time in his life, heard God's voice.

The Child is the Father of the Man

I was born just like everyone else was, or so I thought. But, I am a man unlike any other.

It sounds like one of those riddles, maybe from old China or Japan; like something you need to figure out before you can snatch the pea from the hand of the Master.

What is so different with me, you ask? Well, from the moment I can remember anything; strike that, before I even knew anything I saw myself as I stood just yesterday. Yes, that's right. I am now almost 59 years old and from the moment I was conceived, I believe, I saw myself as I am now. For my whole life I knew that I would make it to at least this age and what I was going to look like when I got here. Tell me; is that a blessing or a curse?

When I was so very young all I could fathom with that picture in my mind was that it would be me some day. That was really a blessing. But over the years, and really many times without the maturity to comprehend the message, I could not only picture myself but catch snippets of the life lessons that put the crinkle at the corners of my eyes, the hitch in my step, and the scars on my heart. Many of those visions felt more like a curse. What really hurt, even when I should have been "grown up," when at an age most people would consider an adult, what really hurt was seeing everything I had to give up to get to where I was going to be.

Every now and then, like in the first grade, or then again the first time I got drunk with a bunch a buddies, and even when I first fell in love with my wife; every now and then I'd ask someone if they had the same vision of themselves as I do. Most times the response was something akin to, "Are you crazy?" On occasion, the recipient of my query would seriously consider the question, but never told me that they had the same vision. The best answer I got was just the other day. A Pastor at my church, somewhat reeling back on his heels with the question, replied, "God knew you before you were born. Perhaps…just perhaps…He shared that with you."

We grew up, my older sister and I, in Kalamazoo, Michigan. Mom and Dad were great. We were the typical family. My sister got her driver's license the week before the first big snow storm when I was just 9 years old. What was different from this storm was that it started as rain but the temperatures plummeted so rapidly, that the rain on the ground turned to ice before being covered by an inches deep blanket of tiny-flaked snow. I was in the back seat; we didn't use seat belts back then like we do today. She was driving and Dad was coaching; he was teaching her how to drive in the snow because up here in Kalamazoo you drive in the snow for what feels like most of the year. The light was green but my sister pushed too hard on the gas and the tires began spinning on the snow camouflaged ice. So, spinning, swerving and with Dad yelling, we lazily entered the intersection. That was when we saw a big truck, barreling down on us fast, pretty much sideways with every one of its tires locked up, skidding. My Dad and sister freaked. But, I felt wrapped in comfort because in that moment I could see me 50 years in the future and I knew I wasn't going to die that day. I could feel that we were all going to survive the impending crash because I perceived that both my father and sister were to influence my life later on. What I couldn't predict was that the accident would result in both of my legs being broken, and the left leg so bad it would take several operations to make it close to good again.

In my teens the image of my older self took on more meaning, a deeper richness. Not only could I see the picture of me with graying temples, and Yes!, still with a full head of hair, I was able to see more about me, the person. I was able to begin to sense personality traits. I could see kindness and gentleness in my eyes; I had the grandfatherly face that anyone would be drawn to at any age. I had the feeling that my older self had patience and tolerance and perhaps a bit of wisdom. As a teen I was anything but patient or tolerant, and the closest I got to wisdom was being the "wise fool" in my sophomore year of high school.

I remember during those high school years we had some trouble with cliques. We had the athletes and the cheerleaders, we had the nerds, the band kids, and we had the Rednecks. I kind of felt that I wasn't in a clique, that I was kind of a free agent, or an independent. But, I couldn't stand the "A" crowd, the athletes and cheerleaders. It was from that group that the prom Kings and Queens came from. It was from that crowd that the Yearbook staff came from. It was that crowd that the faculty pushed as the face of the school in any media opportunity. I summed up that group of kids as "stuck up," "snotty," and "entitled." Other than one guy who was a pretty good friend, but also in the "A" crowd, I didn't know any of them individually; but that didn't stop me from hating them.

I was driving back from school one afternoon in a driving rain storm. Ain't the weather in Kalamazoo something? Anyway, I'm driving home and on the side of the road, in full uniform, is this cheerleader. Her car obviously has a flat tire. She has her hazard lights on and is outside in the rain helplessly looking down the road as the cars approach her. As I come up upon her, even in the pouring rain, I can see that she has been crying, probably as hard as it is raining. I even know her; she's in my second period English class. I hate cheerleaders; I hate them all. But, the 59 year old me whispers to me to stop. I keep going. The older me speaks to me louder, and louder, and only quiets, with complete disdain, after I have long passed her and it is obvious I'm not turning around.

Later that night, after I think I'd forgotten that encounter, the old me flashes to my consciousness. I can tell he is not happy with me. What really bothers me is that I can literally feel his dissatisfaction with me. I have let him down; I let me down. I hated someone I didn't even know. I passed by a classmate in complete despair. I didn't even feel a bit of remorse. That high school me wasn't even close to the old me. How was I ever going to get to be that old guy? How was I ever going to get to be that me? In disgust, the old me went back to where ever he resided, but just before he left me I thought I could feel just a hint of hope for the young me. It was kind of like the old me felt he got his message across to the young me.

In college it was the frat boys I couldn't stand. I was still an independent, but I attended, or crashed, my share of frat parties. Many times I went partying with another guy in my dorm. While we were getting intoxicated on the free booze, we'd pick out frat boys and sorority girls and rag on them. If the guys wore designer clothes, or if the girls had too much spray tan, if we thought there was something to pick on, we did it, mercilessly. The more the booze, the more our bravado and the worse our critiques became.

There was one party though, where things went too far, even for me, but I was too afraid to do anything about it, no matter how hard the older me pushed. From what I pieced together, a sorority had a pledge that wasn't up to the standards of the other girls. At the mixer with their fraternity, the top guy in the frat started hitting on her. As he cajoled her with more and more attention, he got her drunker and drunker. The girl was in one of my classes, and we had actually worked together on an in-class assignment once. The guy got her into another room where he managed to get her top off, at which point he kicked her out of the room back into the party. That was when the real hazing began. Sorority girls and frat boys just let her have it as she staggered through the room looking for her clothes or an exit, whichever one she could find first. Me, I just joined in the finger pointing and laughter. When, at last, she found someone's sweatshirt laying on the back of a couch and covered herself, her eyes caught mine mid chuckle and the hurt on her face towards me burns me still.

I knew what I was supposed to do but I still didn't move. Of course, it was confirmed by the older me. Again, he had disdain for me, and if he could have shook his head and walked away, that's what he would have done.

It turns out that I really didn't like female bosses much. I didn't like Democrats much. I didn't like "cat people" much either. I had some neighbors for almost 20 years that I really didn't like. My life seemed to be like a spiral staircase. One side of the staircase is always in the light, in the glow of the room. The other side is always in the shadows, kind of crimped against a wall. I would get to a point where I thought I was quite tolerant of others, regardless of how I really felt about them. But then, infrequent, not like clockwork, but you could depend on it, I would blow up at somebody on my "list" regardless of how wrong I knew it to be. I don't know how the older me kept his patience with me, but he did. I could see it in his eyes. It was sort of like he knew when the crescendo was, when the event that would teach me this lesson would happen. As I got older, as I went through these episodes, I could almost feel the weight of responsibility lessening on his shoulders, like each time I was one step closer to the finish line.

Somewhere along the line my wife dragged me to church. It was probably when our kids got old enough to where that needed to behave in front of other people. We had Sunday School and a Service just like many churches, I learned. I remember a lesson, or maybe it was a sermon, in which it was discussed that God gives us a soul at the moment of conception; that a soul is really like a piece of God. At the time I heard that, in the news of the world, they were looking for what scientists called the "God particle." I remember chuckling about the coincidence of that timing and saying to a couple of people that scientists didn't need to look any further because there is a "God particle" in each one of us.

On occasion I would take my son, or the whole family, down to Detroit to watch the Tigers play. We weren't much for baseball fans but it was always a good time. Around the park though there were always people begging for money, for a hand out. Especially when the kids were young I did my best to steer around the beggars so as not to be confronted by them. I never really thought much about them or homeless people in general, it was just an unpleasant moment to avoid. That is, until a family friend invited my son to join his family on an outing to a Tigers game. When my son returned I asked him about the game and if he had a good time. He was most excited about one part of his outing. His friend's father had put a bunch of one dollar bills in his pocket and as they walked towards the stadium, each time a beggar asked for money he gave each of the boys a dollar bill to hand over. The older me just smiled and smiled and smiled and I just couldn't shake that story for the longest time, it just continued to bounce around in my head.

For a father like me there was never going to be a good time for a daughter of mine to start dating. I had firsthand knowledge of the thoughts that go on in a man's mind, regardless of how he thinks he can hide them from society. It might be biology, or it might be sexual impurity I don't know, but I fight my impulses to keep my thoughts on women as people and not just a physical body to serve my needs. Any heterosexual male, if he is honest, has to admit that looking at a women's eyes when first meeting her might be the third thing he sees, if that high. All that being said, my daughter had little chance to find a boyfriend while I was around. I simply did not trust any guy to treat my daughter as a person. I quickly added teenage males to my list of people I didn't like.

My son was pulling his second tour in Iraq when my wife got ill. The stress of having a child at war was one thing, thousands of miles away, but the stress of your spouse facing cancer in your own bedroom is something else. One day she was fine, coming home from work, just a bit more tired than normal. And it seems the next day she struggled just to get out of bed. And, much too quickly, she was admitted to the hospital for the shots and the treatments and the tubes and needles. Our daughter, now married and living up near the Lake, came back home to tend to her mother during the day, and me at night. The doctors had rarely seen a cancer spread so fast and our son was working through the Armed Forces bureaucracy to get back in time. He had one last mission, the one he didn't live through, before he was to fly home.

It crushed me. I was reeling from losing my wife and now I was just crushed with the loss of my son. My daughter and I sat at home the night we got the message, just in disbelief, just crying, not wanting to open the front door as people we knew, people that loved us, came to visit and support us.

I didn't want to tell my wife that we had lost our son. I didn't think I could do it. I didn't want to, but now I hoped she would pass before the day our son was supposed to be home. It was going to be a race anyway; the doctors gave it a 50/50 chance. My daughter couldn't believe I would hold that back from her, and we argued. It didn't get nasty, but it divided us at a point when we needed each other so much.

My son-in-law was in our house the next morning. My daughter had called him in the middle of the night. He listened to my argument, to me telling both of them I wouldn't burden my wife at this point in her life with this tragedy. He let me scream it all out, the rage, the pain, all of it. He heard me curse at God. And, silently, I cursed at the older me watching me with tears on his heart. My anguish at the older me, how he didn't tell me, mixed with the anger at God.

After I exhausted my rage, my son-in-law told me this, "Dad, I can understand that you don't want to tell Ma about losing her son; not right now. But I want you to think about two things before you make this decision final. First, you are afraid. You have so much on your shoulders, you are so worn down that you fear that her pain from hearing this will be too much for you to bear. You are afraid that you will fail her when she needs you most. Second, by not telling her you will keep her from God. Just like you she needs to vent her anger to Him. Just like you she needs to curse His name. Just like you need to be strong for her, she needs to be strong for you. Don't prevent her from seeking the strength she will find in God and share it with you. Not now, not when she needs God so much and so soon. Not when she needs all of you, not just the pieces you want to show her, but all of you to help her live, to help her die. Don't take this piece of life away from her now when she has so little life left."

The older me sorrowfully felt so much compassion for my son-in-law, felt so strong about his words that it caused me to really listen to them. I was deflated and felt defeated but I knew his words rang true. I agreed and later that morning I told my wife that she would not meet our son again in this world, but the next.

It was a couple of weeks after both of the funerals, my daughter and her husband had returned to their home and little ones, and I caught my reflection in the mirror. My appearance was getting closer to the older me I had always seen. But, the current me had eyes full of pain and hurt and anger and loneliness and abandonment and incompleteness. None of those traits existed in my vision of the older me; that vision of genuineness and kindness and wholeness and compassion and competence. How was I going to make it to the man I was going to be? What did the older me have left to teach me?

The medical bills from my wife's treatments were staggering. The house, so cozy with a family of four just a few years ago now echoed as I sat lonely on the couch each night, afraid to turn on the TV and catch a show that might have been a favorite of my wife's. The military sent a check for the loss of my son, which sat at my wife's desk collecting dust next to the stack of bills representing the last days of her life. I found a very small home south of Kalamazoo that appealed to me. So, I sold my big house and put a down payment on this new home for me. I was able to clear most of the debt, at least an amount that the collectors could live with. And I wondered what I could do with the money left over, and also wondered what I could do with the rest of my life, alone.

The older me wanted to see the Tigers play again and I really didn't have an argument that could stop him, so, I went. After I parked, I started walking to the stadium and there were the beggars again, just like they hadn't left from 20 years ago when my son gave them dollar bills. That's what the older me wanted me to see. That's why he brought me here. I don't remember much of the ballgame, but I do remember the plans we made that night.

The next morning I sent a check to my daughter from a good portion of the house sale and my son's military check. With the rest of the money I went shopping. First thing I did was to trade in my two cars for a gently used catering truck. Next, I stocked that truck with sandwich makings and drinks and fresh fruit. With no direction, I headed off to Detroit, to some side streets near the stadium. The older me told me where to turn and where to stop; I don't know how he knew where to go but he did. I could tell he was excited, and to be honest, I was either as excited, or awestruck, as he was. I found a spot that seemed a central gathering point for the downtrodden, the suffering, the hungry, the homeless. I parked, opened the side window and began making sandwiches. I had about 20 of them laid out on the counter, with apples or bananas and bottles of water. Then, I rang the dinner bell, an iron triangle with an iron rod dangling from a string next to it and yelled out, "Lunch!"

For the next several months I drove down to Detroit on Mondays, Wednesdays and Fridays and served free lunches to as many people as I could. On Tuesdays, Thursdays and Saturdays I went to as many businesses and churches and people as I could to get donations, either money or food, to support my mission. On Sundays I attended my church, learned a lot about God and grace and love and compassion.

Last night was a rainy Friday night and I was driving back home from Detroit. Yes, the weather in Kalamazoo is something. But when it's sunny, more than one person has called this land God's Country. Anyway, ahead of me there was a line of brake lights slowing down all of us wanting to rush home. As I got closer to the cause of all of this I saw a cheerleader crying next to her broken down car on the side of the road. Everyone had slowed because her car had not limped far enough off the road to pass it easily. But, no one had stopped. I did.

I had her pop the hood but I couldn't figure out what was wrong. I was pretty much drenched when it occurred to me to ask her to check the fuel gauge. It was empty. I told her to get into the cab of my truck and I hopped in behind the wheel. She was sobbing. Getting a name and a place to go and directions out of her was a struggle. The rain poured hard on the roof, but eventually I calmed her enough to find the way to help her. That was when I saw me as I had all of my life, through her eyes. I was the man, the grandfather-like man, with patience and compassion and love that had stopped to help her. That was when the older me and I meshed, when we came together as one. That was when all of my life, the loves and the losses, made me the man I knew I would become when I was a child.

So I Will Recognize His Voice		The Child is the Father

Final Exam

It was a long, long road. Undergrad, Grad School, Medical School; I feel like I'd been studying for decades. There was just one test left, one final exam. For this final exam, all of us Med Students were to be separated into the specific areas of medicine we wanted to pursue. We had all been on numerous rotations the last couple of years. I had started out interested in Emergency Room medicine, but then really liked my Pediatrics rotation too. But, for some reason, not understandable at all to me, I really liked my experience with cancer patients and my Oncology rotation. There were only five of us in this field and our Professor, Dr. Pruitt, was a living legend.

Dr. Pruitt was a tall woman, closer to sixty than fifty if I had to guess by the graying of her hair. She had a great reputation as a surgeon, but her legend was made of more than that. Patients, long cured of their ailments from her treatment, would come by years later just to stop in and say a hello. Many times that hello turned out to be a long conversation about what they'd been up to, how their family was, and more, all lead by the questions from Dr. Pruitt. It was as if she had a steel-trap mind and could remember every patient's name, and the name of all their family members. On top of that, more than once, I saw members of families not so fortunate to have their loved ones survive their ordeal stop by to visit as well.

The five of us were called to a meeting with Dr. Pruitt a couple of weeks before the final. This was to be a prep meeting, to direct us to what was important, what we should study, where we should concentrate our efforts. After we finished asking all of our questions, she had one last closing remark for us. She told us that the final would be comprised of only one question; that we should be prepared to rely on all of our education, on all of our experience, and on the techniques she had modeled for us during our six months of rotation under her. Our final exam was slated to last four hours, but she told us that it wouldn't matter if we needed more time than that. With that, she walked out of the room.

That was daunting! All of us started talking at once. "One question! If we get it wrong do we fail?" "…more than four hours?" "How do we study for only one question?" "What does she mean by all of our education? How far back do we go?"

Those questions, and many more, took up too much of our study time together. And, to be honest, might have taken up too much of my study time alone as well. But, for two solid weeks we poured over our books and we quizzed each other endlessly. Working in a hospital we were used to going without sleep for long periods of time. We used that skill and studied for days on end. Near the end of the two weeks, the last thought I had before finally succumbing to sleep was, "I wonder what that one question will be."

The day of the final arrived, and we were all seated in the exam room. Some of us appeared to need more sleep than others, but we all showed up on time. Dr. Pruitt was sitting behind a small desk at the front of the room. She had told each of us to bring our own computers and now instructed us to turn them on and bring up the word processing application. We were on our honor to only use this application, and not use any other part of the computer, with the exception to email her our final essay. She told us that she had a story to tell us before she would divulge the final exam question. Here is her story:

Three cancer patients came to me on the same day. They had all been referred and their cancers were confirmed. It was my job to inform them of the severity of their condition, the prognosis, and the recommended course of treatment. After reviewing each patient's files, and doing some testing on my own, I determined that each of them had only about three months to live.

I called in the first patient and told him that he had lung cancer and though we could make him more comfortable he had only about three months to live. Of course the news was devastating and I did my best to console him. I laid out my plan for treatment and he told me that he needed to go home to speak with his wife and he would be back tomorrow to let me know how he wanted to proceed.

I called in the second patient and told her that she had ovarian cancer and though we could make her more comfortable she only had about three months to live. She was devastated and I did my best to console her. I told her my plan of action and she told me she needed to go home and speak to her husband and she would be back tomorrow to tell me how she would like to proceed.

I called in the third patient and told him that he had liver cancer and we could make him feel more comfortable but that he only had about three months to live. He was devastated and I did my best to console him. He needed to tell his wife and he would come back tomorrow to let me know how he wanted to proceed with the plan I had explained to him.

The first patient came back the next day and I could tell that he was still smoking cigarettes; he just reeked of tobacco smoke. He said he might try some of my treatments but that he wasn't going to give up smoking. If he was going to die soon anyway he figured he didn't need to quit now. His last comment to me, "I'm already a smoker and that's just the way it is."

The second patient came in and her eyes were like deer's eyes in the headlights. She was flustered and could barely speak in sentences. She had told her husband, and he was out in the waiting room if she needed him. He wanted her to do anything she could, anything "the doctor ordered" to get through this. She, on the other hand, didn't know what she wanted to do. She had stayed up all night fretting over everything but just couldn't decide what to do. Her last comment to me, "I've already had a pretty good life, I think, but I'm just not yet ready to go through all of this."

The third patient came in and he was smiling. He had told his wife and they spent hours together crying and supporting each other. They spent time reminiscing about all of the wonderful things they had done together. They decided that together they would tackle this head on. In fact, his wife was there holding his hand. His last comment to me, "I've already lived a very good life and I am ready for this challenge. I say, 'Bring it on!' Let's see where it takes us and if the Lord takes me, then I'm ready for that too."

Your final exam question: How would you treat each of these patients?

Four hours flew by and I was still typing. So was everyone else. I started off by not accepting the assumptions of the referring doctors and running all new tests. I then went into all of the latest treatments for each type of cancer. I listed qualifications that each patient would need to meet in order to try new treatments, even those that hadn't yet been accepted; that were still in trial periods. I covered the side effects of each treatment I recommended and what would be needed to be done for each. Then, I went into the normal deterioration patterns of patients in the last stages of each cancer and wrote about how to minimize pain and discomfort. I even went on a short tangent about quality of life.

I thought I was nearly done. I had re-read my essay several times. I checked it against the outline I first planned when I heard the question and verified that I hit on all of the issues. I took a moment to reflect on all that I had learned and experienced. And I remembered just two weeks ago when Dr. Pruitt prepared us for this exam. I recalled one thing she had said, "…to remember the techniques she had modeled for us during our rotation with her."

When I had first heard her say this I had thought about surgical techniques. But then I started thinking about all of her visitors. She was loved because of her personality not her surgical skills. It was her bedside manner that had made her a legend. Her story told us about the lives of three different patients and not so much about the cancers they had. In fact, she had done little to discuss the ramifications and effect of the cancers other to just name them. She had told us more about each patient's character, before and after learning the bad news. So, I spent another hour or more addressing the person in each story and their families.

A week had gone by and I was now with Dr. Pruitt reviewing the results of my exam. She was quite pleased with all of the medicine I had covered in my essay. She brought up a couple of examples where she thought I was right on, and a few in which she thought I could have looked a little deeper. But she was more impressed that I had caught the fact that these patients are people first. She went on to tell me:

Life is the moment stuck in-between the Already and the Not Yet. For example, you have already been through Med School but you are not yet a doctor. All of the patients in my story for the final already had been diagnosed with cancer, but none of them had yet lived with cancer.

You will find that some people want to live in the past, even if that past was awful, just because they know what it is, they have experienced it and don't have to face anything new. And some people get paralyzed when faced with something that is new to them; something not yet to happen. And, few people will be very motivated to get to the new phase in their life. They are done with the 'already' and are so looking towards the 'not yet.'

The purpose of this exam is for you to determine which person you are. Are you stuck in the past, frozen in the present, or striving towards the future? Outside of medicine, ask this question in your walk with God. God always seems to have us in that in-between phase. He knows where we are but loves us too much to leave us there. We know where we have already been but are not yet sure what God will bring next.

When you can face not yet, and do so with the grace of God, then you can doctor patients.

Serial Killer

Paul knew that this time he was going to be caught. He suspected that that stupid old man with his stupid old dog saw him take this one and must have called the police. Even though he thought they were coming he couldn't stop. Part of him wanted to be caught. He lay there in bed with her, lifeless, just holding her as he had always done; afraid to stay, afraid to leave, loving the rawness of emotion.

He liked killing. He liked the search, the hunt, the capture, the comfort and finally the killing. He liked all of it. This time, just knowing that the cops were due any minute just made it more exciting.

According to all of the crime drama TV shows he watched, he knew he had been escalating. In ways, that scared him. In other ways it was fine because he needed for other people to know. In one way he knew he had to be caught.

xxxxxxx

Paul's mother was a tramp. Everyone called her that. She even called herself that. Paul didn't know a father but instead a steady stream of weekly, monthly or seasonal boyfriends that his mother would trade her body with for room and board. She was a dirty blonde, and dirty mostly. When she could get a job it was waitressing at whatever dive was close to the current boyfriend's digs.

When Paul was about ten… It was strange that he couldn't remember exactly how old he was but he could remember every time; he had the pictures, the video stored in his memory and they would never leave him. When he was about ten his mother was staying with a really rough guy. It seemed to Paul that the guy never had to go to work. As he thought back on it later in life he figured out that drugs had to play into it somewhere. When Paul's mother would leave for work, usually the evening shift, and if Paul was unlucky enough to be home, the man would abuse Paul. Mostly what Paul remembered was the end of each encounter, lying in bed, with the man cradling Paul in his arms, spooned so to say, holding Paul tight, and nose in his hair. One night either his mother came home early or the abuse went too long. The man squeezed Paul even tighter and put his hand over Paul's face suffocating him. Paul remembers blacking out and waking up in his own bed some time later that night.

xxxxxxx

Paul had a job, he was a dental technician. He was hoping to become a dentist, but for now was basically a tooth cleaner. The office he worked at put in ten hour days Monday to Thursday and took Fridays off. And, he was married. Not the greatest of marriages; not the greatest gal, but then again he wasn't the best husband either; he always chuckled when he thought that. She was a night time manager at a local restaurant. She had dirty blonde hair.

xxxxxxx

Amy Weathers was nine when Paul found her. She was the first. On Friday mornings he would drive around the local neighborhoods and watch the school buses pick up students. For months he had been "shopping;" looking for just the right girl. She had to be about ten. She had to have dirty blonde hair, straight down. She had to be standing at the bus stop without a parent. Paul had shopped for months before he found her, and then watched her for weeks before he got up his nerve.

It was nearing the end of the school year and Paul figured he had to move now or he'd have to wait until summer vacation was over and that felt like just too long a time. One afternoon, he followed Amy back to her house. As she turned down her driveway, out of view from any classmates, who were all long gone in their parents' cars anyway, he pulled up quickly behind her. The squeak of his tires startled her into turning around. Instead, she should have run. Paul leaped out from behind wheel, grabbed her, shoved her into the passenger seat well and sped back to his own garage just a couple of blocks away.

xxxxxxx

Paul disposed of Amy's body before his wife came home from work that night. He was hyped up but his wife was just too tired to notice and went straight to bed. She was too tired to notice that the bed was better made than she usually found it. Paul thought he had done a good job of hiding his emotions, and the evidence of his captive and subsequent murder.

The high from killing Amy lasted him most of the summer, but by the time the school buses started yellowing the streets each morning, he was hungry again.

xxxxxxx

Tricia Downs was just entering the fifth grade. The new school year was just a few weeks old. She was terrified. She'd been grabbed right out of her own yard and brought to a bedroom in someone else's house. The man had been very rough with her and now she was in a bed, on her side, with that man behind her, his chest to her back, arms engulfing her. He said very little. He did very little. But she didn't move either. She thought it odd that he kept smelling her hair; it was like he was trying to figure out what shampoo she used. She really started to struggle when he clamped his hand over her mouth and nose and she couldn't breathe anymore; but that struggle didn't last long.

xxxxxxx

By Christmas time the local news was going crazy. The Dirty Blonde Killer had just snatched his fourth girl. Paul's wife had even made a comment one night, at home, when she was off work about how sick a man must be to do that to young girls.

xxxxxxx

Paul had grabbed a girl pretty much each month of the school year. Though, this last time, it was just one week since the last Friday's abduction. The girl was ten year old Patty Smythe and she got out a scream before he shoved her into his car. That was why the old man, that stupid old man walking his stupid old dog, turned and saw him. He had hoped that the old man's eyes were too bad to see what kind of car he drove; to see his license plate. Part of him had hoped that the man's eyes were still good enough and his memory too, to go back and make a phone call to 911.

He had her in his bed, clutching her to his chest as was his custom. She was terrified, breathing so fast, hyperventilating. He just wanted to hold her for a while, at least until she calmed. He liked to just lay with his girls, nice and quiet, back to chest, nose to hair. In the distance he could hear the police sirens and with that sound, she quieted some.

The screech of tires in the driveway. The pounding on the door. He just wanted to lay there and hold her. He wanted them to see that he was a good man; that he never really meant to hurt her, to hurt any of them. The police burst into his house and Patty tried to scream. He didn't want to, but he put his hand over her mouth to suffocate the noise. With guns drawn the police entered his room and Paul and Patty just lay on the bed. Cops pulled Paul away from Patty, roughly throwing him to the floor, searching him, cuffing him and reading him his rights. Other cops were performing CPR on Patty, trying to bring her back. Serenely, Paul looked on from his spot on the floor.

xxxxxxx

The trial was quick. Before Paul could make a deal to save his life by telling the police where the bodies were hidden, the police had found them. Patty had survived and was able to tell her story in court. The judge, the jury, the public all had no sympathy for Paul. His wife had left him and filed for divorce as soon as she heard the news. He had no character witnesses' stand up for him. He had no family, other than his mother who declined to come to the trial.

The sentencing hearing took place in just a week after the guilty verdict. The families of all of the dead girls had their moments to speak to the court, to bare their pain to Paul. Mr. Smythe was livid. Anger poured from him and the guards had to restrain him before he finished. Mrs. Downs mostly cried. Her question, "Why, why, why?" went unanswered.

Mr. and Mrs. Weathers stood together in front of the court and told stories about their girl, Amy, and how much they would miss her. You could tell they loved each other the way they held each other; the way they looked in the other's eye when he or she spoke. Mrs. Weathers finished meekly by saying, just above a whisper, "We hope to one day forgive you." The death penalty was the court's decision and Paul was escorted to death row at the penitentiary to await his date.

Upon leaving the court, the other families, and especially Mr. Smythe confronted the Weathers asking them how they could forgive such an animal. The press picked up on it and the Weathers needed assistance from the police just to make it to their car.

xxxxxxx

When Peter told people he was a Prison Chaplain he mostly heard silence. If he went first in the conversation, he rarely even got to hear what the other person did for a living. The easiest way to describe Peter would be to simply say, Friar Tuck! But, his dowdy appearance would lead one to miss the intelligence stored behind those cheery eyes and portly cheeks. Peter went to school starting to be a Psychologist specializing in the criminal mind, but along the way, God had a different plan and he became an ordained minister instead. He and God agreed to a compromise and Peter set up his church in the state prison.

xxxxxx

Paul had eighteen months to wait before his penalty was to be carried out by lethal injection. At first prison scared him, but it was pretty quiet on death row and he settled in. Peter would stop by about once a week, and after a bit they started having conversations. Peter got permission for Paul to come to his office for scheduled appointments. They had nothing in common, at first, but Peter's fascination with Paul's history and subsequent murders. Over time, Peter was able to put some of the pieces together in such a fashion that Paul could make sense of his driving factors towards his behavior. The revelation didn't make it easier to accept, in fact, it made it harder and that's when Peter brought Jesus into the picture.

xxxxxx

It was just about a month before Paul's date with the needle. Peter had started taking Paul through the gospel of Luke, on purpose, with trying to time the crucifixion of Jesus, and the two criminals, to come up in discussion soon. Paul had made great progress in understanding the why's of what he had done. He had also, painfully, accepted what he had done and the effect it had on all of the girls' families. Peter had spent many a day helping Paul through that torment.

As the date loomed closer, Paul felt closer to God. He wasn't entirely sure of everything but he knew that he now believed. In that light he felt as if God had told him not to ask his lawyers for a stay of execution; for the sake of the families. Paul had worked hard with Peter to come to a sense of acceptance, or contentment, about his fate. He found that he was able to hand over to God his fears about the upcoming day.

The night after Peter and Paul read and discussed the end of Luke, Paul knelt bedside in his cell until the sun came up the next morning. Through steady, hard prayer, Paul had felt the presence of God. He accepted Jesus as his savior and asked to be baptized the next day by Peter.

xxxxxxx

The day of Paul's execution came. Peter escorted him to the chamber. In the viewing room, many of the parents of the girls he had killed sat. He noticed that Mr. and Mrs. Smythe sat on different sides of the room; he assumed that they must have separated in the year and a half since he had last seen them. He noticed that Mr. and Mrs. Weathers were huddled close, tears in their eyes, his arm around her. They had gold cross on a gold chain, held in both their hands, together.

As Paul was led to the table, Mr. Smythe got up and started screaming. Paul couldn't hear him through the glass but he could imagine what he was yelling. Once again the guards had to take Mr. Smythe away.

There was a lot of anger in that viewing room, Paul could sense it. But, he sensed something completely different when he looked at the Weathers. Paul had prepared a statement that Peter now took out to the viewing room to read. It spoke of his sorrow and his apologies for the loss he had created for them all. It finished with Paul's asking for forgiveness and this last line, "Father God, into your hands I commit my soul."

When the Weathers heard that they looked up and caught Paul's eyes. It wasn't a smile, but the tension eased from their faces for just a moment and Paul knew that they had forgiven him.

Tapestry

It was typical, she thought; a long, dark tunnel with a very bright, white light at the end. Leave it to her to have an average experience, no different than some of the stories in the Reader's Digest she read as a kid. It seemed like everyone that had a near death experience...

"Wait a minute!" she screamed, only inside her own head. "Why am I having a near death experience? Where am I? What happened to me? Why can't I remember anything? I hope my bare bottom is not sticking out of some hospital gown."

She couldn't remember if she was to go towards the light, or retreat from it; so, she stayed where she was, which wasn't that easy of a chore because everything was kind of swirling around. It wasn't quite like that rotating black and white spiral back in the days of Twilight Zone on TV, but it wasn't much different either she thought. She did recall some horror movies she stayed up late to watch as a kid, past when her parents had turned out the lights for the night; she recalled characters shouting to stay away from the light. But she also saw that movie, Ghost, with Demi Moore and Patrick Swayze, and in that movie he was supposed to go towards the light. As usual, she was over thinking things again; "paralysis by analysis" one of her professors had called it back in college.

She could faintly make out a silhouette of a person closer to the end of the tunnel, nearer to the light. If she had to guess, it was a young girl, maybe ten or eleven, and she was waving her to come closer. She wasn't sure she wanted to, but her feet starting shuffling in that direction, that being easier than standing in one spot for some reason.

"Hi Lisa! I'm Breeze," said the girl. Her voice was prepubescent and more tom-boyish than girlie. Breeze was a good name Lisa thought as her loose fitting, all white dress rippled and swayed. Her eyes were electric blue, clear as crystal. Straight brown hair, hair tinted here and there with some auburn and some blonde, wisped around a young face that when grown up to be a woman would be quite striking. Lisa tried not to think of her as grown up, to continue her first impression as that of a child, but Breeze had a presence about her that portrayed maturity; wisdom, stature and experience, such that Lisa could not ignore.

Lisa replied, "Breeze? That's an odd name. How did you come by it?"

"It's not so much a name, but more about what I do. I kind of flit in and out, sometimes I stay when needed, but often I just breeze by. I wish people would ask me to stay more frequently, but, as I said, I often just caress them with my touch and go and find another person," Breeze said all of that, reaching up for Lisa's hand, given freely, leading her towards the light.

"Breeze, why am I here?"

"Oh, you figured it out pretty quickly; you're in a near death experience."

"What?" Lisa almost yelled, pulling back on her hand, which Breeze gently grabbed again. "What did you say?"

"Oh Lisa, I wish I could tell you more, but it is not yet my place to do so. Your memory will return, that I promise you. But first, I am to take you to see Weaver. She has your story and you need to hear it first," Breeze responded, light on her feet, but in no hurry. If anything, she ebbed and flowed, generally in one direction, with a purpose but without care or haste.

"So I'm supposed to meet this Weaver and she is going to tell me a story and then I'll be all better? Is this some really strange dream? It's not a nightmare is it?" Lisa asked, starting to look around here and there to find the Bogey Man if there was one. In looking around, Lisa sensed that this was a place of peace and serenity. Quickly her concerns of fear abated and Breeze could sense that through her hand holding.

Breeze went on, "Weaver is not going to tell you any story. She is going to show you parts of your story. She is the crafts person behind the whole tapestry; and I mean the whole tapestry and that's no small feat!"

"Tapestry? My story? I don't understand," Lisa said.

"She can explain it much better than I can, but think of it this way," started Breeze. "Every person is a string. Some people might be a red thread, others might be a blue yarn, whatever, but everyone is a string. As you live your life, your string gets involved with other strings. Sometimes your string and their string stay close to each other a long time, kind of intertwine. Sometimes the two strings just intersect for a second. Weaver, it's her job to weave all of those strings together into one big, huge, beautiful tapestry. I've seen it and I can tell you, WOW!"

It wasn't really a room they came to, but more of a place, a smaller place similar in look and feel to the much larger place she was now in, but a place of its own. Lisa could see what had to be described as a gigantic loom and billowing out in all directions was this immense tapestry. In many places the weaving was stunning, in other places quite plain. At the base of the loom sat a woman. She wore … she wore, maybe Lisa would call it a frock, but that really wasn't it either. Whatever it was it was covered in bits and snippets of string and yarn and twine. She was surrounded by spools and spools, many of which seemed to exist on the periphery of Lisa's vision, but they were there. The woman hummed as she sat there; her hands held out towards the loom, not on it per se, but hovering above it, more in reverence to the tapestry.

Breeze whispered to Lisa, "That's Weaver. Normally her hands move so fast that they are just a blur and threads and strings just fly from them and the tapestry just grows right in front of your eyes. I think that this might be the first time I've seen her hands not move."

Lisa didn't know what to say, but did reply, "Why, then, is she so still?"

"Weaver?" Breeze tried just louder than her previous whisper to Lisa. "Weaver?" just a bit louder this time.

"Yes Breeze," Weaver answered. "Who is your friend here?"

Weaver seemed to have the same crystal blue eyes as Breeze, but that is where the physical similarities ended. Weaver looked like a very healthy and energetic grandmother, like the ones on TV commercials for retirement planning. Her hair was short and neat, not quite salt and pepper yet but also containing flecks of gold and bronze. There wasn't a wrinkle on her face, but the carry of her body made Lisa sense that she was getting up in years. Lisa felt as comfortable with her as she had immediately felt with Breeze.

"This is Lisa. I've brought her to hear her story from you," Breeze said.

"Ohhh, this is Lisa is it? I don't usually get to meet the person that is the subject of the tapestry I'm working on. Maybe that's why the spools stopped spinning. Maybe that's why the tapestry just rests in front of me."

Lisa looked up at the tapestry and asked, "What do you mean by I'm the subject of your tapestry?"

Weaver smiled and her eyes crinkled, "This tapestry tells your story. This is why Breeze brought you here. I'm to show you your tapestry. You have some decisions to make and you best have all the information you can get before you make them; don't you think?"

Breeze added, "Every person has a tapestry. Weaver is in charge of everyone's story. She and I work together. I blow this way and that and Weaver shows the path that you've taken and that you're gonna take. This tapestry is only yours. Remember, everybody has a tapestry too, and they are all joined together. Weaver just took your piece out to make it easier for you to see."

"Everyone has one just like this?

"Lisa, everyone has a tapestry, but no two are alike. Yours is bigger than some, smaller than many. Some have more threads and thousands of colors; some are plainer to the eye. What's really neat is seeing how they all mesh together. That's where God comes in," said Weaver.

"God? God! I knew God was going to show up somewhere in this. I'm not sure that I believe in God, or Jesus. Who told you to do this to me? I'm not sure…" Lisa ended without really finishing.

Breeze chimed right in, "That's why you're here Lisa. That's the decision you're here to make. But you don't have to make it just yet. Listen to Weaver tell your story first. OK?"

"Okay, but I'm not sure I'm gonna like this," Lisa shot back.

"Lisa, let me first explain a little bit about your tapestry, OK?" Weaver asked. Lisa nodded.

"As Breeze told you, everyone in the world, past, present and future is represented in the bigger tapestry I work on. Everyone has their own color, their own kind of thread. To you, many of the threads, or strings, look the same. But, when you can see like God sees, you can tell the difference between each and every one of them. And God empowered me to see the differences too so that I can work on his masterpiece." Weaver paused.

Lisa, chewed on this for a moment and then alighted on, "You said every person, past, present and future, right? How can that be?"

"Lisa, it gets very complicated, but let me try the simplest answer I can give you. Everything you do has an effect on everyone around you. And like a ripple on a lake, or perhaps Breeze would prefer to call it the 'butterfly effect,' your one action directly affects some and indirectly affects many. For example, Henry Ford invented the car. From the car came the ambulance. So, decades after Henry died he is still affecting the lives of hundreds of people that need an ambulance, and the thousands of people they are related to, every day. A time that you hold a door open for a person in need and you put a smile on their face, they may turn around and help the next person, and so on and so on. Get it?"

"Yes, pretty simple really."

Weaver only chuckled. "Pretty simple when you think of just one person moving through life in the present. Now, multiply that by 7 or so billion people over more than 2,000 years and take linear time out of the equation and tell me what you can do with that?"

Lisa raised her hand to start a reply, but, after thinking a moment, really had nothing to say, so she didn't.

Weaver continued, "So, this tapestry is your life laid out. For you, I have only showed the before and during of your lifetime. I have not shown you the future because that just gets way too complicated. Come over here. This splash of silver intertwined with that thin little red thread coming out of that pretty purple line, that's when you were born. The silver is Jesus putting just a tad of Breeze into you in your mother's womb. She's the purple. The red is you. You can trace your life, and all of the other people that have made an impact on you, by following your red thread through the tapestry. See?"

Lisa piped right in, "Jesus is silver? How is he with me when I don't believe in him? And what do you mean that Breeze is inside of me?"

"Whether or not you believe in Jesus doesn't mean that he doesn't exist. He is there at every birth and he gives every baby of piece of him. That piece of him is the Holy Spirit, or Breeze as she likes to be called here!"

Breeze added, "That's why it was so easy for you to trust me in the tunnel, Lisa. You already know me because I've been with you for your whole life. Now, you don't listen to me all of the time, but I know you do hear me, don't you?"

Lisa, looking back and forth between Weaver and Breeze replied, "Huh? I mean, yes I do hear a voice inside my head at times. I didn't know what it was. Are you telling me that it was you, Breeze?"

"Yep, that's me!"

"So, Lisa, you came here to have me show you your story. Are you ready?" asked Weaver.

"I think I am," Lisa said.

Weaver began her first story: "Come over, closer to your tapestry. See this nice tan thread right here? It starts well before you were born and then just wraps itself around the purple thread of your mother just before it wraps around yours. Well, that's your father. You can see where he met your mother and see that they are a significant part of your thread line for your earlier life. I'm sad to say that you can see here, with another burst of silver, when he passed away. I want you to think about that now. Breeze and I will help you see that part of your life."

"My father died?" Lisa moaned. "How come I can't remember anything? I don't remember anything before meeting Breeze and then you."

"All in good time, but first remember this…"

Lisa could see the farm where she grew up. It was near Broad Run, Virginia, out on Hopeland Mill Road. She was about fourteen. Her hair was back in a ponytail and she remembered that she kept it that way pretty much all of the time. It was late summer, maybe early fall because the trees were shedding their orange, yellow and red leaves. She had on Hawk Ridge Middle School track shorts and matching running top, with some perspiration showing in dark stains. She was on the school's cross country team. Even though it was pre-season, she was out "putting down the miles" as her father had called it.

Her father, lean, tan, tall, with hard, calloused hands and warm, gentle eyes, was out back of the house working on some farm equipment. She jogged back there as part of her cool down, stopped next to him and began stretching her quads and hamstrings. She knew he knew she was there, but she waited for him to speak first; she didn't want to interrupt him. After a bolt was tightened and the wrenched laid down, he looked up, "LiLi! You look like you've run from here to Dulles Airport! You sure you're not pushin' it too hard, Hon?

Sometimes she thought that he tried to baby her too much. Other times she liked it that he cared for her so. This time she had other things on her mind. "Daddy," *she began,* "the girls on the team want to go to the football game tomorrow night. We're playin' Heritage and we just hate them. But, they want to have a sleep over and then hang out all Saturday morning doin' stuff. Do I have to go? Saturday mornings are my long run days and you were gonna take me out to the trails at Banshee Nature Preserve. Do you think I can skip it?"

Her Daddy now straightened up and brushed his hands on the seat of his blue jeans. He looked her right in the eye and loved her with a smile that never moved his lips. She could feel his warmth and hoped that her rosy cheeks hid the blush she knew was coming. "Lisa, you have to enjoy life girl. Cross Country is great, and you're great at it, but it is a lonely sport. You out there runnin' mile after mile everyday all by your lonesome. I worry about you, not about you gettin' hurt, but about becomin' a loner. You got to socialize some, you gotta make some friends. You haven't had a close friend since Rachel moved away last year."

Lisa shook her head and blinked her eyes and Weaver and Breeze were still standing right there. Weaver gave her a little wink and she began to remember another piece:

It was her senior year in high school, the day before the Prom. Lisa's mother had bought her a new dress, mostly without Lisa's involvement. Lisa was wrapped up in first the Cross Country County Championships, where she'd won, and then the State Championships where she'd won again and was hoping for a college scholarship to UVA. She was sitting in the living room with her Daddy. Her mother, flabbergasted with her, had left for her best friend's house just a couple of miles down the road.

"But I don't want to go. Why should I have to go just because she wants me to go? I'm not a baby!"

"LiLi, you'll always be our baby," he said with a big, false grin on his face.

It worked. It cracked just the smallest of smiles on her face. She didn't want to smile; she wanted to hold onto the anger, to make her point, to win another race, this time against her mother. But, the smile let down her guard, "dissolved her resolve" as her father would say. "Daddy, why does she want me to go so bad? Just because she had a great time at her Prom it doesn't mean I will at mine."

"Honey, it's not about the dance. It's about the people and the memories. Don't you want to go with your friends? Don't you want to have a fun night?"

Lisa slumped more into the couch, "I'm just not comfortable with all of those people. I'm not a people person."

"That boy, Joey, he seems to really like you. I see the way he looks at you at church. I see the way he looks at you during your meets. I don't see him with any other girls. Why don't you go and hang with him?"

"He's probably still mad at me because I said 'No' when he asked me to the Prom," Lisa replied, staring off remembering the afternoon he asked her, after one of her meets, when she was too elated with winning to think of anything else.

"Why'd you say 'No'?"

She really didn't know why, but came up with an excuse that she thought would work, "Daddy, he's kind of a loser. I mean he's not even gonna go to college. I have plans, Daddy. I want to go to UVA and I want to go to the Olympics and I want to get a job when I get out. All Joey is gonna do is stay here and work on his farm."

Her Daddy paused a moment, "So you're tellin' me that working a farm is just for losers? What do you think I do all day, Hon?"

Lisa quickly tried to think of a way to retract that last statement, but couldn't find any way out of it. Her blush now showed bright red on her face; she hated it that she was so transparent.

"LiLi, you know Joey's father split with his mother and left her a single mom with three young kids all smaller than Joey. If you look real hard, Hon, you'll see that Joey is not a loser, you'll see that he is a young man trying to grow up fast to take care of a family that no kid should be burdened with."

Lisa took that in silence, a long, pregnant pause her Lit teacher would say. Then, "I know Daddy. I know. But I still don't want to go to that dance."

"Lisa, it's your decision and I know you'll do what's right. But remember, your Ma bought you a new dress. Both Ma and I love you and only want what's best for you. You might trust us now and then to listen to what we think might be good for you. But, all said, it's your choice."

Again, just as Lisa's eyes began to focus on the present instead of the past, Weaver winked:

Hopeland Mill Road was a long, lonely road and had one very sharp turn wrapping around the corner edge of Lisa's family property. There were no street lights, and on moonless nights, like this one it was very dark. Lisa's father had been working on a tractor that broke down as far from the barn as possible and had finally got it working again. It was too dark to drive it back through the fields, so he took it out on the road. A pickup truck with a drunk driver took that one turn too fast and too wide and ran up and over that tractor.

Lisa was in her dorm room trying to study, trying harder to ignore her roommate whispering with her boyfriend in her bed across the room. The phone ringing down the hall was just another annoyance, until a girl knocked on the door and told Lisa it was for her. Lisa couldn't believe it, didn't want to believe, but her mother told her what had happened twice now. Her father was clinging on to life in Loudon County Hospital. Joey was the only person her mother could think of to drive the two hours down to Charlottesville to get Lisa and drive her back. Lisa barely could pack a bag so her roommate, after kicking out the boy, helped her do it.

It was the middle of the night when Joey's pickup parked outside of the Emergency Room at the hospital. Lisa ran from the truck and rushed her way to her father's room. Everyone she saw was downcast; with eyes so low she could barely see anyone's face. Her mother stood by her Daddy's bed with her hand resting on his arm. Doctors and nurses and tubes were covering her father and he didn't see her at first. But then, somehow, he knew she was there waiting for him to speak first.

His voice caught at first, he cleared his throat, and then in a voice louder than the machines around him, "LiLi, how did you get here? Aren't you supposed to be studying away down there at UVA? You playin' hooky Hon?" The smile lit his eyes and just barely curled his lips.

"Daddy," she cried and walked to his side. With one hand she held her mother's hand, with her other she tried to hold his but had to settle for placing it on his shoulder.

Her father looked at the doctors and nurses and with a nod that Lisa could only remember years later, they left the room. Her mother gently let go of her hand and went to the other side of the bed. Her Daddy winked at her mother and then turned to face her. With everyone gone she could see that his body was crushed, she could see that one of his legs was missing under the covers, she could see that he was quite pale, without his farmer's tan he bragged about.

"Daddy," *she mumbled as tears began to well up and then roll down her cheeks.*

"Aw, LiLi, I'm so sorry. I have so much I want to tell you…how proud I am of you, how much both your Ma and I love you, so much more."

"Daddy?"

"Lisa, listen to me now. I want you to keep on runnin'. You're so good at it. You just keep on runnin' more and more, okay? I want you to know that I will be with you every time you run. I'll be there watchin' you so do your best just like you've always done, okay?"

Through the tears now freely flowing, Lisa nodded her head.

"And, Lisa, you've got to spend as much time with people as you do running alone. You like to judge people as a cover on a book. You think you can tell who they are by what they look like. Honey, spend some time, turn some of their pages, try to see life like they do, through their eyes. You have so much to give, and so much to learn from other people. LiLi, promise me you'll try."

Lisa took a quick look at her mother, she too with tears, and then back to her Daddy and nodded again, "Yes, Daddy."

"LiLi, give me a few minutes with your Ma now, okay?"

Lisa was crying now, sobbing. Breeze came close and wrapped herself around Lisa. Weaver waited a long minute and then said, "Lisa, you can see here where your father's thread stops in your tapestry. You can see his thread mixed in with yours and right there a whole lot of silver thread too."

"How can you say God was there at that moment? Why would God take my father from me? Why? I didn't see him there," she almost yelled with more anger than she thought she had.

Weaver let out just a little sigh and with it softly said, "Yes, God was there, but let's wait on that talk for just a bit. I want to give you a little gift. I want you to see your father's thread in some of this…just a few glimpses," and with that Weaver winked again.

He saw the pickup truck much too late, but still had time to think how stupid he was to be driving his tractor this late at night on a dark road with no lights. He thought of how angry his wife was going to be with him. And, he thought, he worried, that he might not get to see his LiLi again.

He found himself on the ground and knew immediately his injuries were serious. It seemed as if his left leg was missing and he could barely breathe because it hurt so much. He undid his belt and tied a tourniquet on his leg above where most of the damage appeared to be. Then, he lay back down and began to pray. He'd had a long relationship with God so talking with him was nothing new. He prayed that he would be found in time to say goodbye.

He was just so very tired, so very sleepy but there were doctors and nurses pounding on his chest so he woke back up. They smiled to see him and he smiled back. He figured he was in the hospital now so he figured that God must have heard his prayer.

His wife was now by his side. She told him that Lisa was on her way and should be there in a couple of hours. He looked up at the clock and marked the time; marked the time that he needed to stay alive.

The doctors wanted to give him morphine to help with the pain. They had already told him that the damage was so bad that it was pretty much a miracle that he was still alive. He said no to the drugs because he wanted to be coherent for his wife, and for LiLi.

In some ways the minutes on that clock moved so slowly. In other ways they rushed much too fast towards death. Lisa was due soon. He knew that he wanted to be the man his daughter had always known. He knew that he wanted her memory of him to be of a full person and not a damaged fraction of a body. He knew that he wanted to be strong for her, so he held on. The pain was intense. He could barely breathe. He felt light headed and so sleepy. He asked his wife to help him stay in the present and she told him stories.

Lisa came and he wanted his voice to be so strong, commanding, as if he could hold off death with his words. He wanted LiLi to see her Daddy as her Daddy one last time.

He could feel LiLi in the room and then turned his eyes and saw her. It hurt him more deeply for her to see him like this than his injuries did. Thinking about LiLi going through the rest of her life without her Daddy put a lump in his throat that was just too hard to clear. He knew he had so little time left he could only give her a couple of pieces of advice, and tell her he loved her. He wanted to tell her so much more, but just couldn't. His last thought of her was as a little girl running to him across the field behind their farmhouse.

Weaver, Breeze and Lisa, all three were sobbing now. Breeze has wrapped herself around Lisa as best she could, and Weaver hugged on both of them. Minutes went by before Lisa gained some sense of control. "I remember everything about my Daddy now. Thanks…I guess."

Weaver, separating from both of them, nodded her head, "You are so welcome, dear."

Lisa looked back up at her tapestry, now with much more interest. She could trace her path, her thread, her life, and see all of the other treads that touched hers. She said, "So, all of these other threads, even some so small I can barely see them, they show where other people came into my life. Is that what you're saying, Weaver?"

"Yes, that is exactly it."

"Whose thread is this one? It kind of twists with mine here, but then it just kind of runs parallel with me, touching me every now and then. Is that someone I know?"

"Yes, Lisa, that is someone you know, and just happens to be a boy I want you to see," replied Weaver.

"A boy?" Lisa inquired.

Breeze let go of Lisa and Weaver once again winked her eye.

Lisa must have been about eight years old or so. She could tell by the sneakers she had on her feet, they still looked new from when her mother had bought them at the Shoe Barn. She was down by the creek, way in the back of their property. Her father was working in a field nearby and she was allowed to wonder off to see what's what.

Joey was his name. He stood in dirty jeans and an even dirtier T-shirt across the creek. He hadn't startled her, but it was a surprise to see him that first time. "Whatcha doin' over there?" she asked.

"Just checkin' out the place. Me and my Mom and Dad just moved here and I wanted to see this creek to see if it was any good for fishin'"

She and Joey became fast friends, for the summer anyway. It turned out that they both went to the same school, and the same church come Sunday. But, it wasn't really cool for girls and boys to mix with each other at either place.

"I remember Joey!" Lisa blurted out. Breeze and Weaver smiled back, and Weaver winked again.

This time memories just seemed to flash by her eyes.

She was twelve, looking in the mirror, practicing her kissing face. She'd seen John Travolta and Olivia Newton-John kiss in the movies and was wondering what that felt like. She wondered what it would feel like to kiss Joey.

She was a couple of years older now and she had won her first cross country race. After being congratulated by her team and coach, she rushed over to where her parents sat. She was so happy, beaming actually. Joey was sitting in the bleachers a couple of rows up from her parents. They caught eye to eye, but that was it, she was off with her parents to the Ice Cream Parlor for a celebration.

In the hallway, near her school locker, a guy from her Math class was giving her grief. They had been paired together in a little competition in the class and Lisa had got a problem wrong, causing them to lose. He was badgering her, calling her dumb and stupid. Joey happened by and stood between him and Lisa, facing him without a word until the jerk left. Joey simply turned to her, sort of nodded and walked off.

She was in church. She and Joey were in the same Sunday School class. She approached the classroom door and saw Joey sitting there. But, she had decided that she didn't believe in God anymore so why go to class. So, she turned on her heel, and walked away hoping that Joey, or the teacher, wouldn't say anything to her parents.

Now, she was all grown up. She even had a wedding ring on. She bumped into Joey, a man now she saw, at the grocery store. It must have been fairly soon after getting married because he congratulated her. They spoke for just a minute or two, and then went in different directions down the aisle, then, awkwardly bumping into each other as they picked out their goods.

It was a tiny little chapel, so small it only had two pews, just enough room for maybe six people. The chapel had no windows, like it was a room within a building. Joey knelt in the front pew, all by himself. Somehow she could tell that he was sad. Somehow she could tell that he was praying very hard.

"I'm married?"

"You were married, you're divorced now, Lisa," Breeze answered.

"How come I can remember Joey but not my husband?"

"Here you go! If you look on your tapestry, here, you can see where your husband came, and went, in your life," Weaver said.

His sadness was palpable. His anger, boiling just beneath the surface. She knew her husband was upset but for some reason that fact didn't really upset her. "So, why did you marry me anyway? Lisa, why?" he fumed.

"I thought that was what I was supposed to do. I thought that's what you expected of me."

Anger quickly flashed in his eyes, but was fast replaced by pain, "Lisa, that's not why I married you. That's not why people get married. I thought I loved you and that you loved me. I feel like you don't even know who I am, and even worse than that, sometimes I wonder if you even care who I am. I think to you I am still just that guy that runs with you and trains with you and that's it."

With that he walked out of their bedroom door.

"That was my husband? That was my marriage?" Lisa asked, sarcasm close to the front.

Both Breeze and Weaver nodded. Breeze responded, "Your marriage didn't last all that long. You thought you were in love. You thought that your husband was going to be very successful and therefore was what you wanted. You thought that the love of running you both had would be enough. But, Lisa, a relationship not founded on true love is no relationship at all. Your husband knew that and sadly moved on."

More awareness of her marriage entered Lisa's memories as she stood there. Most compelling was her memory of how she handled the divorce. She compartmentalized it, closed the book on that chapter. She thought, 'Closed the book, isn't that something my father would have said?'

Weaver waited, giving Lisa enough time to process this thought. Then, she said, "Lisa, look again at your tapestry. I want you to really see how many threads, how many colors, touch yours. Get really close and you can literally see hundreds, if not thousands of them. I want to give you a glimpse of some of these before I answer your questions, OK?"

"I guess. But the more you show me the more questions I have. I need some answers soon."

This time Lisa simply closed her eyes and let the visions, the memories come.

Lisa remembered the dress she was wearing, mostly because she didn't own but two dresses, but also because she wore that dress on the day she got her first real job out of college. She left the interview, walking out of the building so happy. She knew her mother would be proud of her and so happy too. Before she reached her car, parked around the corner, she passed a homeless woman sitting on the ground, back against a building, facing the sun warming her. Lisa could tell she was homeless by the clothes, the filth, the bags and the deadness in her eyes. Lisa opened her purse and took out her last twenty and gave it to the woman and went on. What Lisa hadn't seen that day was the transformation in the woman. With that gift in her hand, the sun now showed a smile on her face and hope in her eyes. She had been so depressed right at the moment, so sad. She had felt utterly alone, that even God had lost sight of her. She had one last prayer in her and that was that she could get just one meal, just something, anything to eat.

It was her senior year in high school, at a cross country meet near the end of the season. Lisa had already qualified for the county championships, but her team needed as many points as they could in this match to make it in. Lisa had sprained her ankle, not seriously, but bad enough that she had considered skipping this meet to better heal for the championships a couple of weeks away. Her mother and father had advised that she skip the meet; her coach was noncommittal but she knew he really wanted her to run. Come time for the race, Lisa had taped up the ankle and was ready at the starting line. On Lisa's team was a freshman girl. She had a lot of promise but really hadn't delivered in any meet yet this season. The coach thought that she was too timid and urged her in practices to become more aggressive, asserting herself to attack other racers when she could gain an advantage. This girl looked over at Lisa before the gun went off and thought, 'If she can run today, then so can I!' The girl finished second, right on the shoulder of Lisa coming in first.

There was a man at her church, he volunteered in the Youth department. She didn't know what he did for a living but it seemed that he was everywhere. Every Sunday morning he was always there with doughnuts and juice for the teens. He also taught Sunday School class. He organized service projects, some of which Lisa participated in so she could log the hours needed for community service on her college applications. He also had a tradition of taking each of his students individually out to lunch, just to get to know them better. During her lunch he was more patient and understanding than she expected when she stepped forward about her not believing in God. He had listened and openly talked about his belief and his faith without trying to persuade her or chastise her in any way. She also learned that he planned his vacations around going to India and work at an orphanage he helped to fund by seeking donations from people and companies here in the States.

She remembered the story her mother found out and shared with her about her track coach. At one time he was a world class long distance runner. He made the US Olympic Team once, but hadn't placed in the event. Many people thought that he would medal at his next Olympics. But, in a freak accident his Achilles' tendon was severed and his running life ended. Her mother was impressed that he was still so involved with running after that. Being a track coach, she had thought, would have been so hard on him.

It was getting close for her to head off to UVA. The summer was nearing an end, her bags were mostly packed, her summer job was over, and, she just couldn't wait anymore. Many of her classmates had received cars, most of them hand-me-downs, when they graduated college. A couple of kids she knew got cars before heading off for college. She had started asking her parents how she was going to get down to Charlottesville, and when down there, how she was to get around. They knew she was hinting at a car. She worked herself up to an agitated state of expectation, so much so that it affected her attitude with her parents. She got up the gumption and approached her father while he was tending to a cow in the barn. He was bent over the animal but knew she was standing there and knew why she had come. Before she could ask he spoke, "LiLi, your mother and I, we don't make a whole lot of money here on this farm. Now, we have enough to send you off to college, especially with the scholarship you earned, so don't you fret none. But, Honey, I've got to tell ya' we don't have the money to get you a car with all the expenses that go with it. It hurts me to tell you that and I'm sorry, I truly am."

Everyone was in black. It was after her Daddy's funeral. So many people had come to the church and then the cemetery. And, so many people were now at their house. Lisa tried to be downstairs, greeting everyone and standing close to her mother. At one point, it just got to be too much and she quietly went up to her room. Lisa sat and watched dust particles floating in a shaft of light from the window. After a bit, her mother knocked on the door and came in. She sat next to Lisa on the bed. She took her hand in hers and they sat for a few minutes. Then, softly her mother said, "I am so grateful to God for the man he gave to me to be my husband, and to be your father. I loved your father so very much, I still do, and I love God for giving him to me. On the night of his accident your father asked God for just one thing. He wanted to be there when you arrived. He and I prayed together that you could get there in time. There came a time when I could see that your father knew he would make it. He knew that God would grant him this last prayer. The peace that came over him...well, I can't thank God enough for that. It made it so much easier for him. He loved you so much, LiLi."

It was after her divorce and she sat at her table for breakfast one morning. She was thinking of being in the hospital with her Daddy that last night. She could hear some of his last words again, "You just keep on runnin' more and more, okay? I want you to know that I will be with you every time you run." Ever since her Daddy had died she had always felt closer to him when she ran. That morning she decided that she wanted to become a marathoner. She figured that the longer she could run the longer she could be with her Daddy. She had ten months until the next Boston Marathon and she thought she could train and qualify to enter in that amount of time.

Lisa slowly opened her eyes again, and still, standing in front of her were Breeze and Weaver. It took a moment for her to digest everything she had just remembered, to come back to the present, if this is what this is. "More and more memories are coming back now," she said.

Weaver simply said, "Good."

"I guess my first question is why am I here? How did I get here? Breeze, you said I am in a near death experience, right?"

Breeze looked first at Weaver, who nodded, and then back to Lisa, "Yes, that's what I said. What was the last thing you recalled, just a second ago?"

"That I was going to train for the Boston Marathon. Did I?"

"Yes, you trained hard and qualified in your first attempt. You were running so well in it too when the bomb went off."

"Bomb!" Lisa almost shrieked at the same moment that memory came back.

At mile marker 24 she had checked her time and she was slightly ahead of her planned pace. She had hit the wall, just a bit, back at mile 20 and had hoped that she had made back her time and was happy to see she had. After the start of the race, when it was so crowded and elbows were flying and racers were careening off of other racers, she was able to settle into her rhythm. For quite a few miles she was on autopilot, in the zone, which she loved because that was when she felt closer to her Daddy. He would be so proud of her now she kept thinking.

She now figured that she had enough gas in her tank to really push hard for the last two miles. She was far ahead of the vast majority of the participants but she was able to pick out a few racers quite a bit in front of her and she set her sights on them. She began to up her tempo and to start picking up her pace. She caught the first racer in front of her, a man about her same age, which made her feel really good. She knew she should feel guilty about that little pleasure but she felt it more important to use it as an adrenaline push.

The third racer she had targeted was just ahead of her, just after mile marker 25. She increased her pace even more because she wanted to blow by this guy. She was feeling really good; pushing hard but still within her capabilities and composure. That was when it all ended.

The next thing she remembered, it was just a flash, but she was laying on the ground and her ears were ringing loudly, so much so she couldn't hear anything else, not even the Police man yelling in her face. She felt sweat roll down her side, under her top. Drip, drip, drip, it went. She was very cold and she thought that odd, sweating so much but so very cold. As the Police man ripped off his shirt and then his T-shirt and compressed it against her side, she closed her eyes.

"I'm so very sorry, Lisa," Weaver softly said.

"Me too," added Breeze.

That was when most all of the pieces fell together for Lisa. She remembered a huge blast just off to her left which knocked her off her feet, scrambling in midair. She felt again the sharp pain in her side before she skidded back down on the concrete road. She thought she remembered her father's face looking down on her. She figured out now why Breeze had said she was in a near death experience. She looked back up to Breeze.

"Your father prayed for another chance for you. He believes that you have yet to experience the real life that was meant for you. He fears that he failed you by not showing you his Father, God. I am here to ask you if you want that second chance. Do you want to live again?"

"My father? My father is dead, how could he be praying for me?" Lisa struggled to get the questions out.

Weaver answered, "Lisa, your father lives here with us. He can see you right now. I bet if you close your eyes and think of him that you will feel him here with you. Try it."

Lisa closed her eyes, skeptical at first, but tried to relax and think of her Daddy. She could see him working in the barn out back of their home. She could see his face above her after the blast. And then, without a doubt, she could feel him right there with him. It was like sitting on the couch with him back home and his genuine love for her made her blush again. She felt him tell her, "LiLi, live to run again, I am always with you when you run."

Breeze broke the silence, "Lisa, would you like the second chance your father hopes for you? Or, should we let nature takes its course?"

"I'm not sure what you're offering me. Are you saying that I am dying, or that I'm already dead? Are you saying that you can bring me back to life? What's the catch?" Lisa replied.

"Your father wants you to come to know his Father. Weaver and I would like you to get to know him too. If you were to die right now you would never know him and that is such a terrible loss. The catch, just open up your eyes and your heart and let God in."

"Breeze, I don't think I even believe in God. How can I do that?"

Weaver stepped forward, "Look at the tapestry again, dear. Look at all of the lives that are involved in your life. Look how much silver there is in just what you can see. God is everywhere. Think of the memories you've just seen here. In every exchange between you and another person, God is there providing gifts. Sometimes that gift is loyalty, most often it is love. Sometimes you can see where a person has denied themselves to provide for you. You have received counsel, understanding and love. You have seen fortitude, charity, prudence, hope, justice, and, faith. Sometimes, it is through you that God gifts the person you touch. God is in everyone, he is everywhere. Your Daddy knows that. That's why he kept telling you to see others in a different light."

Lisa, hugging herself, thinking, replied, "I'm beginning to see what you're saying, sort of."

Weaver moved even closer to Lisa, "Let me show you how I see this tapestry. Close your eyes just for a moment. There, that's good. Now open them again."

Where the tapestry was before, with multitudes of colors going off in all directions, now it glowed brilliantly in most all silver. Silver strands were the rule, but in each thin silver strand there lay lines of colors. It was if silver embraced each of the colored threads she had seen before.

"What happened to all of the threads, and strings and stuff?" she asked.

"Like I told you, this is how I see your tapestry; how I see your life. And, this is how I see everyone's life. Jesus is everywhere. He surrounds every person.

He holds you in his love and embeds himself inside of each of you. To see the world like this is what your Daddy and our Father wish for you."

"I'd like to try to live a life like that," Lisa whispered.

Lisa's mother had kept the TV on in the background as she did her chores the morning of the Boston Marathon. Lisa was running in it and she hoped to keep up with the progress of the race as best she could. She was completely shocked when she heard newscasters break into the coverage to announce the bombing. Calls to Lisa's cell phone went unanswered again and again which added exponentially to her level of anxiety. Finally, after hours of waiting, not knowing anything, the phone rang. Lisa had been admitted to the Massachusetts General Hospital in critical condition. The caller strongly urged her to get there as soon as possible. The only person she could think of to call was Joey.

The drive was long, but fortunately traffic was light. Via her cell phone Lisa's mother was able to keep up with what was happening at the hospital. Lisa had already been in for one emergency surgery and had gone through numerous pints of blood. She was lucky now to have a surgeon that had previous experience with shrapnel. He was trying to stabilize her to undergo another surgery to try to find and repair the damage that was causing her to continue to bleed out. He tried to sound optimistic on the phone but Lisa's mother was not hopeful when she hung up that last time.

She and Joey were due to arrive at the hospital at about the same time Lisa should be coming out of her second operation. That's what her mother hoped. That's what she and Joey prayed for on the drive. Her mother prayed to God and spoke to her deceased husband, running the gambit from pleading and begging to dealing and trading. She finally came to rest and put Lisa's life in God's hands, and asked her husband to watch over her too.

Lisa was exhausted but she wanted to wake up. It was like a dream where she knew she was sleeping and wasn't quite sure how to get out of it. But, she willed herself awake. The room was quiet but bright with lights. She was so cold but could feel the blankets over her. She thought she was alone but could hear the shuffling and rustling of people around her. She quickly realized that her hearing worked again, without any ringing, and that brought her back to the explosion at the race and it jolted her. She could hear her monitors react to the jolt when they started squealing and she jokingly wished her hearing would stop again. That was when she saw her mother, coming out of a chair near her bed and tentatively walking towards her. Her mother looked so worn. She could tell she had been crying and was trying to figure out why. Her cognitive skills seemed to come and go and she had a hard time holding on to the present. She just had to close her eyes and rest.

She came awake much slower this time as her mother held her hand, rubbing the back of it back and forth with her thumb. Her mother thought back to Lisa as a baby and hummed some of the songs she used to sing to her. That was the sound Lisa heard as she came back. She could hear her mother humming. She pictured her mother over the years, from her first memories of warm oatmeal raisin cookies in the kitchen on cold winter days to the dress she begrudgingly wore to her Prom, and was so very happy she had gone, but never did tell her mother. She could both remember all of the love her mother had graced her with throughout her life and the love she was trying to squeeze into her hand right then.

Lisa and her mother talked a bit here and there as Lisa fought her way back to consciousness. Her mother filled Lisa in on the explosion and her operations and Lisa told her about the race and how good she felt running it. They both talked about Lisa's Daddy and how both of them missed him so much.

Lisa's mother was stunned when Lisa said, "Mom, go bring Joey up here. He's down in the Chapel. I want to thank him for driving you all of the way up here. He seems to be our family's angel when we really need one, don't you think?"

"How'd you know Joey was here? I didn't tell you he drove me."

"I saw him in the Chapel. He was sitting in the front pew, so sad looking, and I could tell he was praying, but I didn't know what for," Lisa replied.

"You saw him! When?" her mother blurted out.

Lisa tried to answer but at first she couldn't figure out how she could know. Then she remembered Breeze and Weaver. Then she remembered the tapestry. Then she remembered what they had been telling her. She just smiled, "Mom, it doesn't really matter how I know, just tell him he can come up and be with us now."

A few months later Lisa was back living at home with her mother while she continued recuperating. One day she had gone over to Loudon Outpatient Physical Therapy for her first appointment. There, she met a woman that was to be her therapist. Her name tag read, "Annie, No Pain – No Gain." Lisa started to ask her about it when she thought she recognized the woman.

"Lisa, I don't know if you remember me or not. You and I were on the same Cross Country team back in high school. You were a senior and I was just a freshman so you probably don't remember me, but…"

"Annie? Annie…You were that girl in that last race that just stayed on my tail the whole way. You rode me like a broomstick all the way to second place, right?"

"Yep, that was me," Annie beamed back. "I want to tell you that I learned a lot about myself that day. You were hurt. You had already qualified for the County finals and you were most likely going to win State too. You didn't need to race that day, but the team needed you. I was so impressed I just knew I had to be a fighter like you. I want you to know I've been fighting ever since. I love my job and I had to fight to get here and I want to thank you because you're the reason I made it here."

"You are welcome, I think," Lisa pensively responded.

"Well you are. And now I get to repay you by getting you back in shape. I don't know if you'll ever be the runner you used to be, but I'll work as hard as you on getting you to be the best you can be for now. Are you ready for that challenge?"

Lisa tried to jog a bit, but mostly walked. She ended up on the far end of her family's farm, down by the creek. She had felt a whisper on the breeze telling her to come down to the creek. She remembered Breeze very well and felt compelled to listen to her every time she thought she heard her. She wasn't startled, or even surprised to see Joey on the other side, standing there in old worn out blue jeans and a T-shirt with a few stains of earth and sweat. "What are you doin' down here?" she called over the babble of the creek.

"I'm not really sure, to tell you the truth. I thought I heard a voice and I thought it said to come down here. I was tired with my chores so I thought I'd come," he answered.

They bantered back and forth a bit, getting caught up on the families and telling some old stories. Finally, Lisa asked him, "Joey, how come I never see you with a girl? How come you ain't married off by now?"

Joey hesitated a moment before he spoke. "I've just been waitin', that's all."

It hung out there for a bit; Lisa not really sure what to say about it, so she said nothing. Joey, after a long minute, added, "I've been waitin' for you."

With that, Joey took a hand full of pebbles and tossed them into the still part of the creek, the one spot that you could jump in over your head. When the pebbles hit the water they created what seemed like hundreds of ripples across the surface. It made Lisa think of the tapestry that Weaver worked. It made Lisa think that everyone creates ripples and that sometimes your ripples run into the ripples of other people. She wondered if today, Joey and she just might start to share their ripples together. She thought back to making kissy faces in the mirror and wondered what it would be like to kiss Joey.

The Last Person

Timothy was being transported to the last person. He was up in age now, way up. He had been on his mission for his whole life. I sat with him as the car swayed him in and out of sleep. I became a follower of his years ago, shortly after he had visited me, just like he was coming to visit the last person. I understood and accepted his message, for I truly believed. I was riding with him now because I wanted to learn more about him; to hear his life story, if he would share it with me.

Together, with Timothy's driver, we had been traveling for a few days now. In between visits and naps, sometimes in the car, other times at night in front of a fire to keep his bones warm, Timothy would tell me snippets of his life. As best as I can remember, and put together, here it is.

My Daddy was a Pastor at a Baptist church where I grew up near Chattanooga, Tennessee. I'd been in Sunday School classes and Vacation Bible School as long as I can remember. I was probably twelve or thirteen when I was sitting in a pew listening to one of my Daddy's sermons and it just popped in my head, he was doing it all wrong! The church was doing it all wrong!

In one of my classes we had discussed The Great Commission, and what stuck out in my mind was Jesus telling the Disciples to go out and make disciples of all nations. And he followed that up with we were to teach people to obey everything Jesus had commanded. And, if you got right down to it, Jesus really only had two commandments, to love God and to love each other. In my mind the purpose of the church was to go out of the church and to bring new people to love God by loving them. And since my Daddy was the leader, I didn't think he could do this by standing at the pulpit every Sunday and talking to the same people over and over again. I figured that if these people hadn't gotten the message yet, they weren't gonna git it!

In my mind, I remembered a passage in the Bible that Jesus told us about the Day of Judgment. Basically he said that there are two kinds of people, some are sheep and some are goats. The sheep are the ones that go out and feed the hungry and visit the sick and give their coat to those that are cold. The sheep are going to heaven. The goats don't do any of that and they ain't gonna go to heaven. I felt like I was looking at a church full of goats and I was afraid my Daddy was more goat than sheep.

I talked to my Daddy that night about the revelation I had that day. I asked him why he didn't tell those people what God wants them to do. I asked him why he didn't tell those people to go out of that building right then and find people that don't know God and show them love. I asked him why he only stood up behind the pulpit and didn't go out and be a sheep.

My Daddy was saddened by my questions, and it hurt me some to think that I made him sad like that. But, I was driven more to get answers to my questions. My Daddy said something about "scary Christianity" and how people in church don't like to be made to feel uncomfortable. I really didn't understand his answer but he looked so sad I was afraid to press him anymore.

I can't say that I went out and lit up the world right then, being so young and all. But, I can say that those thoughts have never left me. The Bible tells us that when the gospel has been shared with every person, the end will come. I take that to mean that Jesus will come back and bring heaven on earth. And that's the thought that has stuck with me all of these years. That has been my mission.

Regardless of what I had thought of my father, I grew up wanting to be a Pastor too. A couple of mission trips, through a service organization in high school, cemented that as a personal goal. I went to a Christian college down in North Carolina for my undergraduate work and was set to go to Duke for Seminary when my revelation came back on me but much stronger this time. I had sat through ten more years of sermons thinking most every time that church was being done all wrong. So, I decided that I didn't want to learn how to do it wrong, just like everyone else. I decided I wanted to go out and do it right.

I developed some simple tenants for my new church. God called each one of us to go out and make disciples. This meant that it just wasn't good enough that a person could say that they believed, or had faith, or were even baptized. This meant that a person had to go out and actively search for people to love, people that knew God, but more importantly, people that didn't know God. My goal was to bring Jesus back and to do that everyone had to be told about Jesus. Everyone had to experience Jesus. I looked at people in three ways: sheep were disciples, actively being Jesus here on earth; goats were those that had heard of God, and maybe had accepted God, but didn't really follow God and what he said to do; and the last group was people that had never heard of God. I figured that I needed to show God to everyone, and to do that I needed disciples, just like Jesus had said. I figured that if I truly showed a person who God is through my love for them and they got it, fantastic. If they didn't get it, then they were destined to be goats, but they had been given a choice. I figured that I needed to get God to everyone on earth in order for Jesus to come back. And that's what I set out to do!

My father invited me to speak in front of his congregation one Sunday. I spent days working on my sermon; writing and re-writing, reading aloud in front of a mirror, raising and lowering my voice here and there. I felt aggressive. I felt that I needed to shake up those people that had sat there for years doing it all wrong, listening passively and not doing what Jesus had commanded. I wanted to yell at them and the words I wrote had a sting to them. The night before my speech I had fallen asleep reading my Bible in bed. When I awoke, the Bible was open to Acts and a passage there caught my eye. It spoke about the Fellowship of the Believers. And I felt that God was trying to move me away from hate and towards love. I had been so wrapped up in the past, in my silent frustrations with the people in my Daddy's church that I overlooked what I was trying to accomplish; to what God had lead me to do, and that was to share love.

At the pulpit that morning, with my father sitting behind me and his faithful in front of me, many of the pews full, I started with that passage from Acts:

> *And they were continually devoting themselves to the apostles' teaching and to fellowship, to the breaking of bread and to prayer. And everyone kept feeling a sense of awe; and many wonders and signs were taking place through the apostles. And all those who had believed were together, and had all things in common; and they began selling their property and possessions, and were sharing them with all, as anyone might have need. And day by day continuing with one mind in the temple, and breaking bread from house to house, they were taking their meals together with gladness and sincerity of heart, praising God and having favor with all the people. And the Lord was adding to their number day by day those who were being saved. (Acts 2:42-47)*

I told them that God had shown me a new church; that God had given me a new direction. I told them that Jesus was soon to come back; that all we had to do was to share God's love and he would return. I told them that time, in capsulizing human life, was a pendulum swinging from one extreme to another. We now lived in a time of solitude and entitlement. People communicated today with hundreds of others at the touch of a finger, but they were hundreds of people that they had never met and couldn't more love than the grass outside their door. People today thought that driving an expensive car meant that they could park at the emergency lane outside of a store while they went inside for just a few things. People today thought that their children were anything but normal and deserved specialized and individualized treatment in public school at the cost of every other child. People today were so paralyzed by First World Problems they couldn't relate to a person starving or homeless or dying.

I told them that we were to swing the pendulum back to where God is the center of everything. Our church would be led by God, his love and people like us that truly love and follow him. Our church would be one of fellowship and prayer. Our church would be of members that would sacrifice individual wealth for the greater good of the many. Our church will be spread by love from house to house, through prayers of thanksgiving and praise. Our church will seek all who have known God but not accepted him into their hearts. Our church will seek all who have never known God and show them his love. Our church has one goal, that through sharing God's love we will bring Jesus back and with him heaven on earth. I finished with:

> *And this gospel of the kingdom shall be preached in the whole world for a witness to all the nations, and then the end shall come. (Matthew 24:14)*

In my mind's eye I could see the light of heaven streaming down through the clouds on the day that Jesus would return. It brought tears to my eyes as I finished and blurred my view of the congregation for a moment. It was full quiet as I rubbed my eyes and refocused on the people before me. Full quiet for some time. And, it remained somber as my father stepped back up to the pulpit and thanked me and gently nudged me towards my seat. But, at the end of the service a line of people stood before me ready to start this new church.

Our first meeting was in the gym of my father's church. From there, six couples stepped forward and said they would use their homes as churches. Very simply, we divided up those in the gym to the houses closest to them and they set their meeting times. At first it was just once a week; but many of them added days quickly. Each church was urged to go out and find new members and bring them to God through sharing his love. We spoke about how to listen and empathize and then how to provide. Really, we just talked about how to love.

After a few months, our six homes turned into sixty and we were growing fast. All of our churches were pretty close to each other geographically, but that changed when some families had visitors over the holidays and those visitors went back to their homes and started churches there. I decided that I needed help. I did my best to show up at each church as often as I could, but our growth was so fast that was quickly becoming impossible. So, like two thousand years before, I selected eleven others to help me.

Our prayers were so loud that God must have blessed each and every one of us and every church. Within a couple of years, our churches numbered near a thousand, and we had outposts in several countries. Of course, many people and many organizations worked hard to stop us. From personal attack to formalized efforts to re-zone neighborhoods and home owners' associations to prevent in-home places of worship, the enemy tried everything. And, of course, we had churches that failed and people that fell away. But the sharing of God's love, as genuinely as one human can share it with another, was just too strong and our movement grew and grew.

For a time, bullets would blast into some of our home churches, and our followers were killed and hurt. For a time home churches would have doors bolted shut and set on fire and our followers were killed. But, the love of God had stuck with our followers and we continued to grow.

Our churches ran into opposition from other faiths as well. All I have to say is that our message, to be loved by God and so love each other, was so simple and so powerful that other faiths just couldn't dispel our followers.

I am happy to say that our churches, after decades of both growth and attack, today are generally accepted in peace. Though we have not kept track of who follows and who doesn't, we have kept track of areas we haven't gotten to yet, of people that have yet to hear our message; to hear the gospel. We have identified who we think is the last person to hear the gospel. And, I have been blessed by our churches with the opportunity to share God's love one last time.

On the eve of meeting the last person to hear the gospel, Timothy sleeps. We are in some little village in the back country of China. The home church here is quite small, just a room or two, but the love of God permeates this space like the halls of Notre

Dame. Tomorrow Timothy and I and the couple that lead this church, will go to the last person and speak with him. I have gathered my notes and put together, as best I can, Timothy's story. I have to say I was a bit jittery, a bit nervous. I wasn't sure how Timothy could just sleep so easily at a time like that.

Breakfast met us with the morning sun; a few clouds here and there, but really a brilliant day. After prayers and the cleanup, Timothy grabbed his Bible, torn and weathered, and headed out after our hosts, with me in the rear. It was a short walk for me, but hard on a man of Timothy's age. We rested a couple of times along the way and each time Timothy would read a passage or two out of his Bible. It was like he was preparing for something new, even though he must have had done this a thousand times.

Our last stretch was up hill and Timothy was having difficulty. The husband of our hosting couple went ahead to find the man we were to meet with, to bring him to us. Timothy urged us on nonetheless, and so we plodded ahead. We made it to a stretch where we could see the husband and a man walking toward us, but at that moment Timothy lowered himself not so gently to the ground. Timothy couldn't talk and was quite agitated, trying hard to breathe. I bent over Timothy to make him as comfortable as I could. The husband and the man ran to us; the husband hugging his distraught wife, the man standing uncomfortably, getting more than he bargained for.

Timothy looked at me and then to the man; at me and then him. Then, he handed me his Bible. His finger held a place, and when I opened it, it was at Luke 9, the story of Jesus telling people how exacting discipleship will be. Timothy saw my understanding and weakly pushed the Bible in my hands towards the man one more time. Once the Bible was completely in my hands a beam of sunlight shone more brightly upon Timothy than anywhere else. In the light I swear I saw the wings of angels embracing Timothy as he lay there. The man, by my side, crumbled to his knees and I did too. I had a feeling, if words could invoke a visceral feeling; I had a feeling that I had to tell the story of Jesus to this man right now. As Timothy lay there nonresponsive, I began, meekly at first, voice trembling and unsure, to tell the story of Jesus to this man. The light grew brighter, blinding us as I tried to continue. Outside of that beam so focused on Timothy we all could see angels floating in wait, lifting the soul of Timothy up to heaven. And a voice broke from the sky...

Love and Fame

Benny was your average, everyday kid; medium height and build, brown hair and blue eyes. He was a normal guy, the kind of boy that makes up most of the kids that live in your neighborhood or make up any public school population. He wasn't really anything special and he was okay with that. In his mind there were some kids that were better than him, and he might be better than a few too. And, that was just alright.

He was a Baptist boy, brought up in church on Sundays and Wednesday nights. His parents took him and his brother and two sisters to church every time. He was third oldest, or second youngest, depending on how he told the story. Each of the children were two years apart in age, almost as if their parents planned it that way; but he had heard his mother once, when she didn't think he was there, say it was the glass of champagne she and her husband had each New Year's Eve that brought on the occasion of procreating.

Typically, in the Baptist tradition, children are baptized fairly young. Not so young as infants in the Catholic church, but maybe eight or ten years old; old enough to make their own decision. Each of Benny's siblings had already been baptized, even the youngest one; but not Benny. Benny was fifteen now and was still waiting. His parents, Sunday

School teachers, and even his siblings, had all asked him at one point or another what he was waiting for. He simply told them that he didn't take commitments lightly and that if he was going to make a promise to God, and in front of all of those people, he really wanted to make sure he meant it. He was waiting for the right time.

Well, the right time had come. Benny had read the Bible all of the way through and several sections many times. He had listened to hundreds of sermons, both in Big Church and with the youth. He had been on several retreats and had participated in a few service projects as well. He basically figured out that if God so loved us that he allowed his only Son to be sacrificed and to redeem us of all of our sins then God was really a being of love; and that was pretty cool to him. "If God can love us that much, then I can love him back as best I can and God tells me that to love him I really need to love everybody else," he thought to himself.

The Sunday came and the baptismal was full of water. Benny had asked for the Youth Pastor to conduct his baptism. Benny's family sat in the pews. It was a bit different this time, they all felt, in that Benny was quite a bit older and more somber in his decision than his siblings and that created just a bit of expectancy. Benny was called and he headed down the steps into the water. The Youth Pastor said a few words and then prepared Benny to be lowered. Benny crossed his arms over the forearm of the Pastor, closed his eyes, held his breath and went under.

Very quickly, while he was under, Benny heard, "Do unto others," and he immediately thought of the Golden Rule. In that briefest of moments, in his mind's eye he saw a picture, just a quick video of him treating someone else nicely; treating them as he wished they would treat him.

When he was brought back up he whispered to the Youth Pastor, "What did you say?"

With a quizzical look, and because there was a microphone attached to his collar, the Pastor simply shook his head and raised his eyebrows and shoulders indicating to Benny that he hadn't said anything. Benny thought that odd, stood, regained his balance, and walked out of the water.

As Benny want back to the dressing room to dry off and change back to his dry, Sunday clothes, he came to the realization that it must have been God that spoke to him. He had no other rational idea as to how he could hear those words so clearly underwater. As that thought started to sink in, he started off as quite pensive but then quickly digressed to a sense of giddiness.

All at once he thought, "God spoke to me! Why would God choose me? But he did! He spoke to me! What do I do now? Who do I tell?"

To answer that last question, he quickly formed a list in his head of people he knew that he might tell. He quickly crossed off the church Pastors and Sunday School teachers. Almost as quickly he scratched off his parents. He thought of a few school friends but shook them off too. As much as he wanted to tell someone he feared that they would think him crazy and he didn't want to risk that. He settled on his little sister.

Back home, later that afternoon, he found her alone in her bedroom reading a book. He slinked in and after a "Whatcha doin?" and a few other lines he went about his questioning.

"What'd you think of me being baptized today, huh?"

"Nothing much. You got dunked just like the rest of us," she replied.

"Yeah, I guess so. Was yours like mine, just close your eyes, hold your breath and hope you don't get any water up your nose?"

"Pretty much. What'd you expect?"

"Nothing, really, I guess. So, you just went under, came up and nothing else really happened?

She stopped pretending to read and look at him, "What else was supposed to happen? I mean, if you get all religious and stuff you're supposed to come up reborn. But I ain't seen anyone come outta that water looking any different than when they went in, and that means you and me too."

"OK, just checkin'" he said as he got up and walked out of the room.

That night, Benny took to praying more earnestly. After all, if God was going to talk to him he might as well be serious about his prayers. He did some rote prayers, but they felt a bit stale so he just started talking to God. He thanked him for all that he had and he asked God to watch over his family and other people he knew. Then, he started thinking about the Golden Rule. He took out his Bible and started leafing through it trying to find a passage that addressed the Golden Rule. After a bit of searching he found Matthew 7:12 and read it over and over again several times. As he was getting ready to close the Bible, it flipped over a few pages to Matthew 19 where he saw the line, "You shall love your neighbor as yourself." He finished his prayers asking God to see to it that he loved others as he wanted to be treated. In fact, he closed his prayer by asking God to give him opportunities to do just that.

Benny woke the next morning with his closing prayer still on his mind. For some reason that brought a smile to his face, the fact that he spoke with God in such a direct way, really, to have the confidence to ask God to show him a new world; a world where he was more cognizant of the opportunities to love others. That smile set the tone for the day, even before he got out of bed and dressed for the day. In the kitchen, at breakfast, his brother missed the trash can with a wad of paper towels and Benny picked it up and put it in for him. His father was heading out the door to work and Benny wished him a wonderful day. He even hugged his mother, and lingered long enough for her to give a quick peck, before he headed out for the school bus. At school, he opened doors and picked up pencils; he told his Biology teacher that she looked especially nice today. At the cafeteria he carried a lunch tray for a girl that had too many books in her hand to navigate through the tables without spilling the tray of food on somebody. He even found a poster on the wall from a student organization that was setting up a service project of doing lawn work for some elderly people in the surrounding neighborhoods; and he signed up.

Through high school and community college, Benny continued to search for opportunities to love others as if they were the God that so loved him. He got very good at anticipating when people would need his help. It got to the point that he began to get a reputation of being just a nice guy. He began to stand out a bit from his fellow college students. Mostly that was a good thing, but now and again a few people would openly criticize him, and one even tried to bully him into stopping being so nice. He thought of himself as still an average guy, and his grades leading up to his diploma in Business Administration backed up that assessment.

Upon graduation he took his first job offer, that being working at a big-box retailer, one of those super marts where people can buy most anything at a club discount. He was basically a Stock Boy and sometimes Cashier, but he liked his work. He found a lot of people that needed love and a quick turn of help now and then. And, very soon, his reputation of a "do-gooder" became well known throughout the store, both with fellow employees as well as regular customers.

Ben, as he preferred to be called now, was still living in the same town as his parents and still attending the same church. His church organized a mission trip to Mexico to help with the poor down there. Ben saved up his money, and got a little bit from his parents, scheduled his vacation time, and went on the trip. His co-workers thought he was a bit strange for giving up his vacation time to go and help other people; but those that knew him well didn't think it too strange. Ben was so motivated, so touched from his experience, that upon his return he immediately began planning for his next mission trip. He asked the store's manager if he could put out a donation jar, and got approval to do that.

He did some research and found a shelter for abused women that caught his attention. The shelter was not far from where he lived. He contacted the shelter and asked if he could donate his time there, and bring a donation too. It being a shelter for abused women, the manager said that he wouldn't be allowed in the facility at all, him being a man and all. She said she'd be happy to accept whatever donations he had, but she wasn't sure what he could do on site. He thought for a moment and asked if they were in need of any yard work, or outside painting, or some "fixer up" things on the outside of the building. By the end of the conversation, Ben had garnered a list of things on the outside of the facility that he could work on, under the strict understanding that he would not be socializing with any of the residents there. They scheduled the work for the upcoming spring when the weather would be nicer. Ben set about working out his plans and talking to the store customers as much as he could to get donations.

Ben scheduled his next vacation week so that he could work at the shelter. It turned out that the manager of the shelter had also planned for a full weekend when all of the residents would be on a retreat, and not on site. Ben had gathered thousands of dollars, some of which he spent on supplies and tools for his projects. That first weekend, while the residents were gone, he did yard work and repairs on the inside of the privacy fence around the building. He added one touch of his own, as a surprise, and that was to create a small sitting garden, a place to go for quiet and solitude.

Ben showed up every day that week, never seeing anyone other than the manager who came out once or twice to say hello. Ben washed and painted the fence, and he repaired some holes in the parking lot, and he fixed the gate, and he built an enclosure around the trash bins to keep the animals out, and so on and so on. On his last day he was clearing rubbish and debris from around the back of the fence near where his surprise garden was located on the inside. While he was working there he was able to hear several of the women go on and on about how they loved the garden, that it was so pretty and they loved just sitting there looking at the plants and flowers. The manager was just as happy, just as vocal, when Ben gave her several thousand dollars as he left on his last day.

Every year after that Ben would collect the money from his donation jars in the store and use them to go somewhere in the world and do good; do God's work. It was after one trip, several years later, to an orphanage in Rwanda where the children called him

Father Ben, that the local news got a hold of his story.

She was a young, good looking reporter, though not necessarily seasoned in getting the important part of the story she was after. She interviewed Ben off camera to get a few sound bites, and then filmed him in front of the store he worked at. She had even interviewed his store manager, some co-workers and some customers that knew him and had supported him. The story aired on local TV, and even made it to some regional networks too. However, to many, the story seemed to be more about what a great person Ben was instead of the great things he did for people that really needed help. It was about Father Ben, the enigma, and not Ben, the man. Though he mentioned God frequently in his interviews, God was never mentioned in the clip. The people that had supported Ben over the years were a bit dismayed by how he was portrayed. Unfortunately, when Ben watched it on TV the first time the concerns for honesty and integrity in reporting didn't rise. Instead, he saw himself on TV. He wasn't average anymore. He was close to famous now. All of that hard work, which was how he looked at his gifts now, was finally paying off. Ben loved watching that clip and had it recorded so he could see it over and over again at home.

That clip changed Ben. He changed all of the donation jars to now say Father Ben on them. He greeted people now with a bit of cockiness. He didn't help the elderly out to their cars anymore with heavy burdens. On rainy days, he wasn't there with an umbrella to escort the ladies to their cars. He didn't talk about his causes anymore; he'd rather ask people if they had seen his TV interview. He did all he could do to extract attention from co-workers and customers alike. He was much more extroverted, even breaking into the middle of conversations of other people.

It didn't take long and most everyone was tired of this new Ben. Even his boss had to call him into the office and give him a warning about poor customer service. Ben was confused, how could people not be in love with Father Ben, the guy that helped orphans and widows and the homeless and abused? He thought, "What was wrong with them?"

He had dinner at his parents' house one evening. They, too, had heard enough about Father Ben and his TV interview. They missed their son, Ben, the young man that loved like God loved. During the meal, they let Ben go on and on about how unfair everyone was being. He even went so far as to suggest that they were jealous of him.

Finally, his mother had had enough. "Ben, when you loved other people, it was you giving to them. It was you, using the gifts God has blessed you with to help other people. But, when that interview came on

TV you became famous. Fame is a terrible mistress in that it takes from people. It makes you insatiable for the attention and praise of others; other people, not God. Ben, love and fame can't live in the same place."

Clay

I have a gift. I have two gifts really. I have been blessed with two gifts. Some people don't look at them that way, but I have come to treasure them almost as much as God intended me to. You see, I suffer episodic, infrequent, near death...seizures, for lack of a better word. That's the first gift. You are probably wondering what kind of gift is that. Well, I've learned that it was the best gift I have ever heard of anyone ever getting. It's especially great when combined with the second gift which is having total recall when I'm in the state of near death. Again, you probably think that this woman is really crazy, like one or two of those seizures killed off way too many brain cells or something, right?

Perhaps I should tell you a bit about what happens when I'm in that state, you know, close to death and all.

Well, there I was in my mother's womb... Now I told you I have total recall of every one of my seizures. Well, first, let's call these things something else. I like the word, "trip," better than seizure. You'll see why in a second, Hon.

Okay, I was somewhere late in my second trimester when I took my first trip. For my poor mother, it was awful. She sensed something was wrong. It was definitely Mother's Intuition. Fortunately for us, she was sitting in the doctor's office waiting for our checkup. Anyway, on my first trip I went to this wonderful place, hard to explain, and come to think on it, I've never really described it. Let's see, it was amorphous, meaning no walls and no lights and no furniture, to speak of, kind of misty and I just kind of floated there. Now, I was way too young to think about any of this stuff, but in recollection I have. Anyway, I moved and sort of parted curtains of light, airy, dry, mist and saw a man sitting at a potter's wheel. He introduced himself as Elohim, and welcomed me to come closer.

"Let me show you how I have created you," he says to me.

With that, a blob of that wet, gray clay appeared on the wheel. I wish I could call it something besides "blob" because that blob is me! Anyway, the wheel starts turning and he placed his hands on the blob. Even now I can feel the caress of his hands, stronger than the hug my father gave me that time I fell off my bike when I was going so, so fast…but that is another story, sorry. His hands were softer than the goodnight kisses my mother gave me each night after story time in bed. I turned and turned in his hands and just when I thought I could see a shape forming, he stopped.

He gently picked me up, and by that I mean me as the blob of clay, and whispered to me, "I breathe my life into you." With that he blew the softest breeze, which didn't just cover me, or blow over me like you might think, but I could feel it in me, filling me up.

Then, I was back on the wheel again, turning, with those loving hands just caressing me. He told me, "I am making you to look just like me. You will come back now and then and see my work, my effort on you. I am working hard so that you and I will be brother and sister and when the day comes, you and I will spend eternity together."

That was the last I remember about that trip. I guess I survived because I was born a couple of months later. My Mom and Dad were worried about me, they've told me since. The doctors told them that I was a risk, not only to my own life, but that of my mother's too. Both my Mom and Dad decided that I was worth the risk. Doesn't that make you feel kinda goose-pimply?

In the first two years of my life I took quite a few trips. My parents were quite upset about it most of the time. The doctors couldn't figure out what was wrong. But, I can recall each one of those trips. Each time I'd go, there, just where I left him, was Elohim, turning the clay that was me. And, each time I'd get there, I could just feel the love, the warmth, the embrace of his touch on me. It was still pretty much a blob, if you asked me, but each time it was a slightly different looking blob. I guess it was going to take a long time to make a blob of clay look like Elohim.

The doctors must have worked some magic because just about when I turned three it seemed like my trips were less frequent, really just like two or three times a year for quite a while. And, of course, even throughout those years Elohim sat molding me. As I got to be about eight or nine he began to ask me questions about my Sunday School classes and what I thought about what they were trying to teach me. I remember one time, before I took this one trip I tried praying like they talked about in church. Now my Mom and Dad, they sat with me each night before bed when I was supposed to pray; but more often than not I just thought about what story I wanted to hear that night. Well, before this one trip, for about a week before I went on it, I prayed for a friend of mine in school whose mother just kind of disappeared. I learned later that she divorced the father and left the kids, but at that time my friend and I couldn't figure out how a mother just disappears and she was really sad about it. So, I prayed to God asking him to find that mother and bring her back. On this one trip, when I came to Elohim and we started talking, he said, "I heard your prayers. I can't bring back your friend's mother but you can tell your friend that I am with her all of the time. All she has to do is look for me and I'll comfort her."

I was sort of shocked. How did Elohim know my prayers? I mean, I was praying to God and I wasn't saying it out loud, but silently in my head.

Just a few days before I was baptized I had another trip. I was twelve. By this time my trips were pretty much accepted by my parents and they would just wait me out, praying that I would come back just like every other time. They didn't rush me to the Emergency Room anymore, and I didn't need to spend another night in the hospital either anymore. Well, this trip was when Elohim pretty much told me my suspicions were right, that he was God. That was way cool. We talked about what it meant to be baptized and he told me stories of grace and truth and acceptance and love. And, he told me more about the clay on his wheel.

He said, "I am making you in my own image. I sit with you here, always, molding you to be like me. The stories of grace and love, or truth and acceptance, we just shared…those stories, those qualities come from my hands into you. I can see here in your clay just where I put them. Your clay looks so much like me. But, you don't see that do you?"

"Not really," I replied.

He continued, "That's okay, no one really does, at this point. But what will happen now as you start to become grown up, to really become your own person, when you come back here you will see how your clay changes shape to begin to look a lot more like you than me. Most of the time you'll be changing your clay while you are back on earth. But, I dare say, there will be a time or two when you will take my hands off this blob and you'll try to mold it yourself, in your own image."

"I would never do that!" I huffed. I loved how his hands felt, how his words even caressed my ears down to my soul. I didn't have any intention of messing that up. But, oh, how he was so right.

Well, high school and college came, and so did experiments with alcohol and pot and sex. I knew what I was doing wasn't right, but I knew deep down I was still a good person. I didn't waste a lot of time listening to that voice, Elohim's voice, inside my head.

My parents had told my college roommate, and the Resident Advisor, about my seizures, so they weren't too surprised when I took a trip my sophomore year. Elohim was there at our wheel waiting for me. His hands were still on my turning blob of clay, but I couldn't feel them as good as I had before. And, I could see very subtle changes in the shape of my clay. Other people would miss them I bet, but my shape just wasn't as pretty as I'd remembered it being. It saddened me at first, but then I got a bit angry. Elohim was the same, very loving and warm, asking me this and that, but I didn't pay too much attention. I kept watching my clay turn and didn't like what I was seeing.

My trips the next few years were pretty much the same; Elohim always there, holding and turning my clay and being so damn nice. Me, getting angrier every time because my clay, once quite beautiful I had thought, seemed to be turning into something much less. I clearly remember the trip after I got my first job, which was a sales job for a company I didn't like very much but would look good on my resume. I was selling a product that I thought was substandard, but selling it at a huge profit. To do that it required stretching the truth, that's what I called it, to the customer. Customer complaints were high, but I met my quotas and didn't care much. This trip happened right when I was trying to close a pretty big sale and I was very upset to be floating in to see Elohim right at that moment. And, this time, anybody could see that my clay had taken a very bad turn for the worse.

In a stern, loud voice, I started, "El, what am I doing here now? And why is that clay so ugly? I was right in the middle of something much more important than this right now."

He looked up at me, a bit sad, but still with love in his eyes which hurt me at first but then only fueled the fire more. "Please, just stop turning that blob and let me at it," I ordered as I came over and replaced his hands with mine on the blob.

My clay turned in my hands and I could feel my ebbs and flows during my life, my emotions here and there. If I had tried harder I could have relived some of those moments, the ones that made impressions in the clay. But instead, I had a picture in my mind as to how my clay should look so I started molding and molding. It got to the point that it didn't look anything like Elohim had ever crafted, and that suited me just fine. Then, then, I asked him for a kiln to bake it, to harden my image, to freeze how I thought I should look. Sadly, Elohim showed me the kiln and I fired hard my clay.

Before I left to go back, Elohim turned to me and said, "The life that you are living is not the life that wants to live within you."

You know, as I look back on that trip, it makes me so, so sad. All Elohim had ever done was to hold me, to caress me in his hands, to let me be free to choose my life. I can tell now that it was the anger I felt towards myself that I took out on him. I had let myself down. I had changed my image. I had altered the soul that God had provided me. I had tarnished my trips to see him. And then, in all of the arrogance a human can muster, I tried to stop time and freeze my inadequacies right then for all time, like I never needed to change again because I was who I was and that was good enough for me.

Then, for years, my trips would take me to the same place and Elohim was always there, with my hardened clay on the wheel, standing still in front of him. And you know, he still caressed it in his hands, but I never felt them. It was as if I had hardened my skin as well and wouldn't let his warmth to my heart. We would talk some. At times he'd suggest a church to go to, or a pastor to listen to, or a book to read, or a thought to think. After years, I took him up on a couple of his suggestions.

I was in my late forties when I had another trip. This time it was a new experience. My hard rock of myself was still standing still on the wheel and Elohim was still there, but now, he had a chisel and hammer in his hands. He'd kind of look at me, size me up and down, one way and then the other, and then he would chip off a piece here and there. At first I was aghast. Was he destroying me? Had he finally gotten so upset with me that he was going to crumble me down to nothing?

"What are you doing?" I asked.

Still with love in his eyes, "The same that I've always done. I am making you in my image."

"But how? It was one thing to mold clay, soft clay. But how are you going to mold something as hard as a rock?"

He put his hands to his sides and replied, "The clay I blew my life into is still there. Yes, the appearance of the clay has changed, but you are still who I created you to be, an image of me. All we have to do now, together, is to chip away at what you've made of your life to find again the life I gave to you." With that, he went back to chipping a piece here and a piece there, cradling each piece as it fell from my form and laying it down with reverence, and I went back to listening more closely to where he was leading me.

I'm pretty old now, anyway old enough to talk to you the way I've done, and to do so with no apologies. I took another trip just the other day. Boy, the people in the retirement home where I'm living really freaked on that one! I could hear the sirens of the ambulance they called for me when I came to, and I gotta tell ya, that EMT fellow sure was cute! Anyway, about my trip the other day, Elohim and I have done some mighty fine work on my sculpture. I have to say it looks a lot like him, with just a flare of me to make it mine.

Elohim was the same, as usual. Holding me in his sight, chisel and hammer at the ready, appraising me with love in his face. We looked at each other as people do with a long history between them, a history of hurt and pain and of love and growth. He turned to me and looked into my eyes, pausing to hold my attention, and said, simply, "You are who you have been becoming."

Believe

Joe woke up in a white, shimmering robe, which was funny because he didn't own such a robe. He woke up standing in a line of people, which was also funny because he didn't recognize the place at all and could have sworn he went to sleep in his own bed in his own house.

The people were lined up in front of what had to be the "pearly gates." In everything he had ever read or believed in, these had to be the gates to heaven. After the initial shock of coming to the realization that in order for him to be here he must have died in his sleep; and thinking to himself that heaven must dole out some kind of valium to people standing in the line to keep order from chaos, he was comfortable with the outcome because he knew this was where he belonged.

The line moved none too quickly, he thought, so he decided he'd look around to see if he knew anybody in line with him. He looked as best he could ahead of him, and then turned around to look behind him. He was fairly tall so looking over the heads in line wasn't much of an issue. He was about to give up when he noticed that right in front of him was a lady he thought he recognized. In fact, he was quite certain that she went to the same church as he did. He didn't want to stare at her, or at least he didn't want to get caught staring at her, so he moved from one foot to the other, kind of shuffled here and there trying to get a better angle on her. He turned his head once, just in the nick of time, before she looked up and caught his eyes, but that was the moment he knew where he'd seen her for sure. Indeed, she went to the same church he did. When she attended, he always looked around the pews to check on who was there and who wasn't…when she attended she tended to sit near the back of the church. He hadn't recognized her immediately because he always sat in the front row, which is where he thought the true Christians deserved to be seated.

Well, if these were in fact the pearly gates he'd better prepare himself for the questions Peter should be asking him. He went through a simulated interview in his head. Yes, he attended church every Sunday, many times scheduling vacations so that he could be at his home church every Sunday. In fact, he even went to Sunday School before Service each and every Sunday. And, since his wife divorced him and took the kid with her so many years ago, he had attended most every Wednesday night dinner at church too. Therefore, attendance was a non-issue for passing through the gates. And, he always put his envelope in the offering plate. He knew that he was special in this regard because many of the people that sat near him didn't always put in an envelope; he sort of kept track of that in his head too. So, in his mind, tithing to the church wouldn't be an issue either. He had been baptized, which was another plus for him. And, he had read the Bible, several times, and that had to be a plus. Overall, he felt pretty comfortable and wished that the line would move a bit quicker; he really wanted to see what was waiting for him on the other side of those gates.

Feeling secure about his past, he looked up to check on the progress the line was making. He noticed that Peter invited some people to walk right through the gates while he directed other people off to the side, perhaps into a waiting room. He didn't think that they were destined for Hell; he didn't perceive that going on, but it looked like they weren't permitted through the gates for some reason or another. That gave him a bit of a start, a little concern. But, that anxiety was for just a second or two because he was really sure of himself; really sure that he was a true Christian and that Peter would be able to see that immediately.

Mary knew who Joe was as soon as she saw him. It was his head she could always see above the rest of the congregation at church. She almost caught his eye to at least say hello but she didn't and she was too timid to speak up at the moment. She had always thought that Joe must be a very religious man. He was always in the front row, always dressed in a suit and tie, and always singing when he was supposed to.

Mary had figured out where she was pretty quickly. She had been sort of expecting to be here. Mary had been fighting breast cancer for a long time. She had fought the good fight and had maintained most of her activities but the cancer had spread quickly near the end and the end came so very fast. She did think it funny that even in heaven you had to wait in a line.

Mary spent her time in line praying. She had prayed a lot in her life and had, she thought, a very close relationship with God. She felt comfortable in knowing that she heard him often and clearly; that she was able to get direction from him and she acted according to his will as best as she could determine. Praying right at that moment wasn't much different. She praised God and thanked him for all he had provided her. She prayed for all of those she left behind. She asked God to continue to watch over her loved ones as she would no longer be there with them. She confessed her separateness from God and asked that he forgive her. Then, after her words were through she basked in the love she had for God and the love she knew he had for her. This close to heaven the love radiated almost as bright as the sun she thought. She knew she was in a holy place and that grace abound.

The line had moved quickly for Mary and she now stood with Peter in front of the gates. Joe was next in line behind her; for him the line moving seemed slower. Joe was trying to get as close as possible to Peter and Mary. He wanted to hear Peter's questions first so he could construct the most appropriate answers he could think of so that when his turn came he could impress Peter so much that the gates would open quickly and widely for him. Mary was so focused on Peter, who was holding both her hands in his, that she didn't really notice Joe. If Peter felt that Joe had invaded their personal space, he didn't say anything. Peter started the questioning.

"Mary, I have been waiting a long time to meet you. I have been watching you for your whole life and I have to say I have been so very impressed. Welcome. May I ask you some questions?"

Mary was a bit taken back. She thought to herself, "Peter is impressed with me? He's been watching me?" She replied to Peter, "It is nice to meet you, and thank you for your kind words. Yes, of course, you may ask me some questions. I hope that I can answer them correctly...you know, so I can get into those gates behind you!"

"Oh Mary, as with many questions, there are no right or wrong answers, so please don't worry," he said. After a pause, Peter continued, "Tell me about your experiences at church. Did you like going? Did you learn much? How often did you attend?"

Joe heard that question loud and clear. He knew that his attendance record was near perfection. He also knew that while he didn't specifically look for Mary every Sunday that her attendance was spotty at best, when compared to his. He felt pretty good, that if she would make it through the gates, then so would he.

Still holding Peter's hands, Mary answered, "I love our church. I've gone to church most of my whole life and I have to say the one I've been going to for the last twenty years or so have been wonderful to me and for my family. I don't get to go to Big Church, that's what my family calls going to the adult service; I don't get to go to Big Church as often as I would like. I love to hear our pastor and his sermons. But most Sundays I am down in the nursery looking after the babies so that their parents can go to Sunday School and then Big Church. God told me once to try not to say 'No' when the church calls me to serve and I've been serving in the nursery on and off for a long time."

"You mean that you take care of babies instead of listening to the word of God during service?"

"I feel that I was called to serve others so that they can get to church. I feel that if we weren't there to take care of those babies many of those families would never get to church. Besides, my husband takes good notes during the sermons and the whole family discusses the pastor's sermon each Sunday during our Sunday dinner at home."

Joe didn't see that answer coming, but he still felt very good about his near spotless attendance record.

Peter smiled and then asked Mary, "I don't believe I saw you in church on Wednesday nights. Were you there in Bible study?"

Joe imagined that he licked his finger and stroked a hash mark in the air knowing that he had this one in the bag.

Mary was quick to reply this time, "Oh, I was there every Wednesday night. I worked in the cafeteria dishing out food and then cleaning the pots and pans. My husband worked in the Youth area and our kids hung out with him there."

"Don't you have a job, Mary? I mean there you are on Sundays, working in the nursery, and on Wednesdays, working in the cafeteria. How can you do that if you have a job?" Peter asked.

"Yes, both my husband and I have jobs. I work as a teacher's assistant at our elementary school. My husband is a lawyer. He just recently put out his own shingle, meaning he is working for himself now."

To Joe it appears like Peter mentally checked off the point of Mary working, which then lead right into the next question about tithing. Joe liked how this was going.

"So Mary, both you and your husband have jobs. Tell me about your gifts to the church. Did you put in your envelope every week into the offering plate? How much did you give?"

"A long time ago, when we were first married, my husband and I were in a Bible study and we discussed tithing and offerings quite a bit. We saw where God asked for 10%. We thought that the 10% was more of a guideline. Early on, with jobs just starting and babies and such, we didn't have much money so we did our very best to make our gift $500 a month."

Joe was getting a bit squirmy. He put in $100 a week, every week. He didn't like the 10% figure because he made well over $150,000 a year and 10% of that would be just way too much to give away.

Mary continued, "But as the years went on and we were more successful, we gave more. I think that everything belongs to God anyway. I think that he gives us the resources to live our lives abundantly. I think that it is our responsibility to take that abundance and share it with those in need. So, for the last couple of years we've been gifting about $2,000 a month."

Peter let go of one of her hands and put it up like a stop sign, "Wait a minute Mary. Did you say $2,000 a month? Your husband must be making a lot of money, and you too. That means that you two are making almost a quarter million a year. Is that right?"

Mary blushed a bit, "Oh no, no, no! We don't make anywhere near that. Like I said, we have been blessed with abundance and we are just sharing that through our church."

Peter followed up, "Does that include the money you spend each year on that mission trip to New Orleans? Does that include the money you spend each year on Christmas presents to be sent to orphans your church supports in Africa? Your church built a new sanctuary a couple of years back, does that include money you promised the church for that expense?"

"No, those are extra things. We don't think that they count in our tithing."

Joe was beginning to worry now. How was he going to answer what he did with all of his money? Yes, alimony and child support took a good chuck, but he still lived in the big house they bought, with five bedrooms and six bathrooms and a three-car garage. He even leased a new car every three years. How was he going to answer this question?

Peter paused even longer this time before changing his line of questioning, "Tell me about your kids. Didn't you adopt one of them?"

With this Mary lit up. She went on and on about her three children, and, yes, she and her husband had even adopted one them from an inner city special needs center. As Mary droned on about how wonderful her kids were and all that they did in the Youth department at church, Joe thought back to his only child, his son. When his son was about fourteen he and Joe got into a heated argument about going to church. Joe was insistent that the boy go. The son was questioning if God even existed because he didn't see any evidence of God in his world. Joe basically told his son that if he didn't go to church then he couldn't live at home. As the door slammed to end that argument, Joe yelled through the door, "You are dead to me. I have no son." That was when his wife filed for divorce and took full custody of the boy.

When Mary finished telling about her kids, Peter asked the next question, "Mary, your kids sound just wonderful. You and your husband should be so proud. Can you tell me about your prayer life? Tell me about your relationship with God."

Joe felt good about this question. Like a true Christian should, Joe prayed every day. He had a chair in his study with his Bible on a side table right next to it. Every evening right after dinner he would go to his chair and sit. Since he's read the whole Bible years ago he didn't feel the need to open it up to pray, so he sat in the chair and said a few prayers that he had memorized over the years. In his mind he could always put a mark in the box for daily prayer.

Mary, still gleaming from talking about her kids, went right into this answer, "Oh, God is so wonderful! I mean he has been so good to me and my family. I talk to God almost all of the time. In fact, I was praying to him while I was waiting here in line. My husband used to joke that I had another man in our relationship and that he was just too much for him to compete against. We always got a chuckle out of that one!"

Joe couldn't understand what Mary was saying. "Maybe I misunderstood the question," he thought to himself.

Mary continued, "Anyway, I talk to God a lot. I ask him what I should do about this and that. I try my best to take the stories from the Bible and apply them to my life and my family. I have been so fortunate because God has been so kind as to show me the path. Sometimes I don't listen very well, and sometimes I just can't figure out how I'm supposed to do what he wants me to do, and sometimes I just don't do what he asks. But you know, I ask for forgiveness and I know he gives it to me. But what's funny, even after I know I've been forgiven, he just keeps putting me in the same circumstance until I do things his way instead of my way. You'd think I'd learn after all these years!"

Joe was still confused. He never had a conversation with God. He prayed to God. He praised God and he thanked God but he never really talked to God. And he knew he never asked God a question about what he should do. He made up his mind on every matter and proceeded forward with his decision, hell or high water he always thought. "What was this woman saying?" he mumbled to himself.

Peter, still with Mary's hands in his, seemed to move her just a bit closer to where Joe was eavesdropping, "Mary, one last question, please, if you don't mind. Do you believe God?"

Mary didn't even have to think and blurted right out, "Of course I do…" before Peter interrupted her.

"Thank you so much Mary. Please, please, go right through those gates right there. There are so many people waiting to see you. And, I'll see you very soon too."

And Mary, beaming, walked through the gates and disappeared from view. And now, Joe was next in line. Joe was a bit concerned now about the questions, well not so much the questions, but his answers. Mary had made it look so easy; she had a good answer to every question. Joe wasn't quite as confident now as Peter waved him forward; even though Joe didn't really have but just a step to take he had been so close.

Peter started, "Joe, I am so very happy to meet you. I hope that your wait in line wasn't too long."

"No, it was just fine, thank you. I'm happy to meet you too."

"Joe, I have just one question for you…"

Joe quickly interrupted, "Only one question? Only one? What if I get it wrong? You asked the woman in front of me a lot of questions. You've asked many questions of each person I've seen come to you. Why do I only get one question? Why?"

Peter, tried to sooth Joe with his eyes, tried to calm him by putting his hands on both Joe's shoulders. In as calm a voice as possible, "Joe, as you have heard there are no wrong or right answers here. Your answer is your life, how you lived it. You can't get it wrong here."

Joe took a deep breath and exhaled, "OK, I'm calm, I'm calm. Go ahead."

Peter gave Joe several more moments to collect himself and then asked, "Joe, do you believe God?"

With that Joe smiled and thought, "I've got this in the bag!" Then, he answered, "Yes. Yes, I believe in God. I believe that Jesus is his son and that Jesus sacrificed his life to save us. I accept Jesus as my Savior. Yes, I believe in God."

Peter had to look up into Joe's eyes, "I'm happy that you believe in God and that Jesus is your Savior. But, Joe, that's not the question I asked you. I asked you if you believe God."

Joe's smile left his face, "I don't understand your question. Of course I believe in God. And if I believe in God then I believe God...don't I?" Joe was really perplexed by this and that started his worrying all over again.

"Joe, think on this. Has God ever asked you to do something? Have you ever heard the Holy Spirit guide you, lead you in one direction? Have you ever heard a passage from the Bible that touched you enough to move you from your comfort zone? Have you ever felt the love of God so much that you just had to go and love someone else the same way?

Have you ever trusted God with deciding a path for you to follow? Very simply, have you ever heard God and believed what he told you?"

Joe didn't know what to say. Flashing through his head were many questions, "Didn't he follow all of the rules? Didn't he prove to be a true Christian by going to church, by dropping his envelope in the plate, by being a pillar that other's in the church could admire and emulate? Where did Peter come up with this question?"

As Peter began to lead Joe, not to the gate, but to the side room he saw when he first stood in line, Peter said, "There is a big difference between believing in God and believing God. Joe, find out what that difference is and how you apply it to your life. I will see you again."

Satan's Test

At one moment in the continuum of God's time he breathed his life into the soul of five individuals that were to live on earth. You see, God and Satan had bumped into each enough times that God wanted to see just how successful Satan was becoming. And Satan, well he was always ready to test God in one fashion or another. So, they talked a bit and came up with a test; a trial you might call it. God was to create five lives, as usual in his image and with freedom of choice. It was Satan's hypothesis that if God were to enable each person to get what they wanted, but then took it away by means of molding them, they would walk away from God and then Satan could just grab them up and take them to Hell. God, always the optimist, took the challenge.

God's five children were born in their own places and times and with their own families. As God does, with the help of the Holy Spirit, he looked after those children, nurturing them and loving them. Satan, at first having forgotten that God is also the Holy Spirit and Jesus, tried to call, "Foul," when God enlisted the Holy Spirit. But God simply reminded Satan that he is in fact God and that this is who he is, so Satan relinquished his objection. He didn't think it mattered much anyway; he thought he had this in the bag.

At a critical point in the spiritual development of each person God made sure that they heard a specific message. For most of them that message was preached in a sermon. For one of them they read it in a devotional. Regardless, each one got this message:

> If you are not fully engaged in this great mission of God here on earth, then you will miss the very thing he created you to do.

Instead of getting miffed with this little bit of subterfuge, Satan instead just loved it. He figured that when each soul was lost to God and brought with him to Hell he would show them what God had planned for them, and what they lost out on, over and over again for eternity. He wasn't quite sure how he would know what each person was destined to do, so he asked God.

God thought on the question for just a moment, and then replied, "At the right moment, in each of my children's lives, I will give you just a glimpse, just a fragment of how I see my children. In that way you will know why each of my children was created."

Each person had a dream that initiated their individual test. In each dream Jesus was there. Each person felt as if it were more than a dream; that it was close to real. In each dream, Jesus asked the same question, "What are you looking for?"

xxxxxxx

Teddy was in his mid-thirties when Jesus asked him that question. It didn't take him long to answer it either; "Money" was his answer. When Teddy woke up the morning after that dream he felt like a new man. He felt like nothing could stop him. He had been working for a software development company but had just recently decided to take the entrepreneur route and go it alone. He had learned a lot and had come up with a unique solution that he wanted to develop, market and sell by himself. That dream was the boost of confidence he needed.

By his mid-forties Teddy was a multi-millionaire. He sometimes joked, as the nouveau riche sometimes do, that he had more money than God! His personal accountant was after him on two counts. The first, he needed to generate some tax write-offs. The second, his new plans had leveraged his assets to the hilt, it was a huge risk and personal loss was just one or two bad turns away. Teddy had decided that he would donate heavily to the newly planned children's cancer wing at the local hospital. In fact, the wing would be named after him.

Shortly after he signed the papers to donate some significant cash to the hospital, the first bad turnn popped up. The major client he had lined up, the 20% that was generating the 80% of his total revenue just tanked and went into bankruptcy. That hit Teddy pretty hard, but he figured he could handle it, so he just worked at it harder. He never went to God with his problems, not since that dream anyway, and he wasn't going to start now.

It was just a week or two later when he found out that his lead programmer had made a huge mistake. He had based the entire software on an outdated operating system, thinking that when the time came to go live it would be a simple matter of modifying just a few things. Instead, the new operating system would require a forklift upgrade, a complete overhaul to the entire program. And this was just before they were to announce the product to the market, and just after they had run out of both investment money and operating capital.

That night, Teddy had trouble sleeping. Somewhere in the wee hours, Satan entered his dreams and he asked Teddy, "What are you looking for?"

"Money, money...money!" Teddy cried.

Satan had seen just a glimmer of what Teddy was created for. Teddy was to have established that new wing at the hospital and the doctors there would go on and treat and heal children for decades. In fact, in God's plan for Teddy, Satan could see him much later in life when he had given up on software and instead had applied his business acumen to helping the hospital prosper and become the leading children's cancer care center in the region. That's when Satan told Teddy, "Take back your pledge to that hospital and I'll make sure you get all the money you need."

The next morning Teddy called the hospital and backed out of his pledge. That afternoon, almost out of the blue it seemed a very well-dressed man came to see Teddy. That man was an investor and he had a deal for Teddy to save his company. Teddy barely read the fine print, and didn't even notice the interest rate at which he would need to pay the investment back, and, worst of all, signed the papers without his lawyer reviewing them.

Immediately Teddy's company took off again. There was enough money to correct the mistake by hiring a slew of programmers that worked around the clock for two weeks. Teddy's new software was finally ready and he spent everything he had on a huge marketing campaign and trade shows and traveling around the country making sales calls. The problem was nobody was buying. In six months his first payment, a very substantial sum, was due to the investor and Teddy didn't have the money. Teddy took a second mortgage on his house to make the payment, just barely.

Another month went by and another payment was due. Teddy altered his company's accounting records and took the money that was due for taxes to make that payment. Another month and another payment; this time Teddy talked his parents out of their retirement money. Finally, Teddy wrote a series of bad checks from one bank to another and the house of cards fell and he landed in prison.

In all of that time Teddy never came back to God; never dreamed of Jesus again. He felt unworthy of God, if he really thought hard about it; just too embarrassed or too prideful to ask God for help.

Due to lack of personal care, Teddy passed on a few years later. Satan was there and escorted him to Hell. For all eternity Teddy had to witness children suffering and dying from cancer, and he could do nothing about it.

xxxxxxx

Victoria never thought she was as pretty as all of the other girls. And, she felt she wasn't quite as smart as the rest of the class when she was going through school. But, she knew she had personality, charisma, charm and likability. She did go to college, for a while, taking classes in both marketing and business, but college really wasn't for her. In the work place she was a go-getter and energetic. She moved from one job to a better job every year or two. She finally decided to get her real estate agent license and try that field.

She started off working for a small, local realtor but soon moved up to a national company. She was just coming up to her second year there when she had the dream. It was kind of funny at first, in her dream she was showing a really nice house, much nicer than ones she had ever shown before, and in walks Jesus. She knew it was him immediately; no one else wears that kind of clothing, not in a neighborhood like that one. Jesus looked around a bit and then came up to her and asked, "What are you looking for?"

As quick as lightening, Victoria blurts out, "I want to be successful. I want success and all that comes with it."

Victoria attended church fairly regularly, it was one thing she did with her mother, who was widowed. So, she was quite acquainted with God, which was another reason why Jesus was so familiar to her. Waking up the next morning she knew that God had spoken to her and her day just brightened right at the start.

She continued to work hard and a couple of months later she got her first mega-mansion to list. As far as she was concerned, this was the big time. She prayed that she would be successful in her effort to best represent her client. She recalled her dream and felt confident that God was with her. She ended up doing so well that her client recommended two other rich and famous clients and now Victoria was hanging with the A-listers.

It was about this time that her mother began to slide towards Alzheimer's and dementia. Victoria, not living in a much bigger house than her mother's, persuaded her mother to move in with her. About six months later, after a very long day, Victoria came home to find her front door open and her mother missing. Fortunately, her mother was found by a neighbor down the street who walked her back just as Victoria was frantically about to call the police.

Victoria had four major deals she was working on, all of which were with high class, well known celebrities and she just didn't have time for her mother, so, she put her in a facility. The problem was that Victoria became so successful, and was so busy, so important to her high visibility clientele that she chose not to visit her mother, even once. She didn't pray about it at all.

Satan showed up soon after that in the form of the Vice President of the largest realtor in the country, asking Victoria if she would like to come and work directly under him. He sold houses in destinations around the world and his clientele were all Hollywood. He even told her that he would pay her the lost commissions on the deals she had in the works if she would sign on immediately. Victoria didn't even think about it when he said she'd have to move. She signed the paperwork and left her mother behind.

Victoria's first assignment in her new firm was to locate an estate in the Caribbean for one of Hollywood's brightest stars. All during her travels, the facility where her mother lived continued to call her telling her that her mother, when lucid, had been asking for her. They also told Victoria that her mother was slipping fast. Before Victoria could complete the transaction she felt that she had to fly back to her mother and sort things out. When she did that, the deal fell through, the Hollywood star was infuriated, and her new boss gave her a very stern warning that it was the job and nothing else, take it or leave it.

Victoria rebounded well by going behind a co-worker's back to steal that Hollywood star back by finding an even better estate on a better island and was quickly back on the track to success. She got the news about two years later, on her voice mail that her mother had died. She got the news that her employer had closed the company and had terminated her employment when she was at the funeral.

She went back to her previous employer and sold and sold. By many people's standards she was very successful. But for her, she wasn't flying first class around the world in search of multi-million dollar bungalows anymore. After working almost a week without sleep on a very complicated deal, and then celebrating with colleagues late into the night after the closing, Victoria fell asleep at the wheel and died at the crash scene.

Satan met her there and escorted her to Hell with him. Victoria spent eternity as a little girl calling for her mother, begging for her mother, but her mother failed to even recognize her.

xxxxxxx

Will was in his mid-fifties when he had his Jesus dream. Will was an accountant, had been all of his life, and when they say that accountants have no fun, they were talking about Will. In his dream, Jesus came right up to him, no fanfare and no fantasy, and asked him, "What are you looking for?"

Uncharacteristically, Will said, "Happiness. I'd just like to be happy."

That next week Will's firm decided that they were going to do something to give back to the community; they were going to perform a service project. Will was on a team of people, co-workers that were to go and clean up around and paint the outside of a homeless shelter. It was a fine day and though Will was a bit tentative at first, he ended up diving right in with a paint brush in his hand. By the end of the day, he had a smile on his face; in fact the muscles in his face, unaccustomed to smiling so much, were sorer than his back or arm muscles.

When he got home, he told his wife, "That was really more fun that I could have imagined. I really liked that. If I had just one complaint it would be about some of the other people working with me, but other than that, I'm glad I went."

At church a couple of weeks later, and after a tornado hit hard about a hundred miles away, Will learned of another opportunity to get involved with a service project. On the drive up, he was stuck with three other church members in a car that was part of a caravan of cars and trucks heading to the unfortunate town hit by the storm. He just couldn't believe the stories they were telling, the "drama" that was in their lives. He was glad that the trip was just about two hours long as he didn't think he could have taken much more.

The devastation from the tornado was shocking. Will worked hard all day and found that though he wasn't smiling, he was very happy to be there. Sadly, for him, he had to ride in the same car with the same people back home at the end of a very long day. On top of that, traffic problems made the drive just more than three hours long. That was more than he could take!

Will began to get so turned off by other people, any other person, that he found happiness only when he was by himself. He experienced happiness in the service of others, but found that those others needed to be invisible to him, that if there were other people involved, happiness morphed to misery. He began to change his service projects from ones directed to others to hobbies that made him happy. His wife began to nag him, telling him that he was paying her no attention, that they might as well be roommates as opposed to spouses. The divorce was not long in coming, and a sense of happiness came with that too. His two children, infrequently calling him in the past for help with finances, job choice or their own relationship issues, were now cut off from him; he wouldn't even return their calls.

For the last two decades of Will's life, he lived alone. He retired early, having worked at the same company for over thirty years he had amassed a good retirement package, even after splitting it with his ex-wife. He became a recluse, rarely leaving his house. He stayed in, puttzing around between one hobby or another, happy to be alone.

Satan was there right after the heart attack. Will might have lived, if someone had been there to call 911; but, all in all, he was OK with passing on and doing so all by himself. Satan took him to Hell, where Will was surrounded by masses of people wailing and crying, talking and complaining. And, to top that off, there was a Jack-in-the-Box, with Jack dressed as a clown. The crank would turn by itself, the tinny music would chime out and every time that Jack popped out, he would make the same joke over and over again, for all eternity.

xxxxxxx

Ever since she could remember, at her Nana's hip in the kitchen, Naomi loved to cook. And, better than that, everyone that ate her food loved it. She went from high school to culinary school and got her degree in cooking, as she told people who asked. She worked hard and got her first "real" job as a Sous Chef at a pretty popular restaurant not far from where she lived downtown. Naomi loved working in that restaurant's kitchen; sure she would have preferred the title of Chef, but she loved it just the same.

The restaurant business is an extremely busy one, and like many others in this industry, Naomi worked long hours and it seemed for months on end without any time off. That prevented her from going to her church, where she had grown up with her mother and her Nana, her mother singing in the choir. Her mother said that in her family, artistic talent seemed to skip generations in the women. Her mother's grandmother was a very good singer, but her mother, Naomi's grandmother, was a mighty fine cook. And so, Naomi wasn't a singer like her mother, but a culinary artist like her Nana. Naomi missed going to church, and missed hearing her mother sing, but, in her mind she retained her spirituality and relationship with God.

After several months in her Sous Chef position, the head chef left. The owner's told her that they would be conducting a search for a new Executive Chef. Naomi was a bit dismayed that she wasn't offered the job and went home that night discouraged. She spent quite a bit of time praying that night, telling God, and asking God, that she really wanted that job. The conversation with God calmed her; allowed her to see a bit more clearly and she determined to make a pitch for the job the next morning. God had emboldened her and she brimmed with confidence. During her pitch to the owners, her passion shone through and the decision was made on the spot to promote her to Executive Chef.

As if the restaurant wasn't popular enough already, Naomi's new menu and new flare for sophisticated but oh so rich flavors took off immediately, gaining her accolades in the press and creating a waiting line from five to ten each evening. Things got so good; the owners closed the restaurant one night for a party honoring Naomi and her success. It was during that party she met a man that just seemed to take her breath away each time she glanced at him.

It turned out that he was in the business too, currently as an Executive Chef for an owner of several of the best restaurants in that city. She and Reginald; Reggie when they were by themselves, became a fast couple.

It was only three months later when Naomi found out that she was pregnant. Naomi was a bit skeptical, but Reggie was ecstatic. Naomi started a pre-natal care routine immediately, but kept the news quiet, both at work and with her family and friends. Being unwed, being single and living single and relying only on her own paycheck, she didn't want people to find out until she could package the news and make appropriate plans. Marriage was discussed, up until the sixteenth week when Naomi had her scheduled visit with the doctor and several days later found out that the baby, a boy, would be brought into this world with Downs Syndrome. It was only a couple of weeks after that when Reggie found a new, great, can't pass it up, job on the opposite coast.

Naomi found God again after Reggie left. She prayed and cried, cried and prayed. She first told her mother and Nana the news of her pregnancy, and they couldn't have been more supportive. She then told the restaurant owners and they promised to let her work around her schedule and told her that they would be there for her whenever she needed them.

God blessed Naomi with the most loving child, Bobby. As with most children with Downs Syndrome, Bobby just effused love. Sure, when he was a baby taking care of him was demanding. And, sure, even now, eight years later, his special needs still took a toll on Naomi, especially after long work days. But Bobby was nothing but love shining out like the bright sun behind the last, fleeting cloud of a storm.

Naomi had her routine down, working, taking care of Bobby, visiting with her mother and Nana, both of whom helped with her son. The problem was that during her absences at the restaurant, though still fairly popular, the crowds had begun to dwindle and the reviews were nonexistent because nothing new was going on; the menu and the concept were now almost ten years old, ancient in the restaurant business.

Exhausted one night, after playing with Bobby and finally getting him to bed, Naomi too crashed and fell deep asleep. That was when Jesus showed up in her dream, that was when Jesus asked her, "What are you looking for?"

In was in that dream that Naomi replied, "Fame."

The routine helped and afforded her the time and concentration to re-work the concept at the restaurant. She and the owners had been talking about a new concept for a while, and Naomi was now prepared to dive in. As before, her new menu just took off. The crowds were back. The reviews in the newspaper, and now online, were five stars every time. There was a TV channel dedicated to food and cooking. One night the producer from one of the shows on that channel came to the restaurant and after tasting several of Naomi's dishes, offered her, her own TV show.

Naomi said, "Yes," before she knew the word escaped her mouth. The producer told her all about the concept of the show and how she would be the star. He told her that she would have to move. He told her about the time commitment, not only for the show, writing, taping, recording, editing, and so on, but also the hours required for public relations and marketing and interviews and more. Naomi didn't tell him about Bobby; didn't mention him at all.

It was during that courtship that Naomi's mother died quietly in her sleep one night. Between her death and her funeral, Nana just seemed to age so rapidly, the death of her child taking whatever life she had left and just darkened it. And it dawned on Naomi that she had no one to help her with Bobby.

Naomi could think of nothing else but her own TV show. The producer gave her time to decide on the offer while the funeral was going on, but wanted an answer just days after that. Naomi had the contract in her home and the salary was staggering. She had the marketing plan for the show and the exposure she would be getting, even having an interview on the most watch national morning news show, was just mind boggling.

There was no other choice, she kept telling herself. It would only be for a little while, she kept telling herself. He would be better off, she kept telling herself. No one would think any less of her, she kept telling herself. She would be able to afford much better care for him, she kept telling herself. As she drove away, with Bobby in his new room in a full time care facility; as she drove away with the memory of Bobby waving goodbye, smiling, like he did everyday she went to work; as she drove away with tears streaming down her face, she told herself that this was okay.

The TV show took off and Naomi was a star. In the second season of her first show, she picked up a second show. Her face was on billboards on major highways, it was on the sides of buses. She became so famous that all one needed to say was just her first name and people knew who you were talking about.

With all that fame came two things. She only saw Bobby very infrequently, each time more painful than the last; each meeting with more time in between visits. If she had kept track of such a thing, she would have noticed two things; that Bobby's smile, his love for the world, seem to diminish over time. The second was that she had attracted the attention of a stalker. After some legal work for a restraining order, and after a short stint in jail, the stalker claimed his prey and Naomi was killed on her couch in her own home.

Satan brought the superstar, Naomi, to Hell with him. If the other suffering souls were impressed, they didn't show it. As each day started, she saw Bobby as he was when he lived with her, smiling and effusing love as many Downs Syndrome children do. But as each day ended, due to neglect in a sterile care facility, Bobby's light grew dimmer and dimmer until he sat hugging himself alone in a corner. Day after day, Naomi saw the end of God's light in her son.

xxxxxxx

Chelsea was girl-next-door kind of pretty with fair hair and deep, brown eyes. As a teen, in high school, she just didn't feel like she fit in with most people. Really, what it was, she didn't belong to the clique she thought was the cool clique. Sometimes she hung out in the periphery of those kids, but mostly she found herself in fringe cliques that needed to do other things to be cool. Those other things amounted to alcohol and pot and trouble.

Chelsea was conflicted. Her parents had brought her up right, meaning that they went to church, she was expected to get good grades, that she had to be busy in the afternoons with a sport or a club; that she had to be developing good habits. Her parents caught her a few times coming home late, smelling of beer, or worse, and had grounded her. She wasn't as upset with them as she was with herself. She knew that she didn't want that kind of lifestyle. It took a bit, with a few slips here and there, but she got herself back on the right track.

That right track took her to college, and a couple of small slips, but nothing major. But that college track also brought her to an opportunity to volunteer at a local elementary school. That opened her eyes. That showed her a career path, that of being a teacher. After that revelation, Chelsea had a dream that same night; a dream in which Jesus came to her and asked her, "What are you looking for?"

Satan felt for sure he had Chelsea in his sights, all she had to do was slip a couple of more times and she'd be joining him for eternity.

In her dream, Chelsea was standing at the front of a classroom full of third graders and as she looked over the faces of her charges, she replied, "I am eager to do something that matters."

Chelsea graduated with a degree in elementary education and quickly got a job in a good sized school, teaching third grade. She was nervous starting in her rookie year, but worked hard at her craft and was recognized by her peers, parents and administrators as having great potential as a teacher. Near the end of her first year, she caught one of her students making fun at a special needs child that attended their school. That made an impact on Chelsea, and gave her an idea to include in her curriculum for the next school year.

As the new school year approached, Chelsea had developed a course of study to begin the year she titled, Awareness. However, she was quite apprehensive; not sure if she should try it or not. Tossing and turning one night, wrestling the blankets trying to sleep, Jesus came to her in a dream again. This time she was standing in what must have been an outdoor classroom, lined with benches upright in the green grass. On the benches were children, all of different skin colors and races. Some of the children had easy to see physical handicaps, and some, she could tell somehow, had mental handicaps. Jesus looked over the children sitting quietly, smiling, on the benches, then turned to Chelsea and asked, "What are you looking for?"

Satan perceived a lack of courage, perhaps a lack of trust in Chelsea and knew this time he had her.

And, just like the first time, Chelsea looked in the faces of these children and answered, "I am eager to do something that matters."

The new third grade class in Chelsea's room started the year with something new to them, it was a project called Awareness. The studies were about the fact that the world is made up of all kinds of people, all kinds of different kinds of people. As part of their study, some students would be blindfolded, to learn about blindness, and had to perform tasks aided by a partner. Other students were ear-muffed to be deaf. Other students had to read stories or directions that had all of the letters of words mixed up to simulate dyslexia. Other students had to listen to directions in foreign languages simulating learning disabilities. Students were forced to learn the coping mechanisms other children were challenged with and empathize with them. The culmination of the unit was when a guest speaker, Dr. Tom, was asked to talk with the children about illnesses affecting kids their age and the difficulties those kids had to endure.

Chelsea was surprised by many outcomes of her Awareness study. Parents lauded the impact it had on their children. Other teachers asked her to provide them with her curriculum so that they could use it. The county administration asked her to come present her concept to teachers in a workshop. But, two surprises really stuck with her. The first, her kids decided that they wanted to adopt, or sponsor, a child; a child from another part of the world suffering from poverty. The second, she and Dr. Tom began dating.

The class settled on Kushboo, an eight year old girl, orphaned, living in the Sudan. They determined that if each kid in the class brought one dollar each month then they could adopt Kushboo. By themselves, they wrote a class agreement that each student would bring one dollar a month to Chelsea from now until they graduated from college. Once every student signed that agreement, they posted it to the wall and began writing letters to their new friend half a world away.

Late in that very same school year, Chelsea was visited again by Jesus in a dream. This time, Chelsea was dressed all in white, a flowing gown whispering in the lightest breeze. She and Jesus were surrounded by children again from all parts of the world, and here and there she could see some of her students. Just outside of the circle of children stood Tom; handsome in a tuxedo. She caught the broad smile on his face as Jesus asked, "What are you looking for?" She knew the answer and responded the same as before, and with that Tom began walking towards her as she awoke from the dream. That summer break, Chelsea and Tom were married.

Satan hoped that the marriage would fail. He thought a marriage, in which at least one partner loved something else more than the other partner was doomed to fail. What he didn't know was that both Chelsea and Tom were so confident in their love for each other that the fact that both of them loved Jesus even more was a non-issue.

Several school years went by. The Awareness unit got just better and better each year. On a bulletin board in her classroom, there were postings of the annual class agreements to adopt a child, with the picture of that child above each handwritten and signed agreement. Surrounding the pictures and contracts were copies of letters received from the adopted children. Due to the agreements each child had signed, Chelsea was able to keep up with all of her former students, and many of their parents. They shared stories of letters from their new "classmates" around the world.

Chelsea was preparing for her sixth year of teaching. She and Tom were still madly in love. The only drawback was that they had yet to get pregnant. Both of them worked with other people's children day in and day out. Though they loved their jobs, and the children in their care, they longed for children of their own. One night, Jesus came again to Chelsea in her dream. This time, Chelsea and Jesus stood atop a small hill, surrounded by hundreds of children. Most of these children

Chelsea knew as current or former students, or their brothers and sisters. Some of the children she knew as ones adopted by each of her classes. Jesus asked her, "What are you looking for?"

Satan just knew he had her now. If God couldn't provide her with a child surely her faith in him would crumble.

As much as Chelsea wanted to say, "A child of my own," she didn't. She felt deep in her heart that God had already blessed her with so much that she couldn't ask for anything selfish. Instead, with confidence and a true longing, her answer was, "I am eager to do something that matters."

The next morning she spoke with Tom about adopting a child. Taken aback for just the briefest moment, he quickly agreed and they began the process of adoption.

Ten years later, at the start of another school year, Chelsea brought two eight year old kids, a dark skinned boy and a fair haired, brown-eyed girl, brother and sister, into her classroom and showed them their other sixteen brothers and sisters from around the world. God, simply, smiled.

The Farmer's Sons

Vansi was starving. She was so hungry; so hungry all of the time it seemed. Most every morsel of food she and Zach could scrounge they gave to their son.

Vansi's name was really Vanessa. She had a thing about her name. She thought that she was just so poor that she didn't warrant three syllables in a name; that people just couldn't waste that much breath when they needed to call her. Her husband, Zachery, his name was reduced to just one syllable. It was with this thought that she named her son, Demetrius. Surely a person with four syllables in their name would amount to something. But, alas, even she had succumbed to calling him Deme, just like everyone else.

Deme was almost one year of age. In the agrarian society in which Vansi and Zach lived, due to the very high mortality rate, the celebration of the birth of a child was reserved until their first birthday. At that time it was expected of the parents to invite their friends to a meal to welcome the baby into their community. It was that celebration that was worrying Vansi to no end. She and Zach didn't have any food to feed themselves, let alone invite a slew of people over for a meal.

One Year Prior

And, as with many agrarian cultures there were the land owners that made up the wealthy minority and the workers that made up the vast majority and all dirt poor. Landon owned the best five thousand acres in the valley. He thought he owned the best land anywhere within a week's horseback ride. Landon planted and harvested a wide variety of fruits and vegetables and also raised a few head of cattle, some pigs and a noisy barnyard of chickens. There were a few other farms in the same valley as Landon's but none of them could compete on a commercial scale with Landon. He sold his produce and livestock in the neighboring towns and was a very rich man. He paid workers like Vansi and Zach with very little money; the same money that they had to use to buy their food from Landon to live on. This was the way it had been for generations and Landon had seen no reason to change things. After all, he did provide the workers with a roof over their heads; leaky sometimes, but still…

Landon was getting on in years and was fortunate enough to have three sons. The three boys had been working with him since they could walk. They knew the land, the workers and the tricks of the trade as well as Landon did. And, they were all just about the same age, with only four years separating them. Landon wanted to know which son would be the best to carry on his legacy, so he came up with an idea. He would divide up his land to provide each son with one thousand acres of land and he would also give them a wide variety of plant seeds from his own efforts. He would wait and watch to see how each son used the resources he gave them and then determine which son would be the best to inherit and manage the entire estate. He would give them one year.

Landon called out to the stable boy, Gabe. Now Gabe was both nobody's and everybody's child. No one knew who his parents were, but among the workers, everyone had adopted him and provided for him as one of their own. Gabe made it easy by not burdening any one family for longer than a day or two, and he usually slept in the barn with the cows and chickens at night, with Landon's permission of course. Gabe was a scrappy, dirty, hound dog of a boy of about nine years old, though no one really knew for sure. He was as much a pet to Landon and his sons as he was a child in need to the rest of the valley inhabitants.

"Gabe," Landon bellowed, "go an' fetch me my boys now, you hear me?"

Gabe never spoke much; he could talk, but rarely did. He scampered out from under the stalls he was cleaning and sprinted past Landon so he would know that Gabe had heard him and took off running out into the farmland to find the three men.

Landon had just finished his cool glass of water under the shade of his front porch when he spotted Gabe leading his three boys, Abraham, Benjamin and Christian towards the main house outside of which he sat. Like a sheepdog herding his flock, Gabe, running, circled the three young men with dust off the dry road bed.

Landon asked his boys to sit with him in the protection of the porch while he laid out his plan. Though each son stated that they thought Landon was too young to be thinking of such plans, they all accepted the challenge. At the conclusion, he brought the men out to the barn where, inside, Landon had bagged up thousands of seeds to give to each son. There were tomato and watermelon seeds, corn and cucumber seeds, green bean and onion seeds, squash and strawberry seeds; seeds of so many plants and bushes and trees that one could hardly count them all.

Each son took his seeds and headed out to their respective claims. Each son, with the help of select workers, set out to create and work their land. They knew that they could get two seasons in during the next year and set about their plans.

Abe was the oldest of the sons and had dreams of his own. For his whole life he had worked side by side with his father, well, really, side by side with the workers every day, rain or shine, only enjoying the comforts of his father's home after his work was done. His dreams took him away from dirt, away from working the soil, away from tending needy livestock. In order for Abe's dreams to come true, he needed a lot of money to go as far as he wanted to.

Abe's plan was to grow only the highest priced produce that he could sell. The sons, amongst themselves, had divided up the neighboring towns that depended on the farm so that they wouldn't be competing with each other when selling their produce. Abe picked a couple of towns that were both wealthier and further from home than his brothers. He decided on tomatoes, peppers, watermelon, and strawberries as his main harvest. He didn't bother to grow much, if any, of the staples of life, like corn and green beans and squash. From his first harvest, he selected only the best of his produce and went out to test the market. He let the rest of his crops rot on the vine.

The people in the towns Abe sold to were very impressed with the quality of his produce. Yes, they were a bit upset that they would have to go elsewhere for the staples, but they were happy to pay handsomely for what Abe brought. While Abe was selling he was also busy auctioning off his next harvest. He promised high quality of very select produce to be sold in limited quantity. He played one customer off of another continually raising the price.

Ben was the second oldest son. He too had worked long and hard at his father's call, and to be quite honest about it, he was a bit tired of it. His plan was to simply provide for himself. He chose from the vast array of seeds those that were easiest to grow and that produced food he liked to eat. Even though he had a thousand acres under his control, he planted just two. From his first harvest he found out that he had grown enough produce to sustain him for several months, so he planned an even smaller garden for the next planting. He never even brought any produce to neighboring towns to sell.

Chris was the youngest and loved his father no less than his brothers, he had thought. He planted every seed into every acre he could. He worked the land hard and enlisted as much help from the workers as he could, without over burdening them. He had timed his plantings so that his yield would be spread over weeks enabling him to sell more food for a longer period of time to more towns. His toils paid off very well and during harvest time he could be seen leading a convoy of wagons struggling under the weight of their loads off to towns to sell to the people. Chris had even heard that some of the towns that his brothers were to sell to were complaining about lack of food and he sold in those towns too.

At nights, Chris was exhausted. Even as tired as he was, he sat up most nights planning his next crops. He thought about crop placement and crop rotation. He thought about irrigation and fertilization. He thought about timing and bad weather. He valued the seeds his father had given him and he realized the responsibility those resources imposed on him. He worried not and slept well each and every day.

If Landon was displeased with the efforts of his sons after the first season, he didn't show it. If Landon was happy with their efforts, he didn't say so.

Gabe, on the other hand, was just as curious as he could be. Every moment he could sneak away he would scurry off to one brother's parcel or another's to watch their work. At first, he was impressed with Abe's ability to grow magnificent produce, but he was so very upset when Abe left most of his crop to rot. He had even been caught by Abe trying to take some after days of it just lying there rotting. If he was upset with Abe, he was even more upset with Ben. Ben, who sat on his stoop day after day, watching a few workers tend his few rows of this and that. Gabe just didn't understand that at all. But Chris, now that was a different story. Gabe had even gone on a few junkets with Chris, off to the other towns to sell his goods. Gabe liked working for Chris.

The second planting season was in full swing and each son had his respective plan in operation. Abe had actually taken a risk and planted a bit early. He figured that he would get to his markets while people still had money, money that had not yet been spent on any farmers' produce. He thought if he could manage to get to his customers early that he might even be able to continue his auctioning off of his produce, raising prices yet again.

A couple of weeks ahead of his brothers, Abe loaded his wagons with the best of the best; produce that would gain him top dollar. He had loaded his wagons the night before he planned on leaving, so as to get an early start. In the morning dark, he poured kerosene in place of water in his irrigation system. He gave it some time, and then lit his land on fire, destroying the crops so that no one would gain from them.

Gabe, sleeping in a barn off of Abe's parcel, woke up quick smelling smoke. He rushed out to see the back of Abe's wagons brightly shining in the blaze heading to market. The fire was too big, and Gabe was too small; there was nothing he could do but watch it burn itself out. He did manage to spot one, young tomato plant, with just a couple of small, green tomatoes and many flowers. He rummaged quickly for a burlap sack and then scooped up the plant and root bulb and carefully placed it in the sack. He pack some more dirt around the bulb to make it sturdier, and even mixed in a bit of cow manure with it. When Landon arrived, Gabe, in a combination of single words and hand gestures told him what had happened. Landon was none too pleased. Upon inspection of Abe's living quarters it was obvious that Abe had planned never to come back.

For weeks everyone chuckled when Gabe was around. He was always seen with his new companion, his tomato plant. He cared for and loved on that plant. The flowering buds were turning into little green tomatoes. And, the little green tomatoes were getting bigger and bigger and beginning to ripen. Gabe didn't know if he was happier to have the plant as a companion, or for the expectation of having fresh tomatoes to eat. Even Chris was amused every time he spotted Gabe and his tomato plant.

Ben had underestimated the yield of his second crop. He didn't have enough food to last him until the next harvest. Somewhat apologetically, he went back to his father asking Landon to care for him until the next season. Ben had even brought most of the seeds he had been given back to his father, maybe as a token of payment for his failure.

If Chris thought he had been successful in his first season, this second season was at least twice as bountiful. He had planned his crops to stagger even more than the previous season. When he wasn't working in the fields with his workers he was driving wagons to all of the towns that depended on Landon's farm for food. Chris earned more than enough money to buy the seeds needed to plant the next crops. He had more than enough food for himself, and even gave food to his cadre of workers. In fact, he still had produce left over.

It was at this time, at the end of the second season, that Vansi was starving. It was unfortunate that both she and Zach were selected by Abe to work his parcel. Though Abe didn't abuse them, he had only paid them the wages they were due, that is until he skipped out, and had never let them share any of the produce. It was at this time that Vansi was also dreading the first birthday of Deme. In less than a week, she and Zach were expected to host all of their friends and co-workers in a celebration and they had neither the money nor the food to do so. Their family would be shamed forever, and Demetrius would never be able to have a chance to live the life a name like his might foster.

Gabe could tell that his tomatoes would be ready to eat the next day, or the day after at the latest. His mouth was watering just at the thought. He got called to run an errand and was told to leave the plant. Gabe was distressed, but found a safe place he had thought. Well, unknown to Gabe it wasn't just the people on the farm that had been watching him with his plant, but many of the squirrels and birds had been eyeing those tomatoes too. When Gabe returned there was a bevy of squirrels attacking his plant. There were squirrels surrounding it, each with an orange red tomato in some state of consumption. Gabe rushed in and shooed even the most stubborn of squirrels away. Every tomato, save one, had been taken. Deep within the branches of the plant, still a mixture of green and orange, sat perhaps the largest tomato that plant had borne. Gabe had only one tomato left; only one.

The night before Deme's first birthday party, Gabe was out walking as usual, and of course, carrying his tomato plant. He happened to walk behind the shack in which Vansi, Zach and Deme lived. It was late enough that Deme was sleeping, but not so late that Vansi and Zach were in bed yet. As he past, he could hear crying from inside. It wasn't a baby's cry, it was a woman's. Gabe stepped closer to a small window in the back. There he heard Vansi crying, telling her husband that she didn't know what to do, that tomorrow was Deme's celebration and they had nothing to offer all of their guests. Zach tried to console her but Gabe heard no answers to their dilemma from him. Gabe walked on, somewhat ashamed to have listened in on such an intimate and painful moment. But, the echoes of Vansi's cry stayed with him throughout the night.

It was the day of Deme's celebration. Most of the workers had been talking about the event for weeks now. It wasn't often that they had cause for celebration and they needed something to take their minds off of their situations. Just looking at Vansi you could tell that she had had no sleep the night before, and it didn't take much to see that she had been crying. At the end of the day, people began to gather near Vansi and Zach's shack. At that time, Chris happened by, and was just in time to see Gabe walk up; not with his plant but with the largest, reddest, most beautiful tomato he had ever seen.

Gabe walked up to Vansi. She was so preoccupied, so worried, that she nearly pushed him away. Before she could say anything, Gabe handed her his only tomato. Vansi, when she figured out what Gabe was offering, broke down and wept. Gabe just hugged on her. As the other workers looked on they understood that Vansi had nothing to offer them for her son's celebration. They also understood that Gabe had given her his only tomato to be shared in the celebration. One by one they went back to their own shacks and brought back some food to share. Chris, knowing the custom, was astonished. These people had come expecting to be fed but were now feeding everyone else. Quickly, Chris went back to his storage shed and loaded everything into one of his wagons and this time drove it to Vansi and Zach's shack.

The celebration lasted for hours, into the wee hours of the morning. Everyone had more food than they could eat; in fact, each person went home with more food than they had brought. Chris had stayed for the entire celebration. As he was preparing to leave he happened upon an elder that had been sitting near a fire keeping her bones warm. She caught his eye as he started by, and he said, "I've never seen anything like this, have you? It was great!"

The woman, wrinkles of wisdom and experience across her brow, replied, "We are all made in the image of the Creator. He has generously given us life. He gave his only son to redeem us of our sins. God can do so much when we, too, give our only's to those in need. It is in our soul to be generous. Generosity of this kind is contagious, and tonight, with the help of Gabe you caught it too."

The Hitchhiker

The time it takes me to commute to work every day varies by when I leave and if there are any accidents or not. That's probably the same for most people in metropolitan areas. But yesterday's commute was anything but ordinary.

I woke up with the alarm, and no snooze buttons. I did my morning rituals and was heading out to work right on time, if not a bit early. As I remember it, my wife was still in her robe, so maybe it was just a tad earlier than normal. Anyway, I drove out of my subdivision and headed towards the first of the usual bottlenecks; a stretch of two-lane road, speed limit 50, that connected me to the first major highway. I live out in the suburbs and the typical commute is about thirty minutes for the twenty or so miles I have to drive. Well, thirty minutes if I leave before 7AM and the school buses.

So, I'm driving on this two-lane stretch and traffic is pretty light. It was light enough for me to see quite a bit ahead and that's when I saw her. From the distance I first spotted her she looked young but what really got my attention was that she was walking right down the middle of the road. The other drivers, the sporadic few at that time, thankfully, drove as if they didn't even see her. They didn't swerve; they didn't honk; they didn't even slow down. I came up on her fast and caught a very quick look at a young girl not staggering, not off-keel, but definitely in some sort of trouble. I could see trouble in her body language and in her state of dishevelment.

As quick as I could I drove off to the side of the road, stopped and put my hazard lights on. My first thought, well my second thought after wondering what I was going to do about that girl; my first thought was, "Great, I'm gonna be one of those cars talked about on the morning radio traffic reports!"

The girl just kept walking down the middle of the road, in the direction I had parked, but right down the double yellow line. I walked back perpendicular to where she was on the road, stopped, and tried to get her attention, yelling and waving my arms. Finally, after a rush of several cars, I quickly scampered out to the middle and stood right in front of her. That's when her appearance really struck me. Her shoulder length hair hadn't been washed in a long time and hung down in strings that lined her face. Her eyes were sunken surrounded by dark, dark circles.

There were a line of cars approaching on the horizon, so quickly, "Hey! Where are you going? Can I give you a ride? Are you OK?"

She looked up, and I motioned her towards the side of the road and in the direction of my car. We moved so slowly that the approaching cars had to hit their brakes hard to avoid hitting us. That got the early morning ire of several of them, opening their windows and cursing us out on the way by. I felt lucky to get us both safely into my car. After a short wait, with my blinker on and peering over my shoulder, I made it back out onto the road. Then, I started up my questions again.

Shelby is 13 years old. Her family is quite poor, living in a trailer park about four bus stops from the middle school she goes to. She's a tad overweight and she's a tad not pretty, probably because she can't afford to perform the tasks that transform the ordinary to the attractive. She has been bullied at school, on the bus, and in her trailer park by every other girl she can think of and for as long as she can remember. I try to tell her that she is overstating that a bit, but she just shakes her head, "No." The bullying has gotten worse and she has no one to talk to about it. So, she spotted a jug of anti-freeze her father keeps near his battered Ford pickup truck and drank it. Now, she would like to go to the hospital in the city.

That really caught me off guard. This girl is trying to commit suicide and I'm her only hope!

After a long pause in which I try to regain some sense of normalcy, and truth be told, try not to run off the road, Shelby adds, "I tried talking to Jesus about all of this but I just can't find him. A preacher once told me that Jesus is everywhere and all I have to do is just ask him and he'll help me. But I think that where I live is just so disgusting, so dirty and yucky, that Jesus doesn't ever visit there. I think that I'm just so ugly that he doesn't want to have anything to do with me."

That confession; that intimate revelation just broke my heart; it sickened me. I don't know where my response came from, but this is what I said, "Do you know the Christmas Story? You know the one about Mary and Joseph and no room in the inn and them having to give birth to the baby Jesus in a manger?"

Shelby, for the first time, turned and looked me in the face and answered with a quiet, tentative, "Yes."

"Well, let me tell you, the truth to that story is nowhere near as pretty as it's all made up to be. Mary and Joseph were unwed teenagers and pregnant too. They were forced into town by the government and the only place they could get indoors was basically a barn. They most likely lay down near cows or sheep in the hay or on the hard ground right next to the manure and filth. Jesus was born in a place so dirty, so smelly, and so yucky that I'm sure your trailer park would be like the Taj Mahal in comparison. So, I have to tell you that Jesus is no stranger to nasty places. I know that

Jesus is right there in that trailer park with you, every day, every second, every moment. You have to believe that he is there and that he loves you so much. OK?"

So quiet I could barely hear her, Shelby slipped out an, "OK."

We were coming up to the interchange where I would get onto the four-lane highway into the city. First, we had to go under an overpass. It was early enough that the tunnel was quite dark. When I came out on the other side, and got in the lane to circle up onto the highway, I nearly wrecked the car because Shelby was no longer sitting next to me. Now, in my car somehow was a woman.

As best as I could, between keeping the car on the road and glancing over at my new passenger, I tried to appraise her. The first thing I noticed was the long, red, fresh cuts down the inside of both forearms to her wrists. Immediately I recognized another suicide attempt. She was so pale, like she had lost a lot of blood, "No wonder!" I thought, sarcastically to myself. But still, white as a sheet, she seemed to have a glow about her.

"Okaaay! Who are you?" I asked her.

She seemed so tired, so lackluster that responding was an effort. The traffic slowed to a crawl, meaning that there was a fender-bender or road work up ahead so I didn't need to concentrate too much on driving. I was patient and let my question hang there until she replied, almost in a whisper, "Emma."

"Where do you want me to take you?"

Another long wait, "To the hospital, I think."

Over the next several slow miles I was able to get Emma's story. She was twenty-eight years old and had been living with the same high school sweetheart for twelve years now. Her parents hadn't approved at all. They started their life together living with his parents, in their basement. When they both were able to get something more than minimal wage jobs, they got their own apartment. That was when things got worse. Her boyfriend, even in high school, was a mean drunk, and that only got worse over the years. Sober he was verbally abusive to her; when drunk, sometimes physically abusive. A couple of months back, on another drunken night, after being out with the boys when the home town team lost the Monday Night Football game, he had beaten her bad. The upstairs neighbor in the apartment building heard the ruckus and had called the police. After a night in jail, Emma didn't press charges against him, but he left her the next morning just the same. She had recently heard that he was shacked up with another girl. She had recently received a note from the landlord wanting his back due rent. She had recently slit her wrists.

My eyes welled up, nearly overflowing, and she continued, "I have fallen so far. I used to be a good girl. But I got in with this guy and I got mad at my parents and just left them. Other than arguments, I haven't really spoken with them since before I graduated. I went to a church a couple of times but I felt like such a hypocrite. Why would Jesus help me? I have gone so far down I don't think he can find me. I'm nothing. I have no purpose. Why am I even alive?"

I cleared my throat and before I knew what I was saying, gushed forth with, "Every child of God is of great worth. Sometimes we have to fall so far that we have to stop relying only on ourselves and ask Jesus to step in. When you hit rock bottom, when you are at your lowest, when you have been humbled to nothing, ask Jesus to come into your life. It is at the bottom, where with Jesus to guide you, you will find pure gold. I look at you now and see such a wonderful, loving mother to be. How long have you been pregnant?"

"Pregnant? I can't be pregnant, can I?" She sat back and thought. I could see the calculations in her head and hear her mumbling about calendar dates and forgetting to mark them. With tears streaming down her face, hopefully she asked me, "You think I'm pregnant?"

"Well, as soon as I saw you I could see this glow about you. I remembered that same look with my wife and when she was pregnant with our three kids."

I hadn't been paying enough attention to the traffic in front of me and had to slam on the brakes to avoid running up the back of the car ahead. Coming to such a sudden stop jerked me forward, restrained by the seat belt before I face planted into the steering wheel. Quickly, I looked up to check on Emma, only it wasn't Emma anymore but an old man with what looked like a big gash alongside his right temple.

His name was Winston and he wanted to go to the same hospital. We were inside of the highway that was the perimeter to the city and the hospital was only a few, traffic clogged exits ahead. Winston was seventy-eight years old. He almost said seventy-eight years young but had caught himself. He had been married to the same lovely woman for fifty-five years until she had passed away from cancer just a month back. She was at home, with Hospice taking care of her for the last couple of days. Winston was in bed with her, holding her hand, whispering to her memories of their life together, the night she died. The care workers let him stay with her until the sun came up the next morning. Since then he had been so lonely. He missed her so badly. He had put a gun beside his head and pulled the trigger.

Loud, with anger in his voice he continued, "I am just so stupid. I know my lovely wife is up in heaven waiting for me. I know suicide is a sin, it is the worst sin you can do. And now I won't be going to heaven with my wife, I'll be going to hell where I belong. How stupid of me…how stupid?"

He looked at me, eyes pleading for what I didn't know. Before I could reply with a word, he broke in, "I committed the worst sin of all. How can God forgive me that? How?"

Those pleading eyes looked at me for another start and stop quarter mile. Finally, with the hospital exit just one more green highway sign away, these words came to me, "Do you remember the Bible stories of Jesus in the temples and Jesus speaking with the Pharisees? There are stories of Jesus telling the people that the law is not what he was sent to uphold. He told people that following the law, that even following the Ten Commandments was not what he was here to measure people by. He urged, begged, pleaded and told people to establish a relationship with his Father. He told them that God wanted a relationship with them. I am telling you that God wants a relationship with each of us so badly that he will forgive anything we have done that separates us from him. Jesus is saying that God's rules don't matter near as much as the relationship he wants to create with us."

Winston sat on that for a bit. The ramp to the hospital was clear of traffic and I drove right up to a parking spot very near the main entrance. He got out of the car and waved me to follow him, so I got out too. Together we went into the automatic doors to the main information desk. As I came up to the Candy Striper, Winston just kept walking. The woman at the desk didn't even acknowledge Winston, but stopped me with a question, "Who are you here to visit, sir?"

My call out to Winston coincided with what she thought was my answer. She looked up on the computer screen and found the only Winston in the hospital to be on the fifth floor. When she told me his room number she had such sorrow in her voice. I started after Winston, towards the elevators, but stopped to return to the desk to ask about Winston's last name. That was when I heard her whisper to another woman that the fifth floor was where the people that survived suicide attempts were placed. Instead, I turned and took the elevator to five.

The elevator doors opened and I started down the hallway, following the sign with room numbers and arrows on the wall. The door to the second room on the left was open. My feeling was that I needed to be so quiet and so slow so as to not disturb anyone. As I past the open door, a girl's voice from inside almost yelled, "That's him! That's the guy I told you about from my dream. He's the one that told me that Jesus loves me. Mom, go get him, quick."

What turned out to be Shelby's mother hustled out of the room and almost bumped into me as she turned the corner. Flustered she asked, "Sir? Sir? I'm sorry to disturb you. My daughter seems to think she knows you. Would you come back in the room with me?"

It was Shelby, the dark rings around her eyes were lessened, but it was her; the real her. She told me she had a dream and in it I told her that Jesus had been born with manure all around him and that he was so used to that kind of place that he had no worries about visiting with her at her trailer park. She simply asked to hug me and then went on to tell her parents that her dream was really real and I was the proof. I was able to quietly sneak out of the room.

A couple of doors down on the right an older couple were watching a younger woman take some steps holding onto the railing as if she might fall. I could tell by her hair and the red scar lines on her arms, that it was Emma. I tried to walk past them by giving them a wide berth but Emma saw me. With a stronger voice than she had in the car with me, "You? You, sir? You're the man that told me I was pregnant, aren't you?"

I turned to face Emma and what had to be her parents because they all three looked so much alike. I replied softly, "Yes, Emma, I am."

"I told you! I told you, didn't I? Jesus sent me a messenger and there he stands. This man came to tell me that no matter how far down I fall that if I open up to Jesus I will find pure gold. That's what he told me just before he told me I was going to have my baby. A baby! Can you believe it?"

Emma's father, eyes locked on mine, walked up to me with his hand out to shake. A firm, still hand grasped mine when he said, "Thank you for bringing our little girl back to us. Thank you for giving us the gift of life, and for giving her the gift of life too."

Emma's mother could say nothing so she just hugged me. I could feel her body shake; I could feel the years of fear and hurt and pain wash right out of her. In a bit, she relinquished the hold, looked into my eyes, nodded, and turned back to Emma.

Winston's room was next. He lay in his bed alone, with no one in the room with him. I entered to the whoosh and pings of several machines attached to him. His head was covered in a huge bandage wrap.

A clear tube ran under his nose. I walked up to the side of the bed and looked down on him. I could just imagine the years of living the wrinkles around his eyes portrayed. I reached down to touch his hand, spotted with one arthritic, gnarled finger. Just as I touched him he woke up. The machines made more noise, out of rhythm this time. He opened his eyes and looked at me.

"You're the one, aren't you? You're the one that told me that God wants me to be with him. You said that a relationship with God is stronger than the sins I've committed. You said I might be able to be with my wife in heaven, right? Wasn't that you?"

"Yes, Winston, that was me."

Then, the nurses came bustling into the room, first checking the machines to see what numbers were flashing and then checking Winston, prodding and poking at him. He tried to talk again but one of the nurses stuck a thermometer in his mouth while the other put a cuff on his arm and started pumping.

This time his eyes weren't pleading, they were thankful. I nodded in understanding and left the hospital.

Made in the USA
San Bernardino, CA
21 December 2015